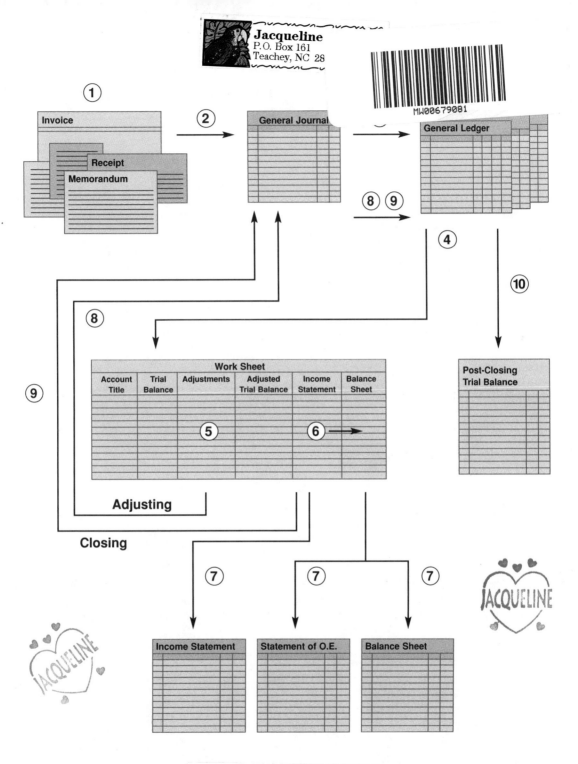

① Invoice, Receipt, Memorandum

② → General Journal

→ General Ledger

⑧ ⑨

④

⑧

⑨

⑩

Work Sheet

Account Title	Trial Balance	Adjustments	Adjusted Trial Balance	Income Statement	Balance Sheet
		⑤		⑥ →	

Adjusting

Closing

Post-Closing Trial Balance

⑦   ⑦   ⑦

Income Statement	Statement of O.E.	Balance Sheet

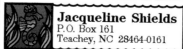

Jacqueline Shields
P.O. Box 161
Teachey, NC 28464-0161

Essentials of
ACCOUNTING

9th Edition

Michael D. Lawrence, MBA, CPA, CMA
Portland Community College
Portland, Oregon

Joan S. Ryan, MS, MBA
Clackamas Community College
Oregon City, Oregon

 **South-Western College Publishing**
an International Thomson Publishing company I(T)P®

Cincinnati • Albany • Boston • Detroit • Johannesburg • London • Madrid • Melbourne • Mexico City
New York • Pacific Grove • San Francisco • Scottsdale • Singapore • Tokyo • Toronto

Acquisitions Editor:	Alex von Rosenberg
Team Director:	Rick Lindgren
Marketing Manager:	Matt Filimonov
Developmental Editors:	Katherine Meisenheimer/Rebecca Glaab
Technology Coordinator:	Lora Craver
Production Editor:	Marci Dechter
Production House:	Navta Associates, Inc.
Internal Designer:	Rokusek Design
Cover Design:	Mike Stratton
Manufacturing Coordinator:	Gordon Woodside
Cover Photograph:	© James Schwaebel/Panoramic Images

Copyright © 1999
by South-Western College Publishing
Cincinnati, Ohio

Library of Congress Cataloging-in-Publication Data
Lawrence Michael D.
   Essentials of accounting / Michael D. Lawrence, Joan S. Ryan. — 9th ed.
     p. cm.
  Includes index.
  ISBN 0-538-86352-8 (alk. paper)
  1. Accounting. I. Ryan, Joan S. II. Title.
HF5635.L367 1998
657'.2—dc21

98-40759
CIP

1 2 3 4 5 6 D 3 2 1 0 9 8
Printed in the United States of America

I(T)P

International Thomson Publishing
South-Western College Publishing is an ITP Company.
The ITP trademark is used under license.

Preface

PURPOSE

Our objective in revising the ninth edition of *Essentials of Accounting* was to make a good text even better. To that end, we have made many changes with the student in mind. Coverage has been condensed in order to present concepts in the most straightforward way possible. All problems and solutions have been double-verified. Our goal is for students to *understand* and *enjoy* reading the material rather than be unnecessarily confused by complicated grammar and vocabulary. The ninth edition continues to take a hands-on approach to teaching accounting. Students take from the course a basic understanding of accounting procedures and the ability to perform basic accounting tasks with confidence.

AUDIENCE

Essentials of Accounting was written to be used in a one-term or one-semester introductory accounting course. Coverage of the entire text will provide the student with a solid understanding of accounting for an office business. Specifically, we focus on professional service businesses that are not involved with inventories of goods for resale or for use in manufacturing products for resale. Chapters 7 and 8 of the text offer an in-depth look at accounting in the legal and medical office environments—they are mini-practice sets that offer hands-on experience.

ORGANIZATION

In the ninth edition, we have organized the text in a more logical progression of concepts. Chapter 1 has been rewritten to include the expanded accounting equation. New tables show different revenue account titles and expense account titles for various types of service businesses. The first four chapters now present the accounting cycle, beginning with analyzing source documents, recording journal entries, and posting. Sample transactions are presented and traced through the accounting records so that students can see how information flows through the cycle. We conclude by presenting the end-of-period adjustments, the work sheet, closing entries, and the financial statements.

In Chapter 5, we turn to cash accounting—receipts and payments, use of a change fund, use of the petty cash fund, and banking procedures. Students learn how to reconcile a bank account and record the journal entries that accompany it. In Chapter 6, we explain payroll and the taxes, tax forms, and journal entries that accompany it.

Chapters 7 and 8 are unique in that they offer students the opportunity to use all of the information they have been building on in the earlier chapters. In Chapter 7, students follow along as the accounting cycle for Wilson Simmons, Attorney at Law, is completed. In Chapter 8, students observe the accounting cycle for Cole and Martin, Physicians and Surgeons. These two demonstration problems give students a hands-on look at the accounting procedures required in these two office environments.

GENERAL FEATURES

In the ninth edition, not only have we made the text more accessible by dividing chapters into modules, but the end-of-chapter materials are now more accessible as well because we have used a logical numbering system. Each of these learning units begins with a list of learning objectives and presents a concise, easy-to-read body of information. Each module concludes with a set of concept questions so students can check their comprehension before going forward.

"Key Point" headers continue throughout the text. Typically, the headers indicate pivotal material that can lead to confusion later if forgotten. Students are alerted by this header to pay close attention.

Throughout the text, we use color to highlight numbers in illustrated transactions, journals, and financial statements. As they read, students can see at a glance what number is being discussed in the text.

At the end of each chapter, we present Exercises, A and B Series Problems, and a Challenge Problem. Students working through an A Series Problem in class can try the B Series Problem on their own at home. These problems are intentionally similar in order to offer an opportunity for additional practice. Challenge Problems encourage students to apply all of the information they have learned in the chapter.

New to this edition are two comprehensive review problems, located after Chapters 2 and 4. These problems are designed to cover the whole accounting cycle.

A full glossary at the end of the book contains all key terms and their definitions, together with other words that are used often or that may be confusing or difficult to remember.

A Check Figures Appendix at the end of the text provides quick solutions to many of the problems. Students can check to see if they have arrived at the correct solution and, if not, set out to discover their error.

ANCILLARIES

The following ancillaries are available with the ninth edition of *Essentials.*

For the instructor:

Instructor's Resource Guide. More than a solutions manual, the Instructor's Resource Guide is a complete teaching resource. This item includes chapter summaries, teaching transparency masters that can be used as overheads or notes for the chalkboard, chapter outlines that are keyed to the teaching transparencies, teaching suggestions, and answers to the Concept Questions, Exercises, and Problems.

Test Bank and Achievement Tests. The test bank for this edition contains over 500 true-false and multiple-choice questions and problems. A computerized version of the test bank is also available.

Included in the printed test bank are achievement tests that correspond to each chapter in the text. These tests are perforated for easy removal and photocopying. Each test includes both matching questions and problems.

For the student:

Study Guide and Working Papers. For this edition of *Essentials,* the Study Guide contains a variety of learning aids, in addition to the working papers needed for the end-of-chapter exercises and problems. For each chapter, we have included a variety of review questions (true-false, multiple-choice, and fill-in-the-blank). In addition, each chapter includes at least one demonstration problem. Students work through the problem and then check the solution for immediate feedback.

General Ledger Software. With this edition the General Ledger Software has been expanded, and problems have been added from Chapters 2 through 6 as well as for Chapters 7 and 8. It has been carefully prepared to offer the beginning accounting student a thorough, but basic, introduction to computerized accounting. For a more thorough introduction to computerized accounting, students re-visit the narrative of transactions for Wilson Simmons, Attorney at Law, and Cole and Martin, Physicians and Surgeons. In these versions, however, the narratives have been re-written to include step-by-step instructions for using the data disk. Students can continue to practice their automated accounting skills by solving the problems that follow each narrative—again, following the step-by-step instructions.

Practice Sets. Two practice sets are available with *Essentials of Accounting*. Both practice sets are designed to give students a review of the complete accounting cycle and require approximately 12 to 15 hours to complete.

Norma Staples, Attorney at Law, covers the transactions for the last month of the fiscal year in the office of an attorney. It contains special journals, office dockets, collection dockets, and other auxiliary records unique to an attorney. This practice set reviews the entire accounting cycle, including the preparation of the financial statements. It is designed for use following Chapter 7.

James Collier and Karen Wray, Physicians and Surgeons, provides practice in recording the transactions for the last month in the fiscal year in a physician's office. It contains special journals, a daily service record, a patient ledger, and other auxiliary records unique to a medical practice. This practice set reviews the entire accounting cycle, including the preparation of the financial statements. It is designed for use upon completion of Chapter 8.

ACKNOWLEDGMENTS

We would like to thank many individuals for their comments and insightful feedback throughout the development of this edition.

A special thank you to Rosemarie Afflick, CPA, of San Bernardino Valley College, San Bernardino, California, for her terrific work in verification, and to Candace Gentry of Pierce College, Lakewood, Washington for her advice and comments.

Michael D. Lawrence   Joan S. Ryan
Portland Community College   Clackamas Community College
Portland, Oregon   Oregon City, Oregon.

Table of Contents

Chapter ONE

The Nature of Accounting

The following modules will be covered in this chapter:

Module 1A
The Accounting Equation and Financial Statements
Understanding the basic Accounting Equation and preparing a basic set of financial statements.

Module 1B
The Double-Entry System of Accounting
Applying the double-entry system of accounting using T accounts.

The Accounting Equation and Financial Statements

Module 1A Objectives
Careful study of this module should enable you to:
1. Understand the process of accounting.
2. Show the effects of selected business transactions on the accounting equation.
3. Prepare a simple income statement, a statement of owner's equity, and a balance sheet.

Accounting is the language of business. Its purpose is to provide useful information to a variety of users so they can make informed decisions. These users of accounting information may include owners, managers, creditors, government agencies, customers, labor unions and competitors.

THE ACCOUNTING PROCESS

Accounting is the process of (1) analyzing, (2) recording, (3) classifying, (4) summarizing, (5) reporting, and (6) interpreting. These six major phases of the accounting process are described below.

Analyzing is the first phase of the accounting process. The accountant must look at a transaction or event and determine its importance to the business.

Recording these transactions is the second phase. Traditionally this meant writing something by hand. Even today, much of the record keeping in accounting is done manually. However, some major changes in the business world have been caused by the introduction of computers. Even though the method of entering or recording accounting information has changed, the concept behind the process has not.

Classifying, phase three of the process, relates to the grouping of like transactions together rather than keeping a narrative record of many transactions. Like items are grouped in separate accounts.

Summarizing is the process of bringing together various items of information to determine or explain a result.

Reporting involves communicating results. In accounting it is common to use tables of numbers rather than narrative-type reports. Sometimes, however, a combination of tables and narratives is used.

Interpreting the reported results is the final phase of the process. At this time, attention is directed to the significance of various matters and relationships. Percentage analyses and ratios often are used to help explain the difference among accounting periods. Footnotes and special captions also may be valuable in the interpreting phase of accounting.

Accounting and Bookkeeping

An accountant is a professional with the education and experience to design an accounting system, prepare reports, and interpret their results. A person who solely records accounting information is referred to as a **bookkeeper**.

Accounting Elements

Before the accounting process can begin, the organization must be defined. A **business entity** could be an individual, association, or other organization that engages in business activities. This definition separates personal from business finances of an owner.

The three **basic accounting elements** are assets, liabilities, and owner's equity. They exist in every business entity.

Assets. An item of value that is owned and will provide future benefits is called an **asset**. Such items include cash, office supplies, office equipment and land. Another type of asset is an account receivable. This is an unwritten promise by a customer to pay for services rendered.

Liabilities. A **liability** is an amount owed to another business. Liabilities are usually paid in cash.

The most common liability is accounts payable. An account payable is an unwritten promise to pay at a later date.

Owner's Equity. The amount by which business assets exceed business liabilities is called **owner's equity**. If there are no liabilities, the owner's equity is equal to the total amount of the assets. Owner's equity is increased with revenue, and decreased by expenses or an owner's withdrawal.

A business that is owned by one person is a proprietorship. The owner of the business is known as the proprietor.

The Accounting Equation

The relationship between the three basic accounting elements—assets, liabilities, and owner's equity—is expressed in the **accounting equation**, shown as follows:

$$\text{Assets} \quad = \qquad\qquad \text{Equities}$$

$$\text{Creditors} \qquad \text{Owner}$$

$$\text{Assets} \quad = \quad \text{Liabilities} \quad + \quad \text{Owner's Equity}$$

This equation shows assets are equal to equities. Equities are divided into liabilities and owner's equity. When the amounts of any two of these elements (assets, liabilities, or owner's equity) are known, the third can be calculated. The following are variations of the accounting equation:

$$\text{Owner's Equity} = \text{Assets} - \text{Liabilities}$$
$$\text{Liabilities} = \text{Assets} - \text{Owner's Equity}$$
$$\text{Liabilities} + \text{Owner's Equity} = \text{Assets}$$

Any activity of a business which affects the accounting equation is a **transaction**. Transactions are recorded in the accounting records using the **cost principle**. The actual amount paid or received is the amount recorded. Buying and selling assets, performing services and borrowing money are common business transactions.

The effect of any transaction on the accounting equation may be indicated by increasing or decreasing a specific asset, liability or owner's equity element. To illustrate, assume the following transactions took place during January, 200X, for Dick Ady, Dentist. The effect of these transactions on the accounting equation can be analyzed as follows:

Transaction (a): Owner invested $30,000 cash in the business.

Effect on Accounting Equation. An increase in an asset offset by an increase in owner's equity + CASH
+ CAPITAL

Analysis. Ady opened a bank account for his business with a deposit of $30,000. This transaction increased the asset Cash. Since Ady contributed the asset, owner's equity—Dick Ady, Capital—was increased by the same amount. The equation for the business would appear as follows:

Assets	=	Liabilities	+	Owner's Equity
Cash	=			Dick Ady, Capital
(a) +30,000				+30,000

Total Assets: $30,000 = Total Liabilities + Owner's Equity: $30,000

Transaction (b): Purchased office equipment on account, $2,500.

Effect on Accounting Equation. An increase in an asset offset by an increase in a liability + OFFICE EQUIPMENT + ACCTS. PAYABLE

Analysis. Ady purchased office equipment (desk, chairs, file cabinet, etc.) for $2,500 on account. This transaction caused the asset Office Equipment to increase by $2,500. The liability Accounts Payable increased by the same amount. There was no effect on the owner's equity. The accounting equation now looks like this:

	Assets			=	Liabilities	+	Owner's Equity
	Cash	+	Office Equipment	=	Accounts Payable	+	Dick Ady, Capital
Bal.	$30,000						$30,000
(b)			+2,500		+2,500		
Bal.	$30,000	+	$2,500	=	$2,500	+	$30,000

Total Assets: $32,500 = Total Liabilities + Owner's Equity: $32,500

Transaction (c): Purchased office supplies for cash, $350.

Effect on Accounting Equation. An increase in one asset offset by a decrease in another asset + OFFICE SUPPLIES - CASH

Analysis. Ady purchased office supplies (stationery, legal pads, pencils, etc.) for cash, $350. This transaction caused a $350 decrease in the asset Cash. The asset Office Supplies increased by $350. The effect on the equation is as follows:

	Assets			=	Liabilities	+	Owner's Equity
Cash	+	Office Supp.	+	Office Equip.	=	Accounts Payable	+	Dick Ady, Capital

	Cash		Office Supp.		Office Equip.		Accounts Payable		Dick Ady, Capital
Bal.	$30,000				$2,500		$2,500		$30,000
(c)	− 350		+350						
Bal.	$29,650	+	$350	+	$2,500	=	$2,500	+	$30,000

Total Assets: $32,500 = Total Liabilities + Owner's Equity: $32,500

Transaction (d): **Paid amount owed to a creditor, $500.**

Effect on Accounting Equation. A decrease in an asset offset by a decrease in a liability   − CASH
                            − ACCTS. PAYABLE

Analysis. Ady paid $500 on account to the company from which the office equipment was purchased. Earlier, Ady purchased office equipment on account. The office equipment account increased and the liability Accounts Payable increased. Now Ady is going to make a payment on this account. This payment caused both the asset Cash and the liability Accounts Payable to decrease by $500. The effect on the equation is as follows:

	Assets			=	Liabilities	+	Owner's Equity
Cash	+	Office Supp.	+	Office Equip.	=	Accounts Payable	+	Dick Ady, Capital

	Cash		Office Supp.		Office Equip.		Accounts Payable		Dick Ady, Capital
Bal.	$29,650		$350		$2,500		$2,500		$30,000
(d)	− 500						− 500		
Bal.	$29,150	+	$350	+	$2,500	=	$2,000	+	$30,000

Total Assets: $32,000 = Total Liabilities + Owner's Equity: $32,000

Transaction (e): **Purchased office supplies on account, $400.**

Effect on Accounting Equation. An increase in an asset offset by an increase in a liability   + OFFICE SUPPLIES
                            + ACCTS. PAYABLE

Analysis. Ady purchased office supplies on account for $400. This transaction caused the asset Office Supplies to increase by $400 and increased the liability Accounts Payable by the same amount. The effect of this transaction on the equation is as follows:

	Assets			=	Liabilities	+	Owner's Equity
Cash	+	Office Supp.	+	Office Equip.	=	Accounts Payable	+	Dick Ady, Capital

	Cash		Office Supp.		Office Equip.		Accounts Payable		Dick Ady, Capital
Bal.	$29,150		$350		$2,500		$2,000		$30,000
(e)			+ 400				+ 400		
Bal.	$29,150	+	$750	+	$2,500	=	$2,400	+	$30,000

Total Assets: $32,400 = Total Liabilities + Owner's Equity: $32,400

To complete our discussion of the accounting equation, three additional items must be covered: revenue, expense and owner's withdrawal.

The term revenue generally means an increase in assets because a service was rendered. Revenue is one of two ways that owner's equity can be increased:

1. As illustrated in transaction (a), the owner may invest cash. Such an investment increases both assets and owner's equity.
2. Revenue earned from providing services to customers also increases owner's equity.

When revenue is earned, the assets are increased (normally cash or accounts receivable), and owner's equity is increased.

The term expense generally means a decrease in assets (usually cash) or an increase in liabilities (usually accounts payable) in order to earn more revenue. Just like revenue, an expense directly affects the owner's equity and is one of the two ways that owner's equity can be decreased:

1. The owner may withdraw cash or other assets from the business. This type of transaction is charged to the owner's drawing account.
2. Expenses incurred in operating the business also decrease owner's equity.

Common examples of expenses are office rent, salaries of employees, telephone service, and many types of taxes.

If total revenue of the period exceeds total expenses, the result is called net income. On the other hand, if total expenses of the period exceed total revenue, the result is called net loss.

The time period covered for a business may be a month, a year, or some other period of time. Any accounting period of twelve months' duration is called a fiscal year. The fiscal year can also be a calendar year.

Effect of Revenue, Expense, and Owner's Withdrawal Transactions on the Accounting Equation

To show the effect of revenue, expense, and owner's withdrawal, the example of Dick Ady, Dentist, will be continued.

Transaction (f): Owner withdrew $300 for personal use.

Effect on Accounting Equation. A decrease in an asset offset by a decrease in owner's equity   −CASH
                                                                              + DRAWING

Analysis. Ady withdrew cash in the amount of $300 from the business for his personal use. This transaction resulted in a decrease to the asset Cash and a decrease to owner's equity. Owner's equity decreased because of a personal withdrawal of cash by the owner. A *withdrawal*, or the use of the term **drawing**, is used to indicate a personal expense and not a business expense. The effect of this transaction on the equation is as follows:

Assets			=	Liabilities	+	Owner's Equity				
						Capital	−	Drawing	+ Revenue	− Expenses
Cash	+ Office Supp.	+ Office Equip.	=	Accounts Payable	+	Dick Ady, Capital	−	Dick Ady, Drawing		
Bal. $29,150	$750	$2,500		$2,400		$30,000				
− 300								+300		
Bal. $28,850	+ $750	+ $2,500	=	$2,400	+	$30,000	−	$300		

Total Assets: $32,100 = Total Liabilities + Owner's Equity: $32,100
(Notice that owner's drawing decreases total owner's equity by $300.)

Transaction (g): Received cash as payment for professional fees, $3,500.

Effect on Accounting Equation. An increase in an asset offset by an increase in owner's equity   + CASH
                                                                                + REVENUE

Analysis. Ady received $3,500 cash from a client for dental services performed. This transaction caused the asset Cash to increase by $3,500. Since cash was received for services performed, owner's equity also increased. Professional Fees is the account title used for revenue. The effect of this transaction on the equation is as follows:

Assets			= Liabilities +	Owner's Equity			
				Capital – Drawing + Revenue – Expenses			
Cash	+ Office + Office = Supp. Equip.		Accounts + Payable	Dick Ady, – Dick Ady, Capital Drawing			
Bal. $28,850	$750	$2,500	$2,400	$30,000			
(g) + 3,500						+ 3,500	Professional Fees
Bal. $32,350 +	$750 +	$2,500 =	$2,400 +	$30,000 –	$300 +	$3,500	

Total Assets: $35,600 = Total Liabilities + Owner's Equity: $35,600

Transaction (h): Paid office rent $1,000.

Effect on Accounting Equation. A decrease in an asset offset by a decrease in owner's equity   – CASH   + EXPENSES

Analysis. Ady paid $1,000 for office rent for January. This transaction caused the asset Cash to decrease by $1,000, with an equal reduction in owner's equity. Owner's equity was decreased because of rent expense. The effect of this transaction on the equation is as follows:

Assets			= Liabilities +	Owner's Equity			
				Capital – Drawing + Revenue – Expenses			
Cash	+ Office + Office = Supp. Equip.		Accounts + Payable	Dick Ady, – Dick Ady, Capital Drawing			
Bal. $32,350	$750	$2,500	$2,400	$30,000	$300	$3,500	
(h) – 1,000							+ 1,000 Rent Expense
Bal. $31,350 +	$750 +	$2,500 =	$2,400 +	$30,000 –	$300 +	$3,500 –	$1,000

(Total Assets: $34,600 = Total Liabilities + Owner's Equity: $34,600)

(Notice that even though $1,000 is added to expenses, there is a minus sign in front of expenses in the equation, which means that expenses decrease owner's equity.)

Transaction (i): Paid telephone expense, $75.

Effect on Accounting Equation. A decrease in an asset offset by a decrease in owner's equity   – CASH   + EXPENSES

Analysis. Ady paid a bill for telephone service, $75. This transaction, like the previous one, decreased the asset Cash, and also decreased owner's equity. Owner's equity was decreased because of the Telephone Expense. The effect of this transaction on the equation is as follows:

	Assets		=	Liabilities	+		Owner's Equity			
Cash	+ Office Supp.	+ Office Equip.	=	Accounts Payable	+	Dick Ady, Capital	− Dick Ady, Drawing	+ Revenue	− Expenses	
Bal. $31,350	$750	$2,500		$2,400		$30,000	$300	$3,500	− $1,000	
(i) − 75									+ 75	Telephone Expense
Bal. $31,275 +	$750	+ $2,500 =		$2,400	+	$30,000 −	$300 +	$3,500	− $1,075	

Total Assets: $34,525 = Total Liabilities + Owner's Equity: $34,525

Exhibit 1.1
Summary of Transactions

	Assets			= Liabil.	+	Owner's Equity				
						Capital	− Draw. +	Rev.	− Expenses	
Cash	+ Office Supp.	+ Office Equip.	= Accts Payable	+	Dick Ady, Cap.	− Dick Ady, Draw.				
(a) +$30,000					+ $30,000				
Bal. $30,000			=		$30,000				
(b) _____	+ 2,500	+ $2,500			_____				
Bal. $30,000	+ $2,500 =	$2,500	+ $30,000						
(c) − 350	+ 350								
Bal. $29,650 +	350	+ $2,500 =	$2,500	+ $30,000					
(d) − 500			− 500						
Bal. $29,150 +	$350	+ $2,500 =	$2,000	+ $30,000					
(e)	+ 400		+ 400						
Bal. $29,150 +	$750	+ $2,500 =	$2,400	+ $30,000					
(f) − 300						+ 300			
Bal. $28,850 +	$750	+ $2,500 =	$2,400	+ $30,000	− $300				
(g) + 3,500							+ 3,500		Profess. Fees
Bal. $32,250 +	$750	+ $2,500 =	$2,400	+ $30,000	− $300	+ $3,500			
(h) − 1,000								+ 1,000	Rent Exp.
Bal. $31,350 +	$750	+ $2,500 =	$2,400	+ $30,000	− $300	+ $3,500	− $1,000		
(i) − 75								+ 75	Tele. Exp.
Bal. $31,275 +	$750	+ $2,500 =	$2,400	+ $30,000	− $300	+ $3,500	− $1,075		

$34,525   = $2,400 + $32,125

OR

$34,525   = $34,525

The Financial Statements

After the preceding transactions have been analyzed and recorded in the books of a business, financial statements can be prepared. The financial statements must always be prepared in the following order: (1) Income Statement, (2) Statement of Owner's Equity, and (3) Balance Sheet.

The Income Statement. The income statement shows total revenue, total expenses, and a net income or net loss for a period of time. An investment or withdrawal of cash by the owner is not recognized on the income statement. Remember, a withdrawal by the owner is not considered a business expense. The owner's drawing appears on the statement of owner's equity. An income statement for Ady's business is shown as follows:

Dick Ady, Dentist
Income Statement
For the Month Ended January 31, 200X

Revenue:		
Professional fees		$3,500.00
Expenses:		
Rent expense	$1,000.00	
Telephone expense	75.00	
Total expenses		1,075.00
Net income		$2,425.00

The Statement of Owner's Equity. The statement of owner's equity shows what happened to the owner's capital account during the accounting period. A statement of owner's equity for the month of January is shown as follows:

Dick Ady, Dentist
Statement of Owner's Equity
For the Month Ended January 31, 200X

Dick Ady, capital, January 1, 200X		$30,000.00
Net income for the month	$2,425.00	
Less withdrawals	300.00	
Net increase in capital		2,125.00
Dick Ady, capital, January 31, 200X		$32,125.00

The Balance Sheet. The **balance sheet** shows the assets, liabilities and owner's equity of a business as of a specified date. A balance sheet for Ady's business as of January 31, 200X, is shown as follows:

Dick Ady, Dentist
Balance Sheet
January 31, 200X

Assets:		Liabilities:	
Cash	$31,275.00	Accounts payable	$ 2,400.00
Office supplies	750.00		
Office equipment	2,500.00		
		Owner's Equity:	
		Dick Ady, capital	32,125.00
Total assets	$34,525.00	Total liabilities and owner's equity	$34,525.00

The balance sheet shown above is in the account format. Notice that this form resembles the accounting equation. The total assets on the left are equal to the total of liabilities and owner's equity on the right.

All three financial statements have a three-line heading. The first line is the name of the business. The second line is the type of financial statement. The third line is the period of time covered.

Concept Questions

1. What is the purpose of accounting?
2. If assets are $40,000 and liabilities are $30,000, how much is owner's equity?
3. Explain the effect of the following transactions on the accounting equation:
   a. Purchased office equipment on account, $1,200.
   b. Purchased office supplies for cash, $200.
   c. Owner withdrew cash, $400.
4. Name the three financial statements that are prepared at the end of an accounting period.

If you cannot answer the above concept questions, go back and review the module material before continuing to the next module.

MODULE SUMMARY

The purpose of accounting is to provide useful information in order to make informed decisions. The accounting process is composed of six major phases: (1) analyzing, (2) recording, (3) classifying, (4) summarizing, (5) reporting, and (6) interpreting.

The basic accounting equation is Assets = Liabilities + Owner's Equity. Under the business entity principle, the business transactions are kept separate from the owner's personal affairs. As each transaction is recorded, the accounting elements are affected. At all times the accounting equation must be in balance. If it is not, an error has been made.

The five major account classifications are Assets, Liabilities, Owner's Equity, Revenue, and Expenses. An income statement shows the difference between revenues and expenses during a given accounting period. If revenues are larger than expenses, there is a net income. If expenses are larger than revenues, there is a net loss. A statement of owner's equity reflects the changes in the owner's capital account during the same accounting period. A balance sheet shows the ending balance of assets, liabilities, and owner's equity for the last day of the accounting period. All three financial statements should have a three-line heading. The first line is the name of the business. The second line is the type of financial statement. The third line is the period of time covered.

Key Terms

accounting equation, *5*
asset, *4*
balance sheet, *13*
basic accounting elements, *4*
bookkeeper, *4*
business entity, *4*
cost principle, *5*
drawing, *9*
expense, *8*

fiscal year, *8*
income statement, *12*
liability, *4*
net income, *8*
net loss, *8*
owner's equity, *4*
revenue, *8*
statement of owner's equity, *12*
transaction, *5*

Module 1A

Exercises

EXERCISE 1A-1 Homework 8/20

1. Judy Eary has a business with assets in the amount of $60,000 and lia-
    bilities that total $35,000. What is the amount of her owner's equity?
2. Sharla Knox's business has assets of $80,000 and owner's equity of
    $42,000. How much are the liabilities of her company?
3. Mark Himes has a business with liabilities that total $21,000 and
    owner's equity in the amount of $72,000. What is the total of the
    assets?

✓ **EXERCISE 1A-2** Classwork

Using plus and minus marks, indicate the effects on the accounting elements
for each of the business transactions presented.

A	=	L	+	OE			
+ −		**− +**		**Capital − Drawing + Revenue − Expense**			
				− +	+ −	− +	+ −

Example: Owner invested cash

✓ a.   Purchased office equipment on account
✓ b.   Purchased office supplies for cash
✓ c.   Paid amount owed to a creditor
✓ d.   Owner withdrew cash for personal use
✓ e.   Paid office rent
✓ f.   Received cash for professional fees

✓ **EXERCISE 1A-3** Homework 8/23/99

On January 1, 200X, Mickey McCrea, a certified public accountant, had assets
consisting of: cash, $15,000; office equipment, $8,000; and an automobile,
$22,000. Accounts payable was $12,800. The following business transactions
occurred during the month of January.

✓ a.   Paid $400 cash for office equipment
✓ b.   Paid office rent for January, $1,100
✓ c.   Received $4,400 cash for professional services
✓ d.   Paid for telephone service, $210
✓ e.   Paid $3,800 on the account payable
✓ f.   Withdrew $900 for personal use

Required:

1. Calculate the beginning balance for capital and indicate the effect of
    each transaction on the accounting equation by using the form

shown below. Each amount should be preceded by a plus sign if it represents an increase or by a minus sign if it represents a decrease. Calculate the balance in each account after each transaction has been entered to verify that the accounting equation is in balance.

2. Prepare an income statement and statement of owner's equity for January, and a balance sheet, in account form, as of January 31, 200X.

	Assets			=	Liabilities	+		Owner's Equity			
Cash +	Office Equipment	+ Automobile		=	Accounts Payable	+	Mickey McCrea, Capital	− Mickey McCrea, Drawing	+ Revenue	− Expenses	
Bal. $15,000 +	$8,000 +	$22,000		=	$12,800	+	_____				
(a) _____	_____	_____			_____		_____	_____	_____	_____	
Bal. _____	_____	_____			_____		_____				
(b) _____	_____	_____			_____		_____	_____	_____	_____	
Bal. _____	_____	_____			_____		_____				

Module 1A

Problems

PROBLEM 1A-4 ANALYZING CHANGES IN ACCOUNTING EQUATION

Duane Davis is a certified public accountant. As of July 1, 200X, Davis owned the following property related to his business: cash, $13,500; office equipment, $9,200; automobile, $28,700. At the same time, Davis owed business creditors $6,900.

The following transactions were completed by Davis during the month of July.

a. Bought office equipment on account, $1,400
b. Paid $2,300 on account
c. Paid cash for an office safe, $1,600
d. Paid $900 for office rent for July
e. Received $5,100 from clients for professional services
f. Paid utility bill, $700
g. Withdrew $2,800 for personal use

	Assets			=	Liabilities	+		Owner's Equity			
Cash +	Office Equipment	+ Automobile		=	Accounts Payable	+	Duane Davis, Capital	− Duane Davis, Drawing	+ Revenue	− Expenses	
Bal. $13,500 +	$9,200 +	$28,700		=	$6,900	+	_____				
(a) _____	_____	_____			_____		_____	_____	_____	_____	
Bal. _____	_____	_____			_____		_____				
(b) _____	_____	_____			_____		_____	_____	_____	_____	
Bal. _____	_____	_____			_____		_____				

Required:

1. Calculate the beginning balance for capital and indicate the effect of each transaction on the accounting equation by using the form shown on page 16. Each amount should be preceded by a plus sign if it represents an increase or by a minus sign if it represents a decrease. Calculate the balance in each account after each transaction has been entered to verify that the accounting equation is in balance.
2. Prepare an income statement and statement of owner's equity for July, and a balance sheet, in account form, as of July 31, 200X.

PROBLEM 1A-5 PREPARATION OF FINANCIAL STATEMENTS

Dan Pike, CPA, determines the following account balances as of October 31, 200X:

Cash	$ 8,110	Accounts Payable	+ $ 7,700
Office Supplies	600	Dan Pike, Capital, Oct. 1	+ 29,060
Office Equipment	7,200	Dan Pike, Drawing	− 4,400
Automobile	23,600	Wages Expense	− 3,100
Professional Fees	+ 12,000	Rent Expense	− 1,400
Telephone Expense	− 350		

Required:

1. Prepare an income statement and statement of owner's equity for the month ending October 31, 200X.
2. Prepare a balance sheet in account form as of October 31, 200X.

PROBLEM 1A-6 ANALYZING CHANGES IN ACCOUNTING EQUATION

Carolyn Ball is an architect and owner of a business called Carolyn Ball Architect. As of March 1, 200X, Ball owned the following property related to her business: cash, $16,350; office equipment, $14,145; automobile, $36,200. At the same time, Ball owed business creditors $5,200.

The following transactions were completed by Ball during the month of March.

a. Paid $2,000 for office rent for March
b. Paid $3,600 on account
c. Paid cash for an office safe, $1,100
d. Bought office equipment on account, $1,700
e. Received $7,500 from clients for professional services
f. Paid utility bill, $550
g. Withdrew $3,800 for personal use

Assets			= Liabilities +		Owner's Equity			
Cash +	Office Equipment	+ Automobile =	Accounts Payable	+ Carolyn Ball, Capital	– Carolyn Ball, Drawing	+ Revenue	– Expenses
Bal. $16,350 +	$14,145	+ $36,200 =	$5,200	+ _____				
(a) _____	_____	_____	_____	_____	_____	_____	_____
Bal. _____	_____	_____	_____	_____	_____	_____	_____
(b) _____	_____	_____	_____	_____	_____	_____	_____
Bal. _____	_____	_____	_____	_____	_____	_____	_____

Required:

1. Calculate the beginning balance for capital and indicate the effect of each transaction on the accounting equation by using the form shown above. Each amount should be preceded by a plus sign if it represents an increase or by a minus sign if it represents a decrease. Calculate the balance in each account after each transaction has been entered to verify that the accounting equation is in balance.
2. Prepare an income statement and statement of owner's equity for March, and a balance sheet, in account form, as of March 31, 200X.

PROBLEM 1A-7 PREPARATION OF FINANCIAL STATEMENTS

Mary Sue Guild, owner of Guild Trades, hires an accountant, who determines the following account balances as of August 31, 200X:

Cash	$ 9,180	Accounts Payable	$13,200
Office Supplies	1,300	M.S. Guild, Capital, Aug. 1	36,590
Office Equipment	11,400	M.S. Guild, Drawing	6,400
Automobile	28,200	Wages Expense	5,300
Professional Fees	13,600	Rent Expense	1,200
Telephone Expense	410		

Required:

1. Prepare an income statement and statement of owner's equity for the month ending August 31, 200X.
2. Prepare a balance sheet in account form as of August 31, 200X.

The Double-Entry System of Accounting

Module 1B Objectives
Careful study of this module should enable you to:
1. Explain the double-entry system of accounting.
2. Enter selected business transactions in T accounts using debits and credits.
3. Explain the purpose of and prepare a trial balance.

In module 1A, we saw how business transactions cause a change in one or more of the three basic accounting elements. Every transaction affects at least two accounting elements. This forms the basis of double-entry accounting. Accuracy is improved because the accounting equation must balance after each transaction. Luca Pacioli, an Italian monk, introduced double-entry accounting back in 1494. The reason that double-entry accounting has been in existence for over 500 years is because it ensures accuracy. Today we have computer software programs like *Quick Books*® that appear to be single-entry (like your checkbook), but are actually written in a double-entry format.

THE ACCOUNT

The assets of a business may consist of a number of items, such as cash and office supplies. A form or record used to keep track of the increases and decreases in each item is known as an account. Accounts are used to maintain an orderly record of all transactions affecting that item. The following accounts with their account classification were used in the example of Dick Ady, Dentist:

Assets   **Liabilities**   **Owner's Equity**

Cash   Accounts Payable   Dick Ady, Capital
Office Supplies   Dick Ady, Drawing
Office Equipment

Revenue   **Expenses**

Professional Fees   Rent Expense
                        Telephone Expense

A T account is commonly used for instructional purposes. It consists of a two-line drawing resembling the capital letter T.

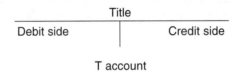

Title

Debit side	Credit side

T account

Debits and Credits

Learning the rules of debits and credits is similar to learning the rules on how to drive a car. You learn to drive your car on the right side of the road. As you learn debits and credits, remember there are established rules that everyone must follow.

To debit an account means to enter an amount on the left side of the account. To credit an account means to enter an amount on the right side of the account. The abbreviation for debit is Dr. and for credit Cr. (based on the Latin terms *debere* and *credere*). Sometimes the word *charge* is used as a substitute for debit. In entering transactions, the debits must always equal the credits.

The rules of debit and credit are based upon the location of the basic elements in the accounting equation. Since left means debit in accounting and assets are on the left side of the equation, increases in assets are entered on the left or debit side of an account. Decreases in assets are entered on the right or credit side. Liabilities and owner's equity are on the right side of the accounting equation. Increases are entered on the right or credit side of an account. Decreases in liabilities or owner's equity are entered on the left or debit side. By following these rules, the basic equality of assets to equities (Assets = Liabilities + Owner's Equity) will be maintained. These basic relationships are shown as follows:

Assets	=	Liabilities + Owner's Equity

All Asset Accounts		All Liability Accounts	
Debit to enter increases **(+)**	**Credit** to enter decreases **(–)**	**Debit** to enter decreases **(–)**	**Credit** to enter increases **(+)**

All Owner's Equity Accounts	
Debit to enter decreases **(–)**	**Credit** to enter increases **(+)**

"Drawing" Accounts		Revenue Accounts	
Debit to enter increases (+)	**Credit** to enter decreases (–)	**Debit** to enter decreases (–)	**Credit** to enter increases (+)

Expense Accounts	
Debit to enter increases (+)	**Credit** to enter decreases (–)

Total Debits   =   **Total Credits**

Use of Asset, Liability, and Owner's Equity Accounts

The next step in learning accounting is to combine the accounting equation with the rules of debit and credit. We will review the same transactions for Dick Ady, Dentist, using T accounts.

Transaction (a): Dick Ady started a business by investing $30,000 in cash.

Cash		Dick Ady, Capital	
(a) 30,000			(a) 30,000

Analysis. The asset Cash and Ady's equity in the business increased. Since Cash is an asset and assets are on the left side of the accounting equation, the Cash account was increased by a debit. Dick Ady, Capital, is on the right side of the equation and to show an increase in this account, Dick Ady, Capital, was credited for $30,000.

Transaction (b): Ady purchased office equipment (desk, chairs, file cabinet, etc.) for $2,500 on account.

Office Equipment		Accounts Payable	
(b) 2,500			(b) 2,500

Analysis. To show an increase in the asset account, Office Equipment, it was debited for $2,500. Since liabilities are on the right side of the equation, increases to liabilities are shown on the right or credit side of the account. To increase the liabilities of the business, Accounts Payable was credited for $2,500.

Transaction (c): Ady purchased office supplies (stationery, legal pads, pencils, etc.) for cash, $350.

Cash		Office Supplies	
(b) 30,000	(c) 350	(c) 350	

Analysis. One asset was increased while another asset was decreased. There is no change in total assets. Office Supplies was debited for the increase and Cash was credited for the decrease of $350. Office supplies are an asset at the time of purchase even through they will become an expense when used. The procedure used in accounting for supplies used will be discussed later.

Transaction (d): Ady paid $500 on account to the company from which the office equipment was purchased. (See Transaction (b).)

Cash		Accounts Payable	
(a) 30,000	(c) 350	(d) 500	(b) 2,500
	(d) 500		

Analysis. The liability Accounts Payable was decreased with a debit, and the asset Cash was decreased with a credit for $500.

Transaction (e): Purchased office supplies on account, $400.

Office Supplies		Accounts Payable	
(c) 350		(d) 500	(b) 2,500
(e) 400			(e) 400

Analysis. The asset Office Supplies was increased with a debit. The liability Accounts Payable was increased with a credit. Assets are on the left or debit side of the accounting equation, and increases to assets are shown on the debit side of the account. Likewise, liabilities are on the right or credit side of the equation, and increases to liabilities are shown on the right or credit side of the account.

Transaction (f): Ady withdrew $300 for personal use.

Cash		Dick Ady, Drawing	
(a) 30,000	(c) 350	(f) 300	
	(d) 500		
	(f) 300		

Analysis. To decrease the asset account, Cash was credited for $300. Remember, a separate account, Dick Ady, Drawing, is used to accumulate withdrawals by the owner. Therefore, to decrease owner's equity, the drawing account was debited.

Use of Revenue and Expense Accounts

Revenue and expense accounts are used to accumulate increases and decreases to owner's equity. By having a separate account for each type of revenue and expense, a clear record can be kept. Also, revenues and expenses can be kept separate from additional investments and withdrawals by the owner. The relationship of these accounts to owner's equity and the rules of debit and credit are indicated in the following diagram:

All Owner's Equity Accounts	
Debit to enter decreases (–)	**Credit** to enter increases (+)

All Expense Accounts		All Revenue Accounts	
Debit to enter increases (+)	**Credit** to enter decreases (–)	**Debit** to enter decreases (–)	**Credit** to enter increases (+)

To illustrate the effect that revenue and expense accounts have on the double-entry process, we will continue to analyze the transactions of Dick Ady, Dentist, using T accounts.

Transaction (g): **Received $3,500 in cash from a client for professional services rendered.**

Cash				Professional Fees	
(a) 30,000		(c) 350			(g) 3,500
		(d) 500			
		(f) 300			
(g) 3,500					

Analysis. This transaction increased the asset Cash, with an equal increase in owner's equity, because of revenue. The asset account Cash was debited and the revenue account Professional Fees was credited. Professional Fees is a temporary account that has the overall effect of increasing owner's equity.

Transaction (h): **Paid $1,000 for office rent for one month.**

Cash				Rent Expense	
(a) 30,000		(c) 350	(h) 1,000		
		(d) 500			
(g) 3,500		(f) 300			
		(h) 1,000			

Analysis. This transaction decreased the asset Cash, with an equal decrease in owner's equity because of expense. Rent Expense was debited and Cash was credited for $1,000. Rent Expense is a temporary account that has the overall effect of decreasing owner's equity.

Transaction (i): **Paid bill for telephone service, $75.**

Cash				Telephone Expense	
(a) 30,000		(c) 350	(i) 75		
		(d) 500			
(g) 3,500		(f) 300			
		(h) 1,000			
		(i) 75			

Analysis. This transaction is identical to the previous one. Telephone Expense was debited and Cash was credited for $75.

THE TRIAL BALANCE

A trial balance is a listing of all accounts showing the title and the ending balance. The trial balance will show if total debits equal total credits. To determine the ending balance, the debit and credit columns of the T account should be totaled. This procedure, called footing the amount columns, is illustrated below.

Cash

(a)	30,000	(c)		350
(g)	3,500	(d)		500
		(f)		300
		(h)	1,000
	33,500	(i)		75
	31,275			*2,225*

Once the columns are totaled, the balance is determined by finding the difference between the footings. This balance should be entered on the side of the account that has the larger total. The footings and balances of accounts should be entered in small figures just below the last entry, preferably in pencil. If there is only one item entered in a column, no footing is necessary.

The normal balance of any account will be on the increase side. Since asset and expense accounts are debited for increases, these accounts normally have debit balances. Because liability, owner's equity, and revenue accounts are credited for increases, these accounts have normal credit balances.

The accounts of Dick Ady, Dentist, are reproduced below and on the next page. The footings and the balances are printed in italics.

Assets			=	Liabilities		+	Owner's Equity	
Cash				**Accounts Payable**			**Dick Ady, Capital**	
(a) 30,000	(c)	350	(d) 500	(b) 2,500			(a) 30,000
(g) 3,500	(d)	500		(e) 400			
	(f)	300		*2,400*			
	(h)	1,000					
33,500	(i)	75					
31,275	*2,225*						

Office Supplies		Dick Ady, Drawing	
(c)	350	(f)	300
(e)	400		
	750		

Office Equipment		Professional Fees	
(b)	2,500	(g)	3,500

Rent Expense	
(h)	1,000

Telephone Expense	
(i)	75

The trial balance of Dick Ady's accounts is shown below. The trial balance was taken on January 31, 200X. This date is shown on the third line of the heading.

Exhibit 1.2
Trial Balance

	Dick Ady, Dentist Trial Balance January 31, 200X				
Account		**Debit**		**Credit**	
Cash		31 2 7 5 00			
Office Supplies		7 5 0 00			
Office Equipment		2 5 0 0 00			
Accounts Payable				2 4 0 0 00	
Dick Ady, Capital				30 0 0 0 00	
Dick Ady, Drawing		3 0 0 00			
Professional Fees				3 5 0 0 00	
Rent Expense		1 0 0 0 00			
Telephone Expense		7 5 00			
		35 9 0 0 00		35 9 0 0 00	

A trial balance is not a formal statement or report. It is rarely seen by anyone other than the accountant. The three financial statements prepared for Dick Ady, Dentist, can be prepared from this trial balance.

Concept Questions

1. Double-entry accounting means that every transaction must affect at least two _____.
2. Are Assets, Expenses, and Drawing increased with a debit or a credit?
3. Are Liabilities, Owner's Equity, and Revenue increased with a debit or a credit?
4. Analyze the following transactions using T accounts:
   a. Purchased office supplies on account, $300.
   b. Paid rent expense, $800.
5. To determine if total debits are equal to total credits, a _____ is prepared.

If you cannot answer the above concept questions, go back and review the module material.

MODULE SUMMARY

A debit increases asset accounts, expense accounts, and the owner's drawing account. A credit increases liability accounts, owner's equity, and revenue accounts. Every transaction affects at least two accounts. This forms the basis of double-entry accounting. A T account has a left side or debit side, and a right side or credit side. The normal balance of a T account is on the increase or plus side of the account. A trial balance shows the ending balance for assets, liabilities, owner's equity, revenue and expense accounts. The left-side column lists the debit balances and the right-side column lists the credit balances. Total debits must equal total credits.

Key Terms

double-entry accounting, *19*   trial balance, *25*

Exercises

EXERCISE 1B-8

Complete the following chart concerning increases and decreases in the accounting elements.

	Recorded on Debit Side	Recorded on Credit Side
a. Increase in cash account	✓	
b. Decrease in accounts payable account	✓	
c. Increase in owner's capital account		✓
d. Increase in owner's drawing account	✓	
e. Increase in expense account	✓	
f. Increase in revenue account		✓
g. Increase in accounts payable account		✓

EXERCISE 1B-9

The expanded accounting equation is:

Assets = Liabilities + Owner's Equity + Revenue − Expense

Required: Set up T accounts under each account classification. Place debit on the left side and credit on the right side of each T account. Under the debit and credit sides, indicate with a plus or minus how each account is increased or decreased.

EXERCISE 1B-10

Required: Prepare a trial balance for LaVonna Tomberlin's Flowers as of October 31, 200X, using the accounts listed below. You will need to calculate the balance in the capital account.

Cash	$ 7,125
Supplies	800
Nursery Equipment	9,120
Delivery Truck	29,800
Accounts Payable	15,100
L. Tomberlin, Capital	32,570?
L. Tomberlin, Drawing	6,000
Income from Services	12,500
Wages Expense	4,600
Rent Expense	1,800
Utilities Expense	925

Problems

PROBLEM 1B-11 T ACCOUNTS AND TRIAL BALANCE   9/7/99

Carl Brown decided to establish an advertising agency to be known as Brownie's Advertising. Brown's business transactions for the first month of operations ending June 30, 200X, were as follows:

   a. Brown invested $40,000 cash in the business
   b. Paid office rent for one month, $1,600

c. Purchased office equipment on account, $11,700
d. Paid cash for office supplies, $700
e. Paid telephone bill, $425
f. Received $5,120 for advertising fees earned
g. Paid $4,000 on account
h. Received $3,200 for advertising fees earned
i. Paid $2,200 wages to office secretary
j. Withdrew $5,000 for personal use

Required:

1. Open T accounts using the following account titles: Cash; Office Supplies; Office Equipment; Accounts Payable; Carl Brown, Capital; Carl Brown, Drawing; Advertising Fees; Rent Expense; Telephone Expense; and Wages Expense.
2. Enter the above transactions in the accounts.
3. Foot the accounts and enter the ending balance on the plus side or larger side.
4. Prepare a trial balance as of June 30, 200X.

PROBLEM 1B-12 TRIAL BALANCE

LaDonna Linscott is new to the job of bookkeeper and has prepared an incorrect trial balance for UpTown Coffee Shop shown below:

permanent accounts {

temporary accounts {

December 31, 200X UpTown Coffee Shop Trial Balance		
Cash		6 2 0 0 00
Office Equipment	18 6 0 0 00	
Accounts Payable	4 1 0 0 00	
Dick Weber, Capital	22 2 5 0 00	
Dick Weber, Drawing		5 0 0 0 00
Income from Services		12 0 0 0 00
Wages Expense	6 0 0 0 00	
Rent Expense	1 8 0 0 00	
Utilities Expense	7 5 0 00	
	53 5 0 0 00	23 2 0 0 00

Required: Prepare a corrected trial balance. All of the accounts have normal balances.

PROBLEM 1B-13 T ACCOUNTS AND TRIAL BALANCE

Michael Eary decided to establish a travel agency to be known as Very Eerie Travels. Eary's business transactions for the first month of operations ending January 31, 200X, were as follows:

a. Eary invested $40,000 cash in the business
b. Paid office rent for one month, $1,700
c. Purchased office equipment on account, $13,400
d. Paid cash for office supplies, $725
e. Paid telephone bill, $445
f. Received $4,700 for services rendered
g. Paid $5,000 on account
h. Received $3,800 for services rendered
i. Paid $1,500 wages to office secretary
j. Withdrew $2,000 for personal use

Required:

1. Open T accounts using the following account titles: Cash; Office Supplies; Office Equipment; Accounts Payable; Michael Eary, Capital; Michael Eary, Drawing; Advertising Fees; Rent Expense; Telephone Expense; and Wages Expense.
2. Enter the above transactions in the accounts.
3. Foot the accounts and enter the ending balance on the plus side or larger side.
4. Prepare a trial balance as of January 31, 200X.

PROBLEM 1B-14 TRIAL BALANCE

Linda Nickerson is new to the job of bookkeeper and has prepared an incorrect trial balance for Tim's Golf Shop shown below:

Trial Balance Tim's Golf Shop August 31, 200X		
Cash	9 1 0 0 00	
Office Equipment		13 6 2 5 00
Accounts Payable		4 2 9 0 00
Tim Harrison, Capital	22 1 3 5 00	
Tim Harrison, Drawing		7 0 0 0 00
Income from Services	9 1 0 0 00	
Wages Expense		4 0 0 0 00
Rent Expense		1 2 0 0 00
Utilities Expense		6 0 0 00
	40 3 3 5 00	30 7 1 5 00

Required: Prepare a corrected trial balance. All of the accounts have normal balances.

Challenge Problem

Michael Conner decided to establish a consulting firm to be known as Mind Research Institute. Conner's business transactions for the first month of operations ending September 30, 200X, were as follows:

a. Conner invested $50,000 cash in the business
b. Paid office rent for one month, $1,400
c. Purchased office equipment on account, $5,500
d. Paid cash for office supplies, $400
e. Paid telephone bill, $260
f. Received $8,900 from cash customers for professional fees earned
g. Received bill for advertising in Journal of Clinical and Consulting Psychology, $700
h. Paid $1,400 on account
i. Paid $1,500 wages to office secretary
j. Paid cash for a new laser printer, $1,425
k. Withdrew $3,000 for personal use

Required:

1. Open T accounts using the following account titles: Cash; Office Supplies; Office Equipment; Accounts Payable; Michael Conner, Capital; Michael Conner, Drawing; Professional Fees; Rent Expense; Telephone Expense; Advertising Expense; and Wages Expense.
2. Enter the above transactions in the T accounts.
3. Foot the accounts and enter the ending balance on the plus side, or larger side, of each account.
4. Prepare a trial balance as of September 30, 200X.
5. Prepare an income statement for the month of September, 200X.
6. Prepare a statement of owner's equity for the month of September, 200X.
7. Prepare a balance sheet as of September 30, 200X.

Chapter TWO

Accounting Procedure

The following modules will be covered in this chapter:

Module 2A
Journalizing and Posting
Journalizing and posting, using the general journal and general ledger accounts, and based on the basic accounting cycle and the chart of accounts.

Module 2B
Trial Balance and Financial Statements
Preparing a trial balance and the financial statements: the income statement, the statement of owner's equity, and the balance sheet.

Journalizing and Posting

Module 2A Objectives
Careful study of this module should enable you to:
1. Explain the basic accounting cycle, the purpose of the general journal, and the chart of accounts, including its numbering system.
2. Journalize transactions in a two-column general journal.
3. Post transactions to general ledger accounts.

In Chapter 1, we introduced the accounting process. Accounting is the process of analyzing, recording, classifying, summarizing, reporting, and interpreting information. Financial data enters the accounting process in the form of transactions (financial events). As transactions are analyzed, we determine which accounts increase and/or decrease. Each transaction begins with a source document—a piece of paper or source of information that contains data that affects the business—such as a receipt, invoice, sales ticket, or cash register tape. Careful study of each source document will determine which accounts are affected. For example, a cash receipt for money spent tells you that some account, perhaps an asset, has increased, while the Cash account has decreased.

This module traces the flow of information from source documents through the accounting system. A general journal is used to record the accounts affected and the dollar amounts of the transactions. The general journal is then posted to the general ledger accounts, which are shown on the chart of accounts. In this chapter, we will illustrate a general service business where we will include accounts receivable transactions.

THE ACCOUNTING CYCLE

The accounting cycle begins with analysis of source documents. When a source document is received, it is examined to determine how it affects the business's financial position. In other words, does an asset increase or decrease? Does a liability increase or decrease? Does owner's equity increase or decrease? After each transaction, the accounting equation must still be in balance (assets equal liabilities plus owner's equity).

2 The second step in the accounting cycle is **journalizing.** First the debit and then the credit of each transaction is recorded in the general journal or **journal** by date and in chronological order. In addition, a brief explanation of the transaction is given. For example, an asset (Cash) account may increase while a liability account (Notes Payable) increases, indicating that money is borrowed and the business will repay it. Notes payable is different from accounts payable in that it usually is for a fixed time period (such as six months), and interest charges will be added.

After journalizing, transactions are posted to the general ledger accounts (such as Cash, Office Supplies, and Accounts Payable). **Posting** is the process of entering the journal amounts into the appropriate general ledger accounts. At the end of the month, each account's ending balance is used to prepare the financial statements that reveal how the business did for the month (profit or loss) and its new financial position.

The Chart of Accounts

Prior to journalizing, the bookkeeper must know which account to use, or which account to debit and which to credit. One of the first things a new business does is to determine what accounts it will use in its day-to-day operations. A separate account is kept for each type of asset and each type of liability, along with the owner's equity accounts. These three types of accounts are called **permanent accounts** because they will have ongoing balances from one accounting period to the next.

In addition to the permanent accounts, there are three types of temporary accounts: (1) revenue, (2) expense, and (3) drawing. These **temporary accounts** are used to match this month's revenues with this month's expenses. These accounts prevent numerous entries to the owner's equity account. At the end of the accounting period, revenues and expenses are totaled. The difference between these two totals becomes either an increase or a decrease to owner's equity. When revenues exceed expenses, it's called net income; when expenses exceed revenues, it's a net loss. Likewise, the drawing account is totaled and subtracted from the total owner's equity. Each of these temporary accounts is, in effect, closed at the end of each accounting cycle (month or year), and reopened at the beginning of the next month or year (with a beginning balance of zero).

The chart of accounts is a list of all accounts used by a business. It is common practice to assign a number to each account and to keep the accounts in numerical order. This numbering system follows a consistent pattern. Typically, asset accounts are 100s, liabilities are 200s, owner's equity accounts are 300s, revenue accounts are 400s, and expense accounts are 500s. A chart of accounts for Ann's Delivery Service Company, a general delivery service, is shown in Exhibit 2.1. (In her business, Ann performs delivery services and bills some customers at the end of the month; therefore, she will have an account called "Accounts Receivable" for accounts billed but not yet collected.)

Exhibit 2.1
Chart of Accounts

Ann's Delivery Service Company
Chart of Accounts

Assets:	**Revenue:**
111 Cash	411 Delivery Fees
121 Accounts Receivable	
131 Office Supplies	**Expenses:**
141 Office Equipment	511 Rent Expense
151 Delivery Truck	521 Salary Expense
Liabilities	525 Utilities Expense
211 Accounts Payable	531 Telephone Expense
221 Notes Payable	533 Advertising Expense
	555 Entertainment Expense
Owners Equity:	560 Truck Expense
311 Ann Moe, Capital	599 Miscellaneous Expense
312 Ann Moe, Drawing	

Some accountants prefer to assign numbers to accounts in alphabetical order, although this procedure is not a requirement of good accounting practice. In expense accounts, the preferred sequence is to assign numbers in order of anticipated dollar amounts. Therefore, the account expected to have the largest amount (Rent Expense) is assigned the first number, and other accounts follow in descending order. Miscellaneous Expense is generally assigned as the last number, even though it may not always be the smallest amount.

The General Journal

The general journal is called a **book of original entry** because it is where the first accounting record of a transaction is made from a source document. The two-column general journal, illustrated in Exhibit 2.2, is the most simple form of journal used in business. General journal pages are numbered consecutively.

Exhibit 2.2
Standard Two-Column General Journal

	Date	Description	Post. Ref.	Debit	Credit	
1						1
2						2
3	**1**	**2**	**3**	**4**	**5**	3
4						4
5						5

General Journal   Page

1. The date column. The year is written once at the first line, together with the month and day. After the first entry, only the day is written until the beginning of the next month's entries.
2. Accounts that are affected by each transaction are written in the description column. A separate line is used for each account title (such as Cash and Accounts Payable). This column may also include a brief reason for the journal entry.
3. The posting reference column (Post. Ref.). This column provides a cross-reference between the journal and the general ledger accounts. Entries in this column are made when journal entries are posted to the ledger accounts.
4. The debit column. The amount being debited to an account is listed in this column.
5. The credit column. The amount being credited to an account is listed in this column.

Some businesses may prefer to use a journal with an additional column between the description column and the posting reference column. This additional column is often titled "Doc. No." (document number) and is used to record the numbers of checks or receipts issued in making transactions. This column provides a simple means of tracing transactions back to their original records (source documents).

Journalizing Transactions

Journalizing begins when a transaction occurs. For each transaction, the entry includes the date, the titles of the accounts affected, the amounts, and a brief description.

For example, assume that on January 1, the owner of Ann's Delivery Service Company, Ann Moe, invested $25,000 cash to get the business started. The general journal entry would look like this:

		General Journal			Page *1*	
	Date	Description	Post. Ref.	Debit	Credit	
1	200X					1
2	Jan. 1	Cash		25 0 0 0 00		2
3		Ann Moe, Capital			25 0 0 0 00	3
4		Initial investment				4
5						5

These four steps are followed in journalizing:

1. The date is entered with the year written above the month. The year is entered only at the top of every journal page.
2. The debit entry is recorded. The title of the account being debited is entered next to the vertical line, in the description column. The debit amount is written in the debit column.
3. The credit entry is recorded. The title of the account being credited is entered (indented one-half inch to the right of the vertical line) below the debited account title. Indenting allows the user to clearly distinguish between accounts being debited and accounts being credited. The credit amount is written in the credit column.
4. A brief explanation may be entered (indented one inch to the right of the vertical line). The explanation should be short, but should clearly indicate the purpose of the journal entry.

As a result of this journal entry, the asset account Cash is increased by $25,000 and the owner's equity account is increased by $25,000. The accounting equation is in balance.

To illustrate the journalizing process, we will enter some transactions similar to those shown in Chapter 1 into the general journal.

On January 3, the business purchased office equipment on account for $1,500. The journal entry shows the day of the transaction (month and year were previously entered), followed by the account being debited and its amount, the account being credited and its amount, and finally, a brief explanation:

6		3	Office Equipment		1 5 0 0 00		6
7			Accounts Payable			1 5 0 0 00	7
8			Purchased equipment on				8
9			account				9
10							10

Analysis. Office Equipment (an asset) is increased, so it is debited for $1,500. Accounts Payable (a liability) is increased, and it is credited. The explanation is brief and clear.

On January 5, office supplies are purchased for $450 cash.

11		5	Office Supplies		4 5 0 00		11
12			Cash			4 5 0 00	12
13			Purchased supplies				13
14							14

Analysis. Office Supplies (an asset) is increased, so it is debited for $450. Cash (also an asset) is decreased, so it is credited.

On January 10, the company paid $700 toward what was owed on a previous obligation (the office equipment purchased January 3):

15		10	Accounts Payable		7 0 0 00		15
16			Cash			7 0 0 00	16
17			Paid on account				17
18							18

Analysis. Accounts Payable (a liability) is decreased, so it is debited for $700; Cash (an asset) is decreased, so it is credited.

On January 12, delivery services were performed which resulted in delivery fees for $500, which will be paid in two weeks.

19		12	Accounts Receivable		5 0 0 00		19
20			Delivery Fees			5 0 0 00	20
21			Services performed on account				21
22							22

Analysis. Accounts Receivable (an asset) is increased, so it is debited for $500; Delivery Fees (a revenue account) is increased because it is earned, so it is credited. Note that Cash will be debited when the actual money is received; however, we will recognize that the revenue is earned now.

On January 15, the business borrows $4,000 at the bank, giving a 30-day note:

23		15	Cash		4 0 0 0 00			23
24			Notes Payable			4 0 0 0 00		24
25			30-day, 13% note from bank					25
26								26

Analysis. Cash (an asset) is increased by the cash borrowed, so it is debited for $4,000; Notes Payable (a liability) is increased since the money must be repaid, so it is credited.

On January 17, the owner withdrew $200 cash for personal use.

27		17	Ann Moe, Drawing		2 0 0 00			27
28			Cash			2 0 0 00		28
29			Withdrawal for personal use					29
30								30

Analysis. The drawing account is increased, so it is debited for $200; Cash (an asset) is decreased, so it is credited. Note that as the drawing account increases, owner's equity decreases.

On January 20, delivery services are rendered for $2,500 cash.

31		20	Cash		2 5 0 0 00			31
32			Delivery Fees			2 5 0 0 00		32
33			Services rendered for cash					33
34								34

Analysis. Cash (an asset) increases, so it is debited for the amount received; the revenue account also increases, so it is credited.

On January 22, the business received $500 cash for services previously performed on account on January 12, when Accounts Receivable was debited and the revenue account was credited.

35		22	Cash		5 0 0 00			35
36			Accounts Receivable			5 0 0 00		36
37			Received payment on account					37
38								38

40

Chapter Two   Accounting Procedure

Analysis. Cash (an asset) increases, so it is debited for the amount of cash received. Accounts Receivable (an asset) is credited because it decreases. Revenue is not affected because it was recorded on January 12 when it was earned.

On January 25, the office rent of $1,000 is paid from cash.

	Date		Description	Post. Ref.	Debit	Credit	
1	200X						1
2	Jan.	25	Rent Expense		1 0 0 0 00		2
3			Cash			1 0 0 0 00	3
4			Paid monthly rent				4
5							5

General Journal — Page 2

Analysis. Rent Expense (temporary owner's equity account) is increased, so it is debited for $1,000; Cash (an asset) is decreased, so it is credited. Remember that as expenses increase, owner's equity decreases and thus the accounting equation is still in balance.

On January 28, the telephone bill of $75 is paid from cash.

			Description		Debit	Credit	
6		28	Telephone Expense		7 5 00		6
7			Cash			7 5 00	7
8			Paid telephone bill				8
9							9

Analysis. Telephone Expense (an expense account) is increased, so it is debited for $75; Cash (an asset) is decreased, so it is credited.

These entries appear consecutively in the general journal, as shown in Exhibit 2.3. You will know that the accounting equation remains in balance because for each debit there is an equal credit. It may be helpful to total the debit and credit columns of the general journal and place small pencil footings at the bottom of each column. This process is called *proving the journal,* and is another way to check that debits equal credits.

Exhibit 2.3
General Journal Entries

	Date		Description	Post. Ref.	Debit						Credit						
1	200X																1
2	Jan.	1	Cash		25	0	0	0	00								2
3			Ann Moe, Capital								25	0	0	0	00		3
4			Initial investment														4
5																	5
6		3	Office Equipment		1	5	0	0	00								6
7			Accounts Payable								1	5	0	0	00		7
8			Purchased equipment on														8
9			account														9
10																	10
11		5	Office Supplies			4	5	0	00								11
12			Cash									4	5	0	00		12
13			Purchased supplies														13
14																	14
15		10	Accounts Payable			7	0	0	00								15
16			Cash									7	0	0	00		16
17			Paid on account														17
18																	18
19		12	Accounts Receivable			5	0	0	00								19
20			Delivery Fees									5	0	0	00		20
21			Services performed on account														21
22																	22
23		15	Cash		4	0	0	0	00								23
24			Notes Payable								4	0	0	0	00		24
25			30-day, 13% note from bank														25
26																	26
27		17	Ann Moe, Drawing			2	0	0	00								27
28			Cash									2	0	0	00		28
29			Withdrawal for personal use														29
30																	30
31		20	Cash		2	5	0	0	00								31
32			Delivery Fees								2	5	0	0	00		32
33			Services rendered for cash														33
34																	34
35		22	Cash			5	0	0	00								35
36			Accounts Receivable									5	0	0	00		36
37			Received payment on account														37
38																	38

General Journal — Page 1

	Date		Description	Post. Ref.	Debit	Credit	
1	200X						1
2	Jan.	25	Rent Expense		1 0 0 0 00		2
3			Cash			1 0 0 0 00	3
4			Paid monthly rent				4
5							5
6		28	Telephone Expense		7 5 00		6
7			Cash			7 5 00	7
8			Paid telephone bill				8
9							9

General Journal *Page 2*

Posting to the Ledger

All amounts in the general journal are posted to the general ledger accounts so that balances may be kept during the month. The general ledger, or **ledger**, is a book of accounts that contains a separate account for each account listed in the chart of accounts. Such posting is done daily, weekly, or at regular intervals. Only when posting is up-to-date will information in the general ledger be accurate.

Posting from the journal to the ledger accounts involves four steps:

1. Enter the *date* of each transaction in the account.
2. Enter the *amount* of each transaction in the account.
3. Enter the *journal page* in the posting reference column of the account.
4. Enter the *account number* in the posting reference column of the journal.

Steps 3 and 4 provide a line between the journal and the ledger known as a **cross-reference**. By checking the ledger account, you can see where the entry was posted from. By checking the journal, you can see which account received the posting.

In Exhibit 2.4, we've posted the first journal entry for Ann Moe where she invested $25,000 in the business to get it started. Step 1 shows transfer of the date; Step 2 shows posting of the debit amount; Step 3 shows posting of the journal page number of the account, and Step 4 shows posting of the account page number to the general journal. This same process is repeated for the credit to the capital account.

Exhibit 2.4

Posting to the General Ledger

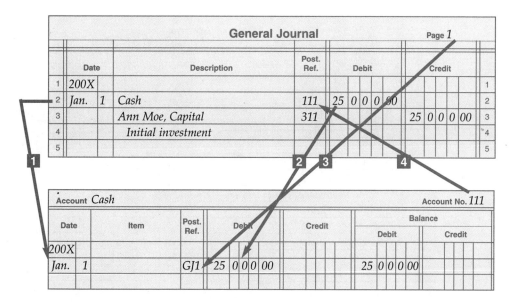

The account you see is called a four-column account. It is different from the T account, but it accomplishes the same purpose. In the T account, you added the left side (debits) and then the right side (credits) to see which was larger. Then you subtracted the smaller from the larger, and the balance remaining was on the side with the larger amount. In the four-column account, you first enter the amount and then compute a new balance. After each entry is posted, the new account balance is computed.

When all of the journal entries are posted, the posting reference column will contain the general ledger account numbers, as shown in Exhibit 2.5.

Exhibit 2.5

The General Journal After Posting

	Date		Description	Post. Ref.	Debit	Credit	
1	200X						1
2	Jan.	1	Cash	111	25 0 0 0 00		2
3			Ann Moe, Capital	311		25 0 0 0 00	3
4			Initial investment				4
5							5
6		3	Office Equipment	141	1 5 0 0 00		6
7			Accounts Payable	211		1 5 0 0 00	7
8			Purchased equipment on				8
9			account				9
10							10
11		5	Office Supplies	131	4 5 0 00		11
12			Cash	111		4 5 0 00	12
13			Purchased supplies				13
14							14
15		10	Accounts Payable	211	7 0 0 00		15
16			Cash	111		7 0 0 00	16
17			Paid on account				17
18							18
19		12	Accounts Receivable	121	5 0 0 00		19
20			Delivery Fees	411		5 0 0 00	20
21			Services performed on account				21
22							22
23		15	Cash	111	4 0 0 0 00		23
24			Notes Payable	221		4 0 0 0 00	24
25			30-day, 13% note from bank				25
26							26
27		17	Ann Moe, Drawing	312	2 0 0 00		27
28			Cash	111		2 0 0 00	28
29			Withdrawal for personal use				29
30							30
31		20	Cash	111	2 5 0 0 00		31
32			Delivery Fees	411		2 5 0 0 00	32
33			Services rendered for cash				33
34							34
35		22	Cash	111	5 0 0 00		35
36			Accounts Receivable	121		5 0 0 00	36
37			Received payment on account				37
38							38

General Journal — Page 1

	Date		Description	Post. Ref.	Debit	Credit	
General Journal						**Page 2**	
1	200X						1
2	Jan.	25	Rent Expense	511	1 0 0 0 00		2
3			Cash	111		1 0 0 0 00	3
4			*Paid monthly rent*				4
5							5
6		28	Telephone Expense	531	7 5 00		6
7			Cash	111		7 5 00	7
8			*Paid telephone bill*				8
9							9

Likewise, the general ledger accounts will reflect new balances as a result of the postings. The posting reference column in each account will show page 1 (or page 2) of the general journal. The general ledger accounts after posting are shown as Exhibit 2.6.

Exhibit 2.6
General Ledger Accounts After Posting

Date		Item	Post. Ref.	Debit	Credit	Balance Debit	Balance Credit
Account *Cash*						**Account No.** *111*	
200X							
Jan.	1		GJ1	25 0 0 0 00		25 0 0 0 00	
	5		GJ1		4 5 0 00	24 5 5 0 00	
	10		GJ1		7 0 0 00	23 8 5 0 00	
	15		GJ1	4 0 0 0 00		27 8 5 0 00	
	17		GJ1		2 0 0 00	27 6 5 0 00	
	20		GJ1	2 5 0 0 00		30 1 5 0 00	
	22		GJ1	5 0 0 00		30 6 5 0 00	
	25		GJ2		1 0 0 0 00	29 6 5 0 00	
	28		GJ2		7 5 00	29 5 7 5 00	

Account *Accounts Receivable*							Account No. *121*
Date	Item	Post. Ref.	Debit	Credit	Balance		
					Debit	Credit	
200X							
Jan. 12		GJ1	5 0 0 00		5 0 0 00		
22		GJ1		5 0 0 00	– 0 –		

Account *Office Supplies*							Account No. *131*
Date	Item	Post. Ref.	Debit	Credit	Balance		
					Debit	Credit	
200X							
Jan. 5		GJ1	4 5 0 00		4 5 0 00		

Account *Office Equipment*							Account No. *141*
Date	Item	Post. Ref.	Debit	Credit	Balance		
					Debit	Credit	
200X							
Jan. 3		GJ1	1 5 0 0 00		1 5 0 0 00		

Account *Accounts Payable*							Account No. *211*
Date	Item	Post. Ref.	Debit	Credit	Balance		
					Debit	Credit	
200X							
Jan. 3		GJ1		1 5 0 0 00		1 5 0 0 00	
10		GJ1	7 0 0 00			8 0 0 00	

Account *Notes Payable*							Account No. *221*
Date	Item	Post. Ref.	Debit	Credit	Balance		
					Debit	Credit	
200X							
Jan. 15		GJ1		4 0 0 0 00		4 0 0 0 00	

Account	Ann Moe, Capital					Account No. 311	
Date	Item	Post. Ref.	Debit	Credit	Balance		
					Debit	Credit	
200X							
Jan. 1		GJ1		25 000 00		25 000 00	

Account	Ann Moe, Drawing					Account No. 312	
Date	Item	Post. Ref.	Debit	Credit	Balance		
					Debit	Credit	
200X							
Jan. 17		GJ1	200 00		200 00		

Account	Delivery Fees					Account No. 411	
Date	Item	Post. Ref.	Debit	Credit	Balance		
					Debit	Credit	
200X							
Jan. 12		GJ1		500 00		500 00	
20		GJ1		2 500 00		3 000 00	

Account	Rent Expense					Account No. 511	
Date	Item	Post. Ref.	Debit	Credit	Balance		
					Debit	Credit	
200X							
Jan. 25		GJ2	1 000 00		1 000 00		

Account	Telephone Expense					Account No. 531	
Date	Item	Post. Ref.	Debit	Credit	Balance		
					Debit	Credit	
200X							
Jan. 28		GJ2	75 00		75 00		

When the posting is complete, the bookkeeper can prepare the trial balance and the financial statements.

Concept Questions

1. What is a source document? Can you give several examples?
2. What is meant by the accounting cycle?
3. Why is the general journal called a book of original entry?
4. What is the purpose of the chart of accounts?
5. What are permanent accounts? Can you list them?
6. What are temporary accounts? Can you list them?
7. Explain how to journalize a transaction (the four steps).
8. Explain how to post from the general journal to the general ledger accounts (the four steps).

If you cannot answer the above concept questions, go back and review the module material before continuing to the next module.

MODULE SUMMARY

In Chapter 1 we analyzed information to determine what accounts would go up or down, and whether those accounts would be debited or credited. In this module, we journalized those transactions. Journalizing is the process of entering transactions into a book of original entry. Each transaction is journalized when appropriate account names are written in the journal, together with amounts being debited and credited. In the general journal, a brief description of each transaction is also required.

The chart of accounts contains a listing of all accounts and their account numbers, consecutively. Assets are usually 100 numbers; liabilities are 200 numbers; owner's equity accounts are 300 numbers; revenues are 400 numbers; and expenses are 500 numbers. Asset, liability, and owner's equity accounts are permanent accounts, while revenue, expense, and drawing accounts are temporary because they start over each month or each year.

Posting is the process of transferring journal entries to the general ledger accounts so that balances can be kept. This is a system of cross-referencing—a vital link between the journal and the ledger accounts.

Module 2A

Key Terms

book of original entry, *36*

chart of accounts, *35*

cross-reference, *42*

journalizing, *34*

ledger, *42*

permanent accounts, *34*

posting, *34*

source document, *33*

temporary accounts, *34*

Module 2A

Exercises

EXERCISE 2A-1

Assign account numbers to the following chart of accounts. While actual numbers may vary, you should be certain you are using the right series of numbers (i.e., 100s, 200s, and so on).

Excel Appliance Repair Company
Chart of Accounts

Assets:

111 Cash

121 Accounts Receivable

131 Office Supplies

141 Equipment

Liabilities:

211 Accounts Payable

221 Notes Payable

Owner's Equity:

311 Jim Mason, Capital

321 Jim Mason, Drawing

Revenue:

411 Repair Fees

Expenses:

511 Salary Expense

521 Rent Expense

531 Telephone Expense

541 Travel Expense

551 Advertising Expense

561 Utilities Expense

571 Miscellaneous Expense

EXERCISE 2A-2

Journalize the following transactions for the month of May, 200X, using a general journal, beginning on Page 4. Use the chart of accounts for Excel Appliance Repair Company for account titles.

May

1 Purchased office supplies on account, $500

5 Borrowed $5,000, giving a 90-day, 10% note

9 Performed services for $200, which will be paid later

10 Owner withdrew $500 cash for personal use

11 Paid the rent, $1,000

13 Paid the telephone bill, $75

19   Received $200 for services previously rendered on May 9 ✓
24   Received $1,500 cash for repair services rendered ✓
29   Paid $100 to a creditor on account (amount previously owed) ✓

EXERCISE 2A-3   Homework 9/14/99

Post these transactions, shown in general journal format, to the general ledger.

	Date	Description	Post. Ref.	Debit	Credit	
		General Journal			Page 9	
1	200X					1
2	May 1	Cash	111	15 0 0 0 00		2
3		M. Smith, Capital	311		15 0 0 0 00	3
4		Owner makes investment				4
5						5
6	5	Rent Expense	511	1 0 0 0 00		6
7		Cash	111		1 0 0 0 00	7
8		Paid monthly rent				8
9						9
10	7	M. Smith, Drawing	312	5 0 0 00		10
11		Cash	111		5 0 0 00	11
12		Withdrawal for personal use				12
13						13
14	10	Cash	111	2 0 0 0 00		14
15		Service Revenue	411		2 0 0 0 00	15
16		Services performed for cash				16
17						17
18	12	Office Supplies	121	8 0 0 00		18
19		Accounts Payable	211		8 0 0 00	19
20		Supplies bought on account				20
21						21
22	14	Telephone Expense	521	7 5 00		22
23		Cash	111		7 5 00	23
24		Paid telephone bill				24
25						25
26	20	Cash	111	5 0 0 0 00		26
27		Notes Payable	221		5 0 0 0 00	27
28		90-day, 8% note				28
29						29
30	25	Accounts Payable	211	5 0 0 00		30
31		Cash	111		5 0 0 00	31
32		Paid on account				32

Problems

PROBLEM 2A-4 CHART OF ACCOUNTS

Richard Miller is setting up a delivery business, and he will need the following accounts: Rent Expense; Telephone Expense; Utilities Expense; Gas and Oil Expense; Advertising Expense; Miscellaneous Expense; Delivery Fees (Revenue); Richard Miller, Capital; Richard Miller, Drawing; Accounts Payable; Accounts Receivable; Notes Payable; Cash; Office Supplies; Delivery Supplies; and Delivery Equipment.

Required: Prepare a chart of accounts for Richard Miller Delivery Company, assigning appropriate account numbers to the account titles.

PROBLEM 2A-5 JOURNALIZING AND POSTING TRANSACTIONS

Patricia Cagney set up her cleaning and maintenance service on July 1, 200X, by depositing $25,000 cash in the business checking account. Her first month's transactions are as follows:

July

- 1 Transferred $25,000 cash to the business
- 2 Paid the office rent, $1,500
- 3 Purchased cleaning equipment, $12,000, on account
- 5 Paid the first month's telephone bill of $100
- 6 Received cash of $2,000 for the first week's cleaning services
- 7 Paid utility bill, $90
- 10 Performed cleaning services of $500 on account (will be paid later)
- 11 Withdrew $500 cash for personal use
- 12 Received cash of $2,200 for the second week's cleaning services
- 16 Borrowed $10,000, giving a 6-month, 10% note
- 20 Received cash of $1,800 for the third week's cleaning services
- 21 Received $500 cash for cleaning services previously rendered
- 22 Paid $500 on account for equipment previously purchased
- 26 Paid $35 to local charity (Miscellaneous Expense)
- 28 Received cash of $1,950 for fourth week's cleaning services

Required:

1. Prepare general journal entries to record Ms. Cagney's transactions.
2. Post the journal entries to the general ledger accounts.

PROBLEM 2A-6 CHART OF ACCOUNTS

Ann Mitchell is setting up an accounting business, and she will need the following accounts: Rent Expense; Telephone Expense; Utilities Expense; Transportation Expense; Advertising Expense; Miscellaneous Expense; Bookkeeping Fees (Revenue); Consultation Fees (Revenue); Ann Mitchell,

Capital; Ann Mitchell, Drawing; Accounts Receivable; Accounts Payable; Notes Payable; Cash; Office Supplies; and Office Equipment.

Required: Prepare a chart of accounts for Ann Mitchell Accounting Services, assigning appropriate account numbers to the account titles.

PROBLEM 2A-7 JOURNALIZING AND POSTING TRANSACTIONS

Mr. Alex McMahon set up his landscaping business on July 1, 200X, by depositing $22,000 cash in the business checking account. His first month's transactions are as follows:

July

1 Transferred $22,000 cash to the business
2 Paid the office rent, $1,800
3 Purchased office equipment, $10,000, on account
5 Paid the first month's telephone bill, $150
6 Received $1,000 for one week's landscaping services
7 Paid utility bill, $80
9 Completed $800 of landscaping services, which will be paid later
11 Withdrew $700 cash for personal use
12 Received $2,400 for one week's landscaping services
16 Borrowed $15,000, giving a 6-month, 10% note
20 Received $1,900 for one week's landscaping services
21 Received $800 for services previously performed
22 Paid $2,500 on account for equipment previously purchased
26 Paid $50 to local charity (Miscellaneous Expense)
28 Received $2,950 for one week's landscaping services

Required:

1. Prepare general journal entries to record Mr. McMahon's transactions.
2. Post the general journal entries to the general ledger accounts.

Trial Balance and Financial Statements

Module 2B Objectives
Careful study of this module should enable you to:
1   Prepare a trial balance from the general ledger accounts.
2. Prepare the financial statements (income statement, statement of owner's equity, and balance sheet) from the trial balance.

In the previous chapter, you prepared financial statements based on balances shown in T accounts. In the first module of this chapter, we journalized transactions and posted them to general ledger accounts. The trial balance is prepared after the posting process has been completed.

THE TRIAL BALANCE

The trial balance is a listing of all accounts and their balances. The purpose of the trial balance is to prove that debit and credit balances in the general ledger are equal. The trial balance can be taken daily, weekly, monthly, or whenever desired. To prepare the trial balance, the following steps should be taken:

1. Complete the heading. The heading contains three parts: (a) the name of the individual or business, (b) the title of the report, which is Trial Balance, and (c) the date reference.
2. For all accounts which have balances, list the account titles in ledger (numerical) order.
3. Enter the account balances, placing debit balances in the left column and credit balances in the right column.
4. Place a single line across the columns below the last entry, add columns, and enter the totals (they must be the same). Place a double line below the totals.

Exhibit 2.7 shows a sample trial balance prepared for Ann's Delivery Service Company. It proves that debits equal credits after posting is complete. It does not prove, however, that there are no errors in the journalizing or posting processes. For example, an amount may have been posted to the wrong account (e.g., Office Supplies may have been debited instead of Office Equipment). Therefore, the accounts could be *in balance* and there still could be errors.

Exhibit 2.7
Trial Balance

Account	Debit	Credit
Ann's Delivery Service Company Trial Balance January 31, 200X		
Cash	29 5 7 5 00	
Office Supplies	4 5 0 00	
Office Equipment	1 5 0 0 00	
Accounts Payable		8 0 0 00
Notes Payable		4 0 0 0 00
Ann Moe, Capital		25 0 0 0 00
Ann Moe, Drawing	2 0 0 00	
Delivery Fees		3 0 0 0 00
Rent Expense	1 0 0 0 00	
Telephone Expense	7 5 00	
	32 8 0 0 00	32 8 0 0 00

FINANCIAL STATEMENTS

While the trial balance shows that debits equal credits, it does not contain all the information an owner would like to know at the end of the month or accounting cycle. Most businesses need to know the results of operations during the month, and the status of the business at the end of the month. Therefore, three financial statements are prepared: (1) the income statement, (2) the statement of owner's equity, and (3) the balance sheet. As illustrated in Exhibit 2.8, each statement builds upon information supplied by the preceding statement.

Figure 2.8
Financial Statements

Ann's Delivery Service Company
Income Statement
For the Month Ended January 31, 200X

Revenue:		
Delivery fees		$3,000
Expenses:		
Rent expense	$1,000	
Telephone expense	75	
Total expenses		1,075
Net income		**$1,925**

Ann's Delivery Service Company
Statement of Owner's Equity
For the Month Ended January 31, 200X

Ann Moe, capital, January 1, 200X		$25,000
Net income for the month	**$1,925**	
Less withdrawals	200	
Net increase in capital		1,725
Ann Moe, capital, January 31, 200X		**$26,725**

Ann's Delivery Service Company
Balance Sheet
January 31, 200X

Assets:		
Cash		$29,575
Office supplies		450
Office equipment		1,500
Total assets		$31,525
Liabilities:		
Accounts payable	$ 800	
Notes payable	4,000	
Total liabilities		$ 4,800
Owner's Equity:		
Ann Moe, capital		26,725
Total liabilities and owner's equity		$31,525

In Chapter 1, you learned the basics about how to prepare these financial statements. In this chapter, the same statements are prepared using the trial balance as the source of information.

The Income Statement

The body of the income statement consists of an itemized list of revenues and expenses during the period. This illustrates the matching concept, which means that the amount of revenue earned during an accounting period must be matched with the expenses incurred to generate that revenue.

The income statement shown in Exhibit 2.9 is prepared from the trial balance of Ann's Delivery Service Company. It follows the same rules shown in Chapter 1 regarding the heading, commas, use of dollar signs, decimals, and rulings.

Exhibit 2.9
Income Statement

Ann's Delivery Service Company
Income Statement
For the Month Ended January 31, 200X

Revenue:		
Delivery fees		$3,000
Expenses:		
Rent expense	$1,000	
Telephone expense	75	
Total expenses		1,075
Net income		$1,925

As previously mentioned, it is good accounting practice to list expenses in descending order. That is, the expense which is the largest should be listed first, and so on. The exception is Miscellaneous Expense, which should always be listed last.

The Statement of Owner's Equity

After the income statement is prepared and net income is computed, the second financial statement to be prepared is the statement of owner's equity. The statement of owner's equity shows changes in the owner's equity during the month. As presented in Chapter 1, owner's equity can be increased in two ways: (1) additional investment by the owner, and (2) revenues. Owner's equity can also be decreased in two ways: (1) expenses, and (2) withdrawals (drawing) by the owner. The body of the statement of owner's equity presents six things:

1. The balance in the capital account at the beginning of the period (beginning balance)
2. Plus additional investments, if any, made by the owner during the period
3. Plus net income (or minus net loss) as shown on the income statement
4. Minus withdrawals, if any, made by the owner during the period
5. The net increase (or decrease) in owner's equity, which is the difference between net income and withdrawals, or the total of net loss plus withdrawals
6. The balance in the capital account at the end of the period (ending balance)

The statement of owner's equity for Ann's Delivery Service Company is shown in Exhibit 2.10. The net income for the month is taken from the income statement which was already prepared. Because net income exceeds the owner's withdrawals, there is an increase in owner's equity for the month of January.

Exhibit 2.10
Statement of Owner's Equity

Ann's Delivery Service Company
Statement of Owner's Equity
For the Month Ended January 31, 200X

Ann Moe, capital, January 1, 200X		$25,000
Net income for the month	$1,925	
Less withdrawals	200	
Net increase in capital		1,725
Ann Moe, capital, January 31, 200X		$26,725

After the statement of owner's equity is prepared, the balance sheet can be prepared. The balance sheet must be prepared last because it shows the ending capital balance, which has been computed on the statement of owner's equity.

The Balance Sheet

The balance sheet is an itemized list of the assets, liabilities, and ending owner's equity of a business on a specified date. Its purpose is to provide information regarding the financial status of the business after the period's transactions. As explained in Chapter 1, the heading of the balance sheet contains the name of the business, the title, and the date of the statement. The account form of balance sheet shown in Chapter 1 is arranged like a standard account with assets on the left side and liabilities and owner's equity on the right side.

The report form of balance sheet is also an acceptable method of presenting the financial position of the business. It lists accounts in order, but does not set them up using a left side and a right side. Nevertheless, it contains the same information and follows the same rules for columns, dollar signs, commas, decimals, and rulings. The balance sheet for Ann's Delivery Service Company, shown in Exhibit 2.11, has been prepared in report form.

Exhibit 2.11
Balance Sheet

Ann's Delivery Service Company
Balance Sheet
January 31, 200X

Assets:

Cash	$29,575
Office supplies	450
Office equipment	1,500
Total assets	$31,525

Liabilities:

Accounts payable	$ 800	
Notes payable	4,000	
Total liabilities		$ 4,800

Owner's Equity:

Ann Moe, capital	26,725
Total liabilities and owner's equity	$31,525

Preparing the financial statements is the last step of the flow of financial information through the accounting cycle. This flow—what we have covered in Chapters 1 and 2—is illustrated in Exhibit 2.12.

Exhibit 2.12

Accounting Information Flow (the Accounting Cycle)

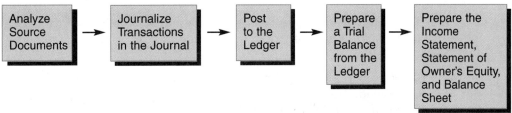

| Analyze Source Documents | → | Journalize Transactions in the Journal | → | Post to the Ledger | → | Prepare a Trial Balance from the Ledger | → | Prepare the Income Statement, Statement of Owner's Equity, and Balance Sheet |

Concept Questions

1. What is listed on the trial balance?
2. What is the purpose of the trial balance?
3. What are the three financial statements, in the order they are prepared?
4. What is the matching concept?
5. Why do business owners need an income statement, a statement of owner's equity, and a balance sheet prepared? (What information do these financial statements provide?)
6. How is the report form of the balance sheet different from the account form of the balance sheet (as shown in Chapter 1)?

If you cannot answer the above concept questions, go back and review the module material.

MODULE SUMMARY

At the end of the month, the account balances from the general ledger are listed on the trial balance. The purpose of the trial balance is to prove that debit and credit balances are equal. Financial statements are prepared from the trial balance; they include the income statement, the statement of owner's equity, and the balance sheet. The report form of the balance sheet differs from the account form presented in Chapter 1 in that accounts are listed below each other rather than side by side.

The accounting cycle has now been presented, from analyzing source documents to journalizing and posting, preparing a trial balance, and preparing the end-of-period financial statements.

Module 2B

Key Terms

account form
  (of balance sheet), *58*
matching concept, *56*

report form
  (of balance sheet), *58*

**Module
2B**

Exercises

EXERCISE 2B-8

Based on the following account balances at the end of January, 200X (from general ledger accounts), prepare a trial balance for B. Cranston Temporary Services.

> B. Cranston, Capital, $13,100
> B. Cranston, Drawing, $1,500
> Placement Fees (Revenue), $7,800
> Rent Expense, $1,000
> Telephone Expense, $80
> Miscellaneous Expense, $20
> Accounts Payable, $1,200
> Notes Payable, $1,500
> Cash, $7,500
> Office Equipment, $10,500
> Office Supplies, $3,000

EXERCISE 2B-9

Based on the following trial balance, prepare an income statement for the month ended March 31, 200X.

		C. Ansel Medical Billing Services Trial Balance March 31, 200X					
Description		Debit			Credit		
Cash	10	5	0	0	00		
Supplies	2	5	0	0	00		
Equipment	9	2	0	0	00		
Accounts Payable						6 0 0 0 00	
Notes Payable						5 4 0 0 00	
C. Ansel, Capital						6 5 0 0 00	
C. Ansel, Drawing	1	5	0	0	00		
Billing Revenue						8 0 0 0 00	
Rent Expense	1	0	0	0	00		
Telephone Expense		1	0	0	00		
Advertising Expense		2	5	0	00		
Entertainment Expense		7	0	0	00		
Miscellaneous Expense		1	5	0	00		
	25	9	0	0	00	25 9 0 0 00	

Problems

PROBLEM 2B-10 TRIAL BALANCE AND INCOME STATEMENT

Beverly Eno operates Eno's Catering Business. For the month ended October 31, 200X, the trial balance for the catering business was as follows:

Account	Debit	Credit
Eno's Catering Business		
Trial Balance		
October 31, 200X		
Cash	22 8 5 0 00	
Supplies	10 4 2 5 00	
Equipment	8 1 7 5 00	
Accounts Payable		5 0 0 0 00
Notes Payable		15 0 0 0 00
Beverly Eno, Capital		20 6 5 0 00
Beverly Eno, Drawing	2 0 0 0 00	
Catering Revenue		7 1 0 0 00
Rent Expense	3 0 0 0 00	
Telephone Expense	2 5 0 00	
Advertising Expense	8 2 5 00	
Entertainment Expense	1 7 5 00	
Miscellaneous Expense	5 0 00	
	47 7 5 0 00	47 7 5 0 00

Required: Prepare an income statement for the month of October.

PROBLEM 2B-11 STATEMENT OF OWNER'S EQUITY

Jack Bellwether owns a deep sea chartering service called Jack's Sea Escapes. After preparing his income statement for the month of June, his business showed a net income of $8,000. His beginning capital balance was $25,200, and during the month, he made withdrawals of $5,500.

> **Required:** Prepare a statement of owner's equity for the month ended June 30, 200X.

PROBLEM 2B-12 BALANCE SHEET

Marian Kilgore owns a dry cleaning service called Kilgore's Cleaners. At the end of March, her statement of owner's equity showed an ending capital balance of $29,750 (after net income was added and withdrawals were subtracted). In addition, she has the following ending balances in the general ledger:

Cash, $12,250
Supplies, $5,000
Equipment, $28,000
Accounts Payable, $8,000
Notes Payable, $7,500

Required: Prepare a balance sheet and report form for March 31, 200X.

PROBLEM 2B-13 TRIAL BALANCE AND INCOME STATEMENT

Richard Ely operates a lawn mowing business called Ely's Lawn Care. At the end of August, 200X, he had account balances in his general ledger as follows:

Cash, $21,550
Supplies, $11,550
Equipment, $7,250
Accounts Payable, $4,000   *Richard Ely, Capital*
Notes Payable, $12,000   *$36,350*
Richard Ely, Drawing, $1,500
Rent Expense, $1,000
Telephone Expense, $150
Advertising Expense, $425
Utilities Expense, $135
Miscellaneous Expense, $40
Mowing Revenue, $5,100

Required:

1. Prepare a trial balance. You must compute the amount of the owner's capital account, assuming there were no additional investments made by the owner during the month.
2. Prepare an income statement from the trial balance.

PROBLEM 2B-14 STATEMENT OF OWNER'S EQUITY

Jane Castlebaum owns a janitorial service called Jane's Clean-up. After preparing her income statement for the month of June, her business showed a net income of $7,500. Her beginning capital balance was $24,800, and during the month, she made withdrawals of $8,500.

Required: Prepare a statement of owner's equity for the month ended June 30, 200X.

PROBLEM 2B-15 BALANCE SHEET

Jeffrey Blackwell owns an advertising agency called Blackwell & Associates. At the end of March, his statement of owner's equity showed an ending capital balance of $32,750 (after net income was added and withdrawals were subtracted). In addition, he has the following ending balances in the general ledger:

Cash, $22,250
Supplies, $4,000
Equipment, $18,000
Accounts Payable, $7,000
Notes Payable, $4,500

Required: Prepare a balance sheet and report form for March 31, 200X.

Challenge Problem ✓ 9|17|99

Bart Adkins has been a research analyst since January of the current year. A chart of accounts for Bart's business is as follows:

Bart Adkins, Analyst
Chart of Accounts

Assets:
111 Cash
121 Accounts Receivable
131 Office Supplies
141 Office Equipment

Liabilities:
211 Accounts Payable

Owner's Equity:
311 Bart Adkins, Capital
312 Bart Adkins, Drawing

Revenue:
411 Research Fees

Expenses:
511 Rent Expense
522 Utilities Expense
533 Telephone Expense
543 Charitable Contributions Expense
555 Salary Expense
577 Travel & Entertainment Expense
599 Miscellaneous Expense

During the month of June, the following transactions were completed:

June 1 Bart invested $25,000 cash in the business.
        Paid office rent for June, $1,250
     2 Purchased office equipment on account from Town Square Company, $1,875
     7 Purchased stationery on account from Level Office Supplies, $350
     8 Received $4,500 in client fees
     9 Paid electric bill, $176
    14 Paid $500 on account to Town Square Company
    15 Paid secretary's salary for first half of month, $700
    16 Paid telephone bill, $82
    19 Received $4,075 in client fees
    20 Gave $500 to the Red Cross Foundation

21 Performed analyst services on account, $2,000
22 Paid to have office windows washed, $50
23 Paid expenses for trip to testify before state legislature, $315
29 Received $1,000 from clients previously billed on June 21
30 Paid secretary's salary for end of month, $700
30 Withdrew $2,000 for personal use

Required:

1. Record each transaction in a general journal. Number the journal pages beginning with Page 8.
2. Post the journal to four-column accounts in the general ledger. Keep running balances in all accounts.
3. Prepare a trial balance as of June 30, 200X.
4. Prepare the income statement for the month of June, 200X.
5. Prepare the statement of owner's equity for the month of June, 200X.
6. Prepare the balance sheet and report form as of June 30, 200X.

Comprehensive Review Problem 1

The following transactions were completed for Anderson Delivery Services for the month of April, 200X.

April 1 Jerry Anderson deposited $10,000 to the business account to start his business. DR Cash CR Capital
2 Office rent of $500 was paid. DR rent cr cash
5 Jerry purchased a delivery truck for $5,000, giving $1,000 cash and the balance on a note payable. DR del tk cr cash . cr notes
6 Jerry purchased office supplies for $300 cash. DR supplies cr cash
7 Jerry purchased office equipment for $1,500 on account. DR equip cr acpay
9 Jerry performed delivery services for $700 cash. DR cash cr fees
10 A bill for $75 telephone installation and service was received and paid. DR telephone cr cash
12 Services were performed on account, $800. Dr acct rec cr fees
14 Gave $50 cash to the local Kidsport Council (charitable contribution). DR cont CR cash
15 Paid $500 to part-time workers for services performed. DR salary cr cash
18 Paid $100 for truck repair expense. DR repairs cr cash
22 Received $400 on account for services previously performed. DR rec cr fees
24 Jerry withdrew $200 for personal use. Dr drawing cr drawing
26 Paid $220 cash to the local newspaper for advertising. Dr ads cr cash
27 Paid $80 for the monthly utility bill.
28 Jerry paid $350 for previous purchase of office equipment on account.
29 Services were performed for $250 cash.
30 Paid $450 on the note payable for delivery truck purchased April 5.

Required:

1. Record each transaction in a general journal. Number the general journal pages beginning with Page 1.
2. Post the journal to four-column accounts in the general ledger. Keep running balances in all accounts.
3. Prepare a trial balance as of April 30, 200X.
4. Prepare the income statement for the month of April, 200X.
5. Prepare the statement of owner's equity for the month of April, 200X.
6. Prepare the balance sheet as of April 30, 200X.

Anderson Delivery Services
Chart of Accounts

Assets:
- 111 Cash
- 121 Accounts Receivable
- 131 Office Supplies
- 141 Office Equipment
- 151 Delivery Truck

Liabilities:
- 211 Accounts Payable
- 221 Notes Payable

Owners Equity:
- 311 Jerry Anderson, Capital
- 312 Jerry Anderson, Drawing

Revenue:
- 411 Delivery Fees

Expenses:
- 511 Rent Expense
- 521 Telephone Expense
- 531 Charitable Contributions Expense
- 541 Salary Expense
- 551 Repairs Expense
- 561 Advertising Expense
- 571 Utilities Expense

Chapter THREE

The End-of-Period Work Sheet

The following modules will be covered in this chapter:

Module 3A
The Accounting Cycle and the Work Sheet
Prepare a ten-column end-of-year work sheet.

Module 3B
Prepare Financial Statements with the Aid of a Work Sheet
Prepare financial statements, using the work sheet as a guide.

The Accounting Cycle and the Work Sheet

Module 3A Objectives
Careful study of this module should enable you to:
1. Understand the accounting cycle.
2. Analyze and input adjusting entries onto the work sheet.
3 Complete a work sheet.

THE ACCOUNTING CYCLE

In the first two chapters of this textbook, you have learned several steps of the accounting cycle. The accounting cycle is the term used to describe the steps involved in accounting for all of the business activities during a time period. These steps are listed below:

1. Analyze source documents.
2. Journalize transactions in the general journal.
3. Post transactions from the general journal to the general ledger.
4. Prepare a trial balance.

End of Accounting Period
5. Prepare a work sheet.
   a. Analyze adjustments and enter onto the work sheet.
   b. Complete the work sheet.
6. Prepare the financial statements, using the work sheet as a guide.
7. Journalize and post adjusting entries, using the work sheet as a guide.
8. Journalize and post closing entries, using the work sheet as a guide.
9. Prepare a post-closing trial balance.

Most of an accountant's time is spent on the first four steps, and in preparing interim financial statements. Interim financial statements are statements covering less than a year. In this module, we are going to cover the preparation of a work sheet. In the next module, the use of a work sheet as a guide to preparing the financial statements will be covered. Chapter 4 will cover the remaining steps of the accounting cycle, journalizing and posting the adjusting and closing entries.

END-OF-PERIOD WORK SHEET

A **work sheet** is used by accountants at the end of the accounting period to make the last steps of the accounting cycle easier. The work sheet lists all the accounts from the general ledger that have a balance or will have a balance after the adjusting entries are entered. The accountant can determine immediately if there is a net income or net loss. A work sheet is not a financial statement. It is normally prepared in pencil.

The chart of accounts and trial balance as of December 31 for Raynette Wray, CPA, are shown as Exhibits 3.1 and 3.2.

Exhibit 3.1
Chart of Accounts

Raynette Wray, CPA
Chart of Accounts

Assets:
111	Cash
121	Office Supplies
123	Prepaid Insurance
131	Automobile
*131.1	Accumulated Depreciation—Automobile
141	Office Equipment
*141.1	Accumulated Depreciation—Office Equipment

Liabilities:
211	Accounts Payable
212	Salaries Payable

Owner's Equity:
311	Raynette Wray, Capital
312	Raynette Wray, Drawing
331	Income Summary

Revenue:
411	Professional Fees

Expenses:
511	Rent Expense
512	Office Supplies Expense
513	Insurance Expense
521	Salary Expense
522	Telephone Expense
523	Automobile Expense
531	Depreciation Expense—Automobile
541	Depreciation Expense—Office Equipment
551	Charitable Contributions Expense
561	Reference Library Expense
580	Miscellaneous Expense

*It is standard practice to use a decimal point in the account number to indicate that it is a contra account. A contra account is discussed on page 74.

The income statement, statement of owner's equity, and balance sheet will be prepared, using the work sheet as a guide.

Exhibit 3.2
Trial Balance

Raynette Wray, CPA Trial Balance December 31, 200X		
Account	**Debit**	**Credit**
Cash	24 8 2 0 00	
Office Supplies	4 5 0 00	
Prepaid Insurance	3 6 0 0 00	
Automobile	14 0 0 0 00	
Accumulated Depr.—Automobile		3 0 0 0 00
Office Equipment	20 0 0 0 00	
Accumulated Depr.—Office Equipment		4 0 0 0 00
Accounts Payable		8 0 0 00
Raynette Wray, Capital		42 3 2 0 00
Raynette Wray, Drawing	30 0 0 0 00	
Professional Fees		116 0 0 0 00
Rent Expense	14 0 0 0 00	
Salary Expense	52 0 0 0 00	
Telephone Expense	2 3 5 0 00	
Automobile Expense	1 3 7 5 00	
Charitable Contributions Expense	1 5 0 0 00	
Reference Library Expense	1 7 0 0 00	
Miscellaneous Expense	3 2 5 00	
	166 1 2 0 00	166 1 2 0 00

The end-of-year work sheet for Wray, CPA is reproduced in Exhibit 3.3. Following is a discussion of the steps that were followed in the preparation of the work sheet. Each step should be studied carefully with frequent reference to the work sheet.

Trial Balance Columns

The trial balance of the general ledger accounts as of December 31 is entered in the first pair of amount columns. Notice that all of the account titles were included in the work sheet even though certain accounts had no balance at this point. (See Raynette Wray, CPA, Chart of Accounts, page 68.)

The Trial Balance Debit and Credit columns are totaled. The totals must be equal. If not, the cause of any error must be found and corrected before continuing.

Exhibit 3.3
End-of-Year Work Sheet

Raynette Wray, CPA
Work Sheet
For the Year Ended December 31, 200X

	Account Title	Trial Balance Debit	Trial Balance Credit	Adjustments Debit	Adjustments Credit
1	Cash	24 8 2 0 00			
2	Office Supplies	4 5 0 00			(a) 2 7 0 00
3	Prepaid Insurance	3 6 0 0 00			(b) 1 2 0 0 00
4	Automobile	14 0 0 0 00			
5	Accum. Depr.—Automobile		3 0 0 0 00		(c) 3 0 0 0 00
6	Office Equipment	20 0 0 0 00			
7	Accum. Depr.—Office Equip.		4 0 0 0 00		(d) 4 0 0 0 00
8	Accounts Payable		8 0 0 00		
9	Salaries Payable				(e) 3 0 0 00
10	Raynette Wray, Capital		42 3 2 0 00		
11	Raynette Wray, Drawing	30 0 0 0 00			
12	Income Summary				
13	Professional Fees		116 0 0 0 00		
14	Rent Expense	14 0 0 0 00			
15	Office Supplies Expense			(a) 2 7 0 00	
16	Insurance Expense			(b) 1 2 0 0 00	
17	Salary Expense	52 0 0 0 00		(e) 3 0 0 00	
18	Telephone Expense	2 3 5 0 00			
19	Automobile Expense	1 3 7 5 00			
20	Depr. Expense—Automobile			(c) 3 0 0 0 00	
21	Depr. Expense—Office Equip.			(d) 4 0 0 0 00	
22	Charitable Contributions Exp.	1 5 0 0 00			
23	Reference Library Expense	1 7 0 0 00			
24	Miscellaneous Expense	3 2 5 00			
25		166 1 2 0 00	166 1 2 0 00	8 7 7 0 00	8 7 7 0 00
26	Net Income				
27					
28					
29					
30					
31					
32					

	Adjusted Trial Balance		Income Statement		Balance Sheet		
	Debit	Credit	Debit	Credit	Debit	Credit	
	24 8 2 0 00				24 8 2 0 00		1
	1 8 0 00				1 8 0 00		2
	2 4 0 0 00				2 4 0 0 00		3
	14 0 0 0 00				14 0 0 0 00		4
		6 0 0 0 00				6 0 0 0 00	5
	20 0 0 0 00				20 0 0 0 00		6
		8 0 0 0 00				8 0 0 0 00	7
		8 0 0 00				8 0 0 00	8
		3 0 0 00				3 0 0 00	9
		42 3 2 0 00				42 3 2 0 00	10
	30 0 0 0 00				30 0 0 0 00		11
							12
		116 0 0 0 00		116 0 0 0 00			13
	14 0 0 0 00		14 0 0 0 00				14
	2 7 0 00		2 7 0 00				15
	1 2 0 0 00		1 2 0 0 00				16
	52 3 0 0 00		52 3 0 0 00				17
	2 3 5 0 00		2 3 5 0 00				18
	1 3 7 5 00		1 3 7 5 00				19
	3 0 0 0 00		3 0 0 0 00				20
	4 0 0 0 00		4 0 0 0 00				21
	1 5 0 0 00		1 5 0 0 00				22
	1 7 0 0 00		1 7 0 0 00				23
	3 2 5 00		3 2 5 00				24
	173 4 2 0 00	173 4 2 0 00	82 0 2 0 00	116 0 0 0 00	91 4 0 0 00	57 4 2 0 00	25
			33 9 8 0 00			33 9 8 0 00	26
			116 0 0 0 00	116 0 0 0 00	91 4 0 0 00	91 4 0 0 00	27
							28
							29
							30
							31
							32

Balance Sheet

Income Statement

Adjustments Columns

The second pair of amount columns on the work sheet is used to record adjusting entries. **Adjusting entries** are needed in order to bring certain accounts up to date. They are done at the end of the accounting period in order to comply with the matching concept. The matching concept, as was mentioned in Chapter 2, states that the amount of revenue earned during an accounting period must be matched with the expenses incurred to generate that revenue.

Five entries are made in the Adjustments columns to reflect changes that took place in the accounts during the year. As you can see, when an account is debited, the amount is entered in the Adjustments Debit column on the same horizontal line as the name of the account. Amounts credited are entered in the Credit column. Each entry on the work sheet is identified by a small letter in parentheses to facilitate a cross-reference. Note that two accounts are always affected by an adjustment, just as two accounts are always affected by a transaction. Again, one account is debited and the other is credited.

Adjustment (a):   **As office supplies were purchased, the asset account Office Supplies was debited. At the end of the year, an inventory of supplies was taken. The ending inventory count was $180.**

The difference between the ending inventory count ($180) and the book balance of Office Supplies that appears on the trial balance ($450) represents the amount of supplies that was used: ($450 − $180 = $270). This amount, $270, is debited to Office Supplies Expense and credited to Office Supplies (an increase in an expense and a decrease in an asset). Using T accounts, the above transaction can be analyzed as follows:

(Balance Sheet) Office Supplies		(Income Statement) Office Supplies Expense	
Unadjust. Bal 450	(Adj.) 270	(Adj.) 270	
Ending Bal. 180			

Notice that this adjusting entry affected one balance sheet account title and one income statement account title.

KEY POINT

All adjusting entries will affect one balance sheet account title and one income statement account title.

Adjustment (b):   **As insurance was purchased, the asset account Prepaid Insurance was debited. At the end of the year, the amount of expired insurance is determined.**

The trial balance shows an unadjusted balance of $3,600. This balance represents the purchase of insurance on September 1, for a one-year policy. On December 31, the end of the current year, $1,200 of insurance ($3,600/12 = $300 × 4 = $1,200) has been used up. This amount ($1,200) is debited to Insurance Expense and credited to Prepaid Insurance. Using T accounts, the above transaction can be analyzed as follows:

(Income Statement) Insurance Expense	(Balance Sheet) Prepaid Insurance
(Adj.) 1,200	Unadjust. Bal 3,600 (Adj.) 1,200 Ending Bal. 2,400

The term **depreciation** refers to the process of allocating the cost of a depreciable asset over its useful life. A depreciable asset is an asset like office equipment or an automobile that will last for more than a year. The formula to calculate the annual amount of depreciation is as follows:

Original cost of asset	$xx
Less: estimated salvage value	xx
Amount to be depreciated	$xx
Divided by estimated useful life	
in years (or months)	xx
Equals annual amount of depreciation	$xx

The estimated salvage value is a guess at what the asset will be worth at the end of its useful life. The estimated useful life in years (or months) is a guess at how long the asset will remain useful. In accounting for depreciation, estimates are not only allowed but are expected to be used. The depreciation method that we are using is referred to as the straight-line method. Each year the same dollar amount of depreciation is used until the asset has been depreciated to its estimated salvage value.

Adjustment (c):   **The automobile cost $14,000 and its estimated salvage value is $2,000 at the end of 4 years. According to the above formula:**

Original cost of automobile	$14,000
Less: estimated salvage value	2,000
Amount to be depreciated	$12,000
Divided by estimated useful life in years	4
Equals annual amount of depreciation	$ 3,000

Therefore, adjustment (c) shows a debit to Depreciation Expense—Automobile and a credit to Accumulated Depreciation—Automobile for $3,000. Using T accounts, the above transaction can be analyzed as follows:

(Income Statement) Depr. Exp.—Automobile		(Balance Sheet) Accum. Depr.—Automobile	
(Adj.) 3,000		(Beg. Bal.)	3,000
		(Adj.)	**3,000**
		(End. Bal.)	6,000

The asset being depreciated, Automobile, is not credited and, in fact, is not credited until the asset is disposed of, either by selling it or by discarding it after its useful life has ended. Instead, a contra-asset account, Accumulated Depreciation, is credited. A **contra asset** is an offsetting or opposite account and should be deducted from the related asset account. Accumulated Depreciation has a normal credit balance. The difference between the asset account and its related accumulated depreciation (contra asset amount) is known as the **book value** of the asset. At this point in our example, then, the book value of R. Wray's automobile would be $8,000 ($14,000 – $6,000).

Adjustment (d):   **This adjustment is similar to adjustment (c). The formula to calculate the amount of annual depreciation for office equipment is given below:**

Original cost of office equipment	$20,000
Less: estimated salvage value	4,000
Amount to be depreciated	$16,000
Divided by estimated useful life in years	4
Equals annual amount of depreciation	$ 4,000

Therefore, adjustment (d) shows a debit to Depreciation Expense—Office Equipment, and a credit to Accumulated Depreciation—Office Equipment for $4,000. Again, using T accounts, the adjustment can be analyzed as follows:

(Income Statement) Depr. Exp.—Office Equip.		(Balance Sheet) Accum. Depr.—Office Equip.	
(Adj.) 4,000		(Beg. Bal.) 4,000	
		(Adj.) 4,000	
		(End. Bal.) 8,000	

Adjustment (e):   **At the end of the accounting period, there may be salaries employees have earned but for which they have not received payment.**

For example, if $750 of salaries is paid every Friday and the end of the year falls on a Tuesday, there is $300 of salaries ($750/week divided by 5 days equals $150/day, times 2 days equals $300) employees have earned but have not received. Therefore, an adjustment is needed to bring salary expense up to date. Also the related liability for salaries owed to the employees must be entered. The adjustment can be analyzed as follows:

(Income Statement) Salary Expense		(Balance Sheet) Salaries Payable	
(Adj.) 300		(Adj.) 300	

NOTE: The first four adjustments: supplies used, insurance expired, and depreciation adjustments, are normally done by all businesses, including professional service businesses that use the *modified cash basis* of accounting. The last adjusting entry, salary accrued, is only done by businesses that use the *accrual basis* of accounting. Under the accrual basis of accounting, revenue and expenses are recognized when earned or incurred, regardless of when cash is received or paid. Under the modified cash basis of accounting, revenue and expenses are recognized only when cash is received or paid. However, adjusting entries are normally done for the amount of supplies and insurance used, and for the depreciation of long-term assets, such as equipment and automobiles. A more detailed explanation of the modified cash basis and accrual basis of accounting can be found at the beginning of Chapters 7 and 8.

Every adjusting entry has an effect on net income. If these five adjustments were not made at the end of the accounting period, then net income would have been overstated by $8,770. This is true because the total of the five expense accounts mentioned in adjustments (a) through (e) is $8,770.

After making the required entries in the Adjustments columns of the work sheet, the columns are totaled to prove that total debits equal total credits.

Adjusted Trial Balance Columns

The third pair of amount columns of the work sheet is used for the adjusted trial balance. When an account balance is not affected by an adjusting entry, simply extend the amount directly from the trial balance to the Adjusted Trial Balance columns. When an account balance is affected by an adjusting entry, the adjustment must be added or subtracted.

There is a rule that can be followed when adding or subtracting adjustments. If there are debits in both the adjustment columns and trial balance columns, the two amounts are added. If there are credits in both the adjustment columns and trial balance columns, the two amounts are added. However, if there is a credit adjustment to a trial balance account with a debit balance, it must be subtracted. Or if there is a debit adjustment to a trial balance account with a credit balance, it must be subtracted.

Adjusted Trial Balance columns are totaled to prove the equality of the debits and credits.

KEY POINT

One method of improving accuracy on the work sheet is to use a ruler when extending dollar amounts across the work sheet. This will ensure that the amount is written on the correct line and in the correct column.

Income Statement Columns and Balance Sheet Columns

The fourth and fifth pairs of amount columns in the work sheet are for the Income Statement and Balance Sheet. Starting at the top of the work sheet, the first account title, Cash, was extended from the adjusted Trial Balance column to the Balance Sheet Debit column. Each account thereafter is extended from the Adjusted Trial Balance columns to either the

Income Statement columns or the Balance Sheet columns. Remember, all revenue and expense accounts appear in the Income Statement columns. All other accounts, including the owner's drawing account, appear in the Balance Sheet columns.

NOTE: Be sure to carry over the *adjusted* trial balance amounts, not the trial balance amounts.

The Income Statement columns and Balance Sheet columns need to be totaled. The difference between the Income Statement debit and credit columns represent either net income or net loss. Expense accounts have a normal debit balance. Revenue accounts have a normal credit balance. If total credits exceed total debits on the income statement columns, the difference is net income. If total debits exceed total credits, the difference is net loss.

The difference in the Balance Sheet columns will be exactly the same as the difference in the Income Statement columns.

Completing the Work Sheet

The difference between the totals of the Income Statement columns and the totals of the Balance Sheet columns should be entered on the next line below the column totals. If the difference is net income, the words "Net Income" should be written, and the amount entered in the Income Statement Debit and Balance Sheet Credit columns. If there is a net loss, the words "Net Loss" should be written, and the amount entered in the Income Statement Credit and Balance Sheet Debit columns. After the net income (or net loss) has been entered, a double line is ruled immediately below the totals.

To help you complete the work sheet, see Exhibits 3.4 and 3.5.

Exhibit 3.4
Illustration of Business with Net Income for Accounting Period

	Account Title	Income Statement Debit	Income Statement Credit	Balance Sheet Debit	Balance Sheet Credit	
		Work Sheet				
18	(Totals)	82 0 2 0 00	116 0 0 0 00	91 4 0 0 00	57 4 2 0 00	18
19	*Net Income*	33 9 8 0 00			33 9 8 0 00	19
20		116 0 0 0 00	116 0 0 0 00	91 4 0 0 00	91 4 0 0 00	20

Exhibit 3.5
Illustration of Business with Net Loss for Accounting Period

	Account Title	Income Statement		Balance Sheet		
		Debit	Credit	Debit	Credit	
18	*(Totals)*	116 0 0 0 00	82 0 2 0 00	57 4 2 0 00	91 4 0 0 00	18
19	*Net Loss*		33 9 8 0 00	33 9 8 0 00		19
20		116 0 0 0 00	116 0 0 0 00	91 4 0 0 00	91 4 0 0 00	20

KEY POINT

When a business has a net income, the amount is added to the outside of the four columns in order to have equal debits and credits upon completion of the work sheet. When a business has a net loss, the amount is added to the inside of the four columns in order to have equal debits and credits upon completion.

NOTE: A net income is placed on the balance sheet credit side because it increases capital. A net loss is placed on the balance sheet debit side because it decreases capital.

Concept Questions

1. What is the term used to describe the steps involved in accounting for all of the business activities during an accounting period?
2. What is the purpose of preparing a work sheet?
3. Adjusting entries are prepared at the end of the year in order to comply with what principle in accounting?
4. If the totals on the income statement credit column of the work sheet exceed the debit column, is this net income or net loss?

If you cannot answer the above concept questions, go back and review the module material before continuing to the next module.

MODULE SUMMARY

The accounting cycle is the term used to describe the steps involved in accounting for all of the business activities during an accounting period. A work sheet is prepared in order to make the remaining steps of the accounting cycle easier. Accounts that need to be adjusted are first analyzed and input onto the work sheet. Adjustments are required by the matching principle. Adjustments can be analyzed with T accounts. Every adjustment must affect one income statement account title and one balance sheet account title. Accounts such as Supplies and Prepaid Insurance need to be adjusted in order to show the correct ending balances. Long-term assets such as automobiles and office equipment need to be adjusted to show depreciation for the time period. Depreciation accounting is the process of allocating the cost of the asset over its useful life. Salary expense needs to be adjusted for the amount of salaries accrued but not paid at the end of the accounting period.

The work sheet is completed by extending the dollar amounts from the adjusted trial balance columns to either the income statement or balance sheet columns. The difference between the income statement debit and credit columns will represent either a net income or a net loss for the accounting period.

Key Terms

accounting cycle, *67*

adjusting entries, *72*

book value, *74*

contra asset, *74*

depreciation, *73*

interim financial statements, *67*

matching concept, *72*

work sheet, *68*

Exercises

EXERCISE 3A-1

Rearrange the following steps of the accounting cycle into the proper order:

1. Prepare a work sheet.
2. Journalize transactions in the journal.
3. Journalize and post closing entries, using the work sheet as guide.
4. Post transactions from the journal to the ledger.
5. Prepare a trial balance.
6. Prepare the financial statements, using the work sheet as a guide.
7. Analyze source documents.
8. Prepare a post-closing trial balance.
9. Journalize and post adjusting entries, using the work sheet as a guide.

EXERCISE 3A-2 10/4

The unadjusted trial balance of Ray Nelson and Mark Duel, Attorneys at Law, on December 31, 200X, includes Office Supplies amounting to $1,300. An ending inventory taken on this day indicates that $410 of office supplies are remaining.

Required: Using T accounts, analyze the above adjusting entry.

EXERCISE 3A-3 HW 10/5

An automobile was purchased by Dr. Carolyn Rogers at the beginning of this year for $39,000. Its estimated salvage value at the end of its estimated useful life of three years is $12,000.

Required: Using T accounts, analyze the above adjusting entry.

EXERCISE 3A-4 HW 10/5

The total amount of medical equipment in the Medical Equipment account of the unadjusted trial balance of Dr. Jason Flint is $48,000. It is estimated to have a useful life of six years with no salvage value.

Required: Using T accounts, analyze the above adjusting entry.

EXERCISE 3A-5 10/4

Using the information on the following page, determine the required adjusting entry for each situation:

a.

Supplies				Supplies Expense	
Beg. Bal.	700	(Adj.) _____		(Adj.) _____	
Purchased	900				
	1,600				

Ending balance of Supplies = $500

b.

Supplies				Supplies Expense	
Beg. Bal.	300	(Adj.) _____		(Adj.) _____	
Purchased	600				
	900				

Supplies used = $400

EXERCISE 3A-6   10/4

At the end of the year, the accounting records of Phil Hehr Company indicate that $1,200 of salaries have been earned by employees but have not been paid.

Required: Using T accounts, analyze the above adjusting entry.

EXERCISE 3A-7

Indicate how a net income of $6,000 would appear in the income statement and balance sheet columns of the work sheet:

	Income Statement		Balance Sheet	
	Debit	Credit	Debit	Credit
Net Income	6,000	_____	_____	6,000

EXERCISE 3A-8

Indicate how a net loss of $4,000 would appear in the income statement and balance sheet columns of the work sheet:

	Income Statement		Balance Sheet	
	Debit	Credit	Debit	Credit
Net Loss	_____	4,000	4,000	_____

Module
3A

Problems

PROBLEM 3A-9

Indicate with an X where each account total should be extended: either to the Income Statement Debit or Credit column, or to the Balance Sheet Debit or Credit column.

	Income Statement		Balance Sheet	
	Debit	Credit	Debit	Credit
Cash			X	
Office Supplies			X	
Office Equipment			X	
Accum. Depr.—Office Equip.			X	
Accounts Payable				X
Owner's Capital				X
Owner's Drawing			X	
Professional Fees		X		
Office Supplies Expense	X			
Salary Expense	X			

✳ PROBLEM 3A-10

Lester Fong started a business called "Fong's Kitchen." After the first month of operations, the trial balance as of June 30 is shown below and on the next page.

		Fong's Kitchen Work Sheet (Partial) For the Month Ended June 30, 200X			
		Trial Balance		**Adjustments**	
	Title	Debit	Credit	Debit	Credit
1	Cash	7 0 0 00			
2	Accounts Receivable	4 0 0 00			
3	Office Supplies	3 1 0 00			1 3 0 0 —
4	Prepaid Insurance	6 8 0 00			4 0 0 —
5	Kitchen Equipment	12 2 0 0 00			
6	Accum. Depr.—Kitchen Eq.				9 0 0 —
7	Accounts Payable		6 0 0 00		
8	Salaries Payable				2 5 0 —
9	L. Fong, Capital		14 3 2 5 00		
10	L. Fong, Drawing	3 0 0 0 00			
11	Income from Services		5 4 0 0 00		

12	Rent Expense	1 2 0 0 00											
13	Depr. Expense—Kitchen Eq.				9 0 0 –			
14	Salary Expense	1 4 0 0 00			2 5 0 –			
15	Utilities Expense	3 7 5 00						
16	Office Supplies Expense				1 3 0 –			
17	Insurance Expense				4 0 0 –			
18	Miscellaneous Expense	6 0 00						
		20 3 2 5 00	20 3 2 5 00					

Required:

1. Analyze the following adjustments and enter them on a work sheet.
    a.   Ending office supplies inventory as of June 30, $180.
    b.   Insurance expired, $400.
    c.   Depreciation of kitchen equipment, $900.
    d.   Salaries earned but not paid as of June 30, $250.
2. Complete the work sheet. *(adjusted trial balance)*

PROBLEM 3A-11

Homework 10/7/99

Indicate with an X whether each account total should be extended to the Income Statement Debit or Credit, or to the Balance Sheet Debit or Credit.

	Income Statement		Balance Sheet	
	Debit	Credit	Debit	Credit
Cash				
Accounts Receivable				
Supplies				
Automobile				
Accum. Depr.—Automobile				
Salaries Payable				
Owner's Capital				
Owner's Drawing				
Income from Services				
Rent Expense				
Utilities Expense				

PROBLEM 3A-12 10/7/99

The trial balance for Marion Martin's Delivery Service as of September 30, 200X, is shown on the following page:

Marion Martin's Delivery Service
Work Sheet (Partial)
For the Year Ended September 30, 200X

	Account Title	Trial Balance Debit	Trial Balance Credit	Adjustments Debit	Adjustments Credit
1	Cash	5 6 0 0 00			
2	Accounts Receivable	9 0 0 00			
3	Office Supplies	8 0 0 00			
4	Prepaid Insurance	7 5 0 00			
5	Delivery Van	36 4 0 0 00			
6	Accum. Depr.—Delivery Van		4 2 0 0 00		
7	Accounts Payable		1 5 0 0 00		
8	Salaries Payable				
9	M. Martin, Capital		26 4 5 0 00		
10	M. Martin, Drawing	30 0 0 0 00			
11	Income from Services		106 1 0 0 00		
12	Rent Expense	35 0 0 0 00			
13	Depr. Expense—Del. Van				
14	Salary Expense	24 4 0 0 00			
15	Utilities Expense	3 6 0 0 00			
16	Office Supplies Expense				
17	Insurance Expense				
18	Miscellaneous Expense	8 0 0 00			
19		138 2 5 0 00	138 2 5 0 00		

Required:

1. Analyze the following adjustments and enter them on a work sheet.
   a. Ending supplies inventory as of September 30, $200.
   b. Insurance expired, $625.
   c. Depreciation of delivery van, $2,300.
   d. Wages earned but not paid as of September 30, $900.
2. Complete the work sheet.

Prepare Financial Statements with the Aid of a Work Sheet

Module 3B Objectives
Careful study of this module should enable you to:
1. Prepare an income statement using the work sheet as a guide.
2. Prepare a statement of owner's equity using the work sheet as a guide.
3. Prepare a classified balance sheet using the work sheet as a guide.

THE FINANCIAL STATEMENTS

In this module, we will review the three financial statements you were shown from the first two chapters, only using the work sheet as a guide to preparing them.

The Income Statement

The **income statement** is generally considered to be one of the most important financial statements. Decisions to continue, expand, or contract a business are often based upon information reported in the income statement.

The income statement and balance sheet columns from the work sheet of Raynette Wray, CPA, are reproduced on the next page.

Exhibit 3.6

Work Sheet (Partial)

Raynette Wray, CPA
Work Sheet (Partial)
For the Year Ended December 31, 200X

	Account	Income Statement Debit	Income Statement Credit	Balance Sheet Debit	Balance Sheet Credit	
1	Cash			24 8 2 0 00		1
2	Office Supplies			1 8 0 00		2
3	Prepaid Insurance			2 4 0 0 00		3
4	Automobile			14 0 0 0 00		4
5	Accum. Depr.—Automobile				6 0 0 0 00	5
6	Office Equipment			20 0 0 0 00		6
7	Accum. Depr.—Office Equip.				8 0 0 0 00	7
8	Accounts Payable				8 0 0 00	8
9	Salaries Payable				3 0 0 00	9
10	Raynette Wray, Capital				42 3 2 0 00	10
11	Raynette Wray, Drawing			30 0 0 0 00		11
12	Professional Fees		116 0 0 0 00			12
13	Rent Expense	14 0 0 0 00				13
14	Office Supplies Expense	2 7 0 00				14
15	Insurance Expense	1 2 0 0 00				15
16	Salary Expense	52 3 0 0 00				16
17	Telephone Expense	2 3 5 0 00				17
18	Automobile Expense	1 3 7 5 00				18
19	Depr. Expense—Automobile	3 0 0 0 00				19
20	Depr. Expense—Office Equip.	4 0 0 0 00				20
21	Charitable Contributions Exp.	1 5 0 0 00				21
22	Reference Library Expense	1 7 0 0 00				22
23	Miscellaneous Expense	3 2 5 00				23
24		82 0 2 0 00	116 0 0 0 00	91 4 0 0 00	57 4 2 0 00	24
25	Net Income	33 9 8 0 00			33 9 8 0 00	25
26		116 0 0 0 00	116 0 0 0 00	91 4 0 0 00	91 4 0 0 00	26
27						27

Everything an accountant needs to prepare the income statement appears in the income statement columns of the work sheet. Notice that even the total expenses are shown in the Income Statement Debit column total.

The income statement for Wray, CPA, for the year ended December 31, 200X, is shown on the following page.

Exhibit 3.7
Income Statement

Raynette Wray, CPA
Income Statement
For the Year Ended December 31, 200X

Revenue:

Professional fees		$116,000

Expenses:

Salary expense	$52,300	
Rent expense	14,000	
Depreciation expense—office equipment	4,000	
Depreciation expense—automobile	3,000	
Telephone expense	2,350	
Reference library expense	1,700	
Charitable contributions expense	1,500	
Automobile expense	1,375	
Insurance expense	1,200	
Office supplies expense	270	
Miscellaneous expense	325	
Total expenses		82,020
Net income		$ 33,980

As was mentioned in Chapter 2, the expenses are listed in descending order of amount, except for miscellaneous expense, which is always listed last.

The Statement of Owner's Equity

The statement of owner's equity summarizes the events that affected owner's equity during the accounting period. The statement of owner's equity shows the amount of net income offset by the amount of withdrawals. If net income exceeds owner withdrawals, there is a net increase in capital. If withdrawals exceed net income, there is a net decrease in capital.

The statement of owner's equity is considered the connecting link between the income statement and the balance sheet. The income statement must always be prepared first. The statement of owner's equity is prepared second.

The statement of owner's equity can be prepared for Wray, CPA, from the information provided in the income statement and balance sheet columns of the work sheet.

Exhibit 3.8
Statement of Owner's Equity

Raynette Wray, CPA
Statement of Owner's Equity
For the Year Ended December 31, 200X

Raynette Wray, capital, January 1, 200X		$42,320
Net income for the year	$33,980	
Less withdrawals	30,000	
Net increase in capital		3,980
Raynette Wray, capital, December 31, 200X		$46,300

Notice that the beginning owner's capital balance as of January 1, was taken from the Balance Sheet Credit column of the work sheet. The net income can be taken from the income statement or it can be found on the work sheet. The owner's withdrawals were found in the Balance Sheet Debit column of the work sheet. The ending owner's capital as of December 31, will be used on the balance sheet.

Alternative Formats of the Statement of Owner's Equity. The following three examples do not relate to the work sheet of Raynette Wray, CPA. They are used to illustrate "what if" situations.

Consider a situation where there is a net loss. Assume that Raynette Wray, CPA, had a net loss of $5,000 for the year. The format of the statement would appear as follows:

Exhibit 3.9
Statement of Owner's Equity (with Net Loss)

Raynette Wray, CPA
Statement of Owner's Equity
For the Year Ended December 31, 200X

Raynette Wray, capital, January 1, 200X		$42,320
Net loss for the year	$ 5,000	
Add withdrawals	30,000	
Total decrease in capital		35,000
Raynette Wray, capital, December 31, 200X		$ 7,320

Consider another situation where the owner made an additional investment during the year. Assume that Raynette Wray, CPA, invested an additional $10,000 during the year. The format of the statement would appear as follows:

Exhibit 3.10

Statement of Owner's Equity (with Additional Investment)

Raynette Wray, CPA
Statement of Owner's Equity
For the Year Ended December 31, 200X

Raynette Wray, capital, January 1, 200X		$42,320
Add: Additional investment	$10,000	
Net income for the year	33,980	
	$43,980	
Less withdrawals	30,000	
Net increase in capital		13,980
Raynette Wray, capital, December 31, 200X		$56,300

Consider one final situation: The owner's withdrawals exceed the amount of net income. Assume that Raynette Wray, CPA, had a net income of only $15,000 for the year. The owner's withdrawals were $30,000. The format of the statement would appear as follows:

Exhibit 3.11

Statement of Owner's Equity (with Withdrawals Exceeding Income)

Raynette Wray, CPA
Statement of Owner's Equity
For the Year Ended December 31, 200X

Raynette Wray, capital, January 1, 200X		$42,320
Net income for the year	$15,000	
Less withdrawals	30,000	
Net decrease in capital		15,000
Raynette Wray, capital, December 31, 200X		$27,320

The Balance Sheet

A formal statement of the assets, liabilities, and owner's equity as of a specific date is a balance sheet.

The balance sheet is of interest to many users for several reasons. The owner or owners of a business are interested in the kinds and amounts of assets and liabilities. Creditors are interested in the amount of owner's equity.

The balance sheet of Raynette Wray, CPA, as of December 31, 200X, in report form, is shown on the following page. The information to prepare the balance sheet was taken from the work sheet in Exhibit 3.3. The ending owner's capital is taken from the statement of owner's equity.

Exhibit 3.12
Balance Sheet

Raynette Wray, CPA
Balance Sheet
December 31, 200X

Assets

Current assets:			
Cash		$24,820	
Office supplies		180	
Prepaid insurance		2,400	
Total current assets			$27,400
Long-term assets:			
Automobile	$14,000		
Less Accumulated Depreciation—Automobile	6,000	$ 8,000	
Office Equipment	$20,000		
Less Accumulated Depreciation—			
Office Equipment	8,000	12,000	
Total long-term assets			20,000
Total assets			$47,400

Liabilities

Current liabilities:			
Accounts payable		$ 800	
Salaries payable		300	
Total current liabilities			$ 1,100

Owner's Equity

Raynette Wray, capital			46,300
Total liabilities and owner's equity			$47,400

Classification of Data in the Balance Sheet. It has become almost universal practice to classify assets and liabilities as either (1) current or (2) long-term.

Current Assets. Current assets include cash, accounts receivable, supplies and prepaid insurance. These assets will be used up within a year. Current assets are listed in liquidity order. The term *liquidity* relates to how quickly the current assets can be converted into cash or can be used up as an expense. Cash is always listed first because it is already liquid.

Long-Term Assets. Assets that will last more than one year are called **long-term assets**. These assets include land, buildings, automobiles and office equipment. The balance sheet of Raynette Wray, CPA, lists long-term assets as an automobile and office equipment. In each case, accumulated depreciation is deducted from the cost of the asset. Remember, the difference between the cost of the asset and its related accumulated depreciation is called book value.

Current Liabilities. **Current liabilities** are debts that will be paid in less than a year. As of December 31, Wray's current liabilities were accounts payable and salaries payable.

Long-Term Liabilities. **Long-term liabilities** are debts that will be paid after one year or more. Reference to the balance sheet of Raynette Wray, CPA, will not show any long-term liabilities. However, one of the more common long-term liabilities is Mortgage Note Payable. A mortgage note payable is a long-term debt, secured by property, that will not be paid for several years.

Owner's Equity. The owner's equity section shows the ending owner's capital balance. Reference to the balance sheet of Raynette Wray shows her ending capital of $46,300. This amount was taken directly from the statement of owner's equity. Notice that the beginning owner's capital amount appears in the balance sheet credit column of the work sheet. If this amount was used, the balance sheet would not balance. The owner's capital must be taken from the statement of owner's equity because this represents the ending owner's equity amount.

Concept Questions

1. What information does the income statement provide?
2. Which financial statement is considered the connecting link between the income statement and the balance sheet?
3. Assets and liabilities on the balance sheet can be further classified into what four categories?
4. What source of information is used as a guide to prepare the three financial statements?

If you cannot answer the above concept questions, go back and review the module material.

MODULE SUMMARY

The completed work sheet can be used as a guide to prepare the income statement, statement of owner's equity, and balance sheet. The three financial statements must always be prepared in the same order: the income statement, first; statement of owner's equity, second; and balance sheet, last. The statement of owner's equity is the connecting link between the income statement and balance sheet. The balance sheet can be further classified into current assets, long-term assets, current liabilities, and long-term liabilities.

Module 3B

Key Terms

current assets, *90*   long-term assets, *91*
current liabilities, *91*   long-term liabilities, *91*
income statement, *85*

Module 3B

Exercises

		Income Statement			Balance Sheet		
	Account	Debit		Credit	Debit		Credit
1	Cash				14 3 5 0 00		
2	Office Supplies				9 2 5 00		
3	Prepaid Insurance				3 1 0 0 00		
4	Medical Equipment				82 0 0 0 00		
5	Accum. Depr.—Med. Equip.						24 0 0 0 00
6	Office Equipment				45 0 0 0 00		
7	Accum. Depr.—Office Equip.						7 0 0 0 00
8	Accounts Payable						1 4 0 0 00
9	Salaries Payable						7 0 0 00
10	Royce Kildare, Capital						90 9 9 5 00
11	Royce Kildare, Drawing				80 0 0 0 00		
12	Professional Fees			275 0 0 0 00			
13	Rent Expense	42 0 0 0 00					
14	Office Supplies Expense	6 9 0 00					
15	Insurance Expense	5 6 0 0 00					

Royce Kildare, M.D.
Work Sheet (Partial)
For the Year Ended December 31, 200X

16	Salary Expense	107	8	5	0	00																							16
17	Telephone Expense	3	9	4	0	00																							17
18	Depr. Expense—Med. Equip.	8	0	0	0	00																							18
19	Depr. Expense—Office Equip.	3	0	0	0	00																							19
20	Charitable Contrib. Expense	2	0	0	0	00																							20
21	Miscellaneous Expense		6	4	0	00																							21
22		173	7	2	0	00	275	0	0	0	00	225	3	7	5	00	124	0	9	5	00								22
23	Net Income	101	2	8	0	00											101	2	8	0	00								23
24		275	0	0	0	00	275	0	0	0	00	225	3	7	5	00	225	3	7	5	00								24
25																													25

EXERCISE 3B-13

From the partial work sheet above, prepare an income statement for the year ended December 31, 200X.

EXERCISE 3B-14

From the partial work sheet above, prepare a statement of owner's equity for the year ended December 31, 200X, assuming no additional investment was made by the owner.

EXERCISE 3B-15

From the partial work sheet above, prepare a balance sheet for Royce Kildare, M.D., for December 31, 200X.

EXERCISE 3B-16

From the partial work sheet above, prepare a statement of owner's equity for the year ended December 31, 200X, assuming that during the year there was an additional cash investment of $40,000 by the owner. The beginning owner's capital balance, before the additional investment, was $50,995.

EXERCISE 3B-17

From the partial work sheet above, prepare a statement of owner's equity for the year ended December 31, 200X, assuming that the owner's drawing was $120,000 instead of $80,000.

Chapter Three   The End-of-Period Work Sheet

10/8/99

Problems

PROBLEM 3B-18

A partial work sheet for Edgar Hoover, Consulting is shown below.

Edgar Hoover, Consulting
Work Sheet (Partial)
For the Year Ended December 31, 200X

	Account	Income Statement Debit	Income Statement Credit	Balance Sheet Debit	Balance Sheet Credit	
1	Cash			21 710 00		1
2	Office Supplies			935 00		2
3	Prepaid Insurance			2 275 00		3
4	Automobile			38 700 00		4
5	Accum. Depr.—Automobile				14 700 00	5
6	Office Equipment			18 600 00		6
7	Accum. Depr.—Office Equip.				9 200 00	7
8	Accounts Payable				7 810 00	8
9	Salaries Payable				800 00	9
10	Edgar Hoover, Capital				24 940 00	10
11	Edgar Hoover, Drawing			50 000 00		11
12	Professional Fees		235 000 00			12
13	Rent Expense	36 000 00				13
14	Office Supplies Expense	3 710 00				14
15	Insurance Expense	4 600 00				15
16	Salary Expense	92 900 00				16
17	Telephone Expense	3 850 00				17
18	Automobile Expense	2 850 00				18
19	Depr. Expense—Automobile	7 350 00				19
20	Depr. Expense—Office Equip.	4 600 00				20
21	Charitable Contributions Exp.	3 500 00				21
22	Miscellaneous Expense	870 00				22
23		160 230 00	235 000 00	132 220 00	57 450 00	23
24	Net Income	74 770 00			74 770 00	24
25		235 000 00	235 000 00	132 220 00	132 220 00	25
26						26

Required:

1. Prepare an income statement for the year ended December 31, 200X.
2. Prepare a statement of owner's equity for the year ended December 31, 200X. Edgar Hoover invested an additional $5,000 during the year. His beginning capital balance was $19,940.
3. Prepare a balance sheet for December 31, 200X.

PROBLEM 3B-19

A partial work sheet for Lisa Kendig, Repair is shown below. 10/8/99

	Account	Income Statement				Balance Sheet				
		Debit		Credit		Debit		Credit		
1	Cash					15 9 2 0 00				1
2	Accounts Receivable					6 8 1 0 00				2
3	Office Supplies					1 7 0 0 00				3
4	Prepaid Insurance					2 5 6 0 00				4
5	Delivery Equipment					46 8 0 0 00				5
6	Accum. Depr.—Delivery Equip.							14 9 0 0 00		6
7	Office Equipment					24 6 5 0 00				7
8	Accum. Depr.—Office Equip.							8 1 0 0 00		8
9	Accounts Payable							3 7 5 0 00		9
10	Salaries Payable							9 0 0 00		10
11	Lisa Kendig, Capital							104 7 9 5 00		11
12	Lisa Kendig, Drawing					20 0 0 0 00				12
13	Repair Revenue			66 0 0 0 00						13
14	Rent Expense	18 0 0 0 00								14
15	Office Supplies Expense	2 4 6 0 00								15
16	Insurance Expense	1 8 7 5 00								16
17	Salary Expense	42 9 0 0 00								17
18	Telephone Expense	2 8 7 0 00								18
19	Delivery Expense	3 4 0 0 00								19
20	Depr. Expense—Delivery Equip.	4 5 7 0 00								20
21	Depr. Expense—Office Equip.	3 4 2 0 00								21
22	Miscellaneous Expense	5 1 0 00								22
23		80 0 0 5 00		66 0 0 0 00		118 4 4 0 00		132 4 4 5 00		23
24	Net Loss			14 0 0 5 00		14 0 0 5 00				24
25		80 0 0 5 00		80 0 0 5 00		132 4 4 5 00		132 4 4 5 00		25
26										26

Lisa Kendig, Repair
Work Sheet (Partial)
For the Year Ended December 31, 200X

Required:

1. Prepare an income statement for the year ended December 31, 200X.
2. Prepare a statement of owner's equity for the year ended December 31, 200X.
3. Prepare a balance sheet as of December 31, 200X.

10/8/99

PROBLEM 3B-20

A partial work sheet for Eric Klobas, Consulting is shown below.

Eric Klobas, Consulting
Work Sheet (Partial)
For the Year Ended December 31, 200X

	Account	Income Statement Debit	Income Statement Credit	Balance Sheet Debit	Balance Sheet Credit	
1	Cash			22 580 00		1
2	Office Supplies			1 690 00		2
3	Prepaid Insurance			2 450 00		3
4	Automobile			29 600 00		4
5	Accum. Depr.—Automobile				11 300 00	5
6	Office Equipment			18 450 00		6
7	Accum. Depr.—Office Equip.				8 200 00	7
8	Accounts Payable				4 470 00	8
9	Salaries Payable				950 00	9
10	Eric Klobas, Capital				10 395 00	10
11	Eric Klobas, Drawing			35 000 00		11
12	Professional Fees		197 000 00			12
13	Rent Expense	34 000 00				13
14	Office Supplies Expense	1 800 00				14
15	Insurance Expense	4 100 00				15
16	Salary Expense	62 200 00				16
17	Telephone Expense	3 275 00				17
18	Automobile Expense	3 290 00				18
19	Depr. Expense—Automobile	5 140 00				19
20	Depr. Expense—Office Equip.	3 820 00				20
21	Charitable Contributions Exp.	4 000 00				21
22	Miscellaneous Expense	920 00				22
23		122 545 00	197 000 00	109 770 00	35 315 00	23
24	Net Income	74 455 00			74 455 00	24
25		197 000 00	197 000 00	109 770 00	109 770 00	25
26						26

Required:

1. Prepare an income statement for the year ended December 31, 200X.
2. Prepare a statement of owner's equity for the year ended December 31, 200X. Eric Klobas invested an additional $5,000 during the year. His beginning capital balance was $5,395.
3. Prepare a balance sheet as of December 31, 200X.

PROBLEM 3B-21

10/8/99 A partial work sheet for Nancy Wilder, Repair is shown below.

	Account	Income Statement Debit		Income Statement Credit		Balance Sheet Debit		Balance Sheet Credit	
1	Cash					15 8 5 0 00			1
2	Accounts Receivable					4 3 0 0 00			2
3	Office Supplies					1 8 2 0 00			3
4	Prepaid Insurance					2 7 0 0 00			4
5	Delivery Equipment					46 4 1 0 00			5
6	Accum. Depr.—Delivery Equip.							12 7 4 0 00	6
7	Office Equipment					24 9 0 0 00			7
8	Accum. Depr.—Office Equip.							8 3 0 0 00	8
9	Accounts Payable							4 4 0 0 00	9
10	Salaries Payable							6 3 0 00	10
11	Nancy Wilder, Capital							111 7 2 0 00	11
12	Nancy Wilder, Drawing					27 0 0 0 00			12
13	Repair Revenue			73 0 0 0 00					13
14	Rent Expense	29 0 0 0 00							14
15	Office Supplies Expense	8 7 0 00							15
16	Insurance Expense	1 6 2 0 00							16
17	Salary Expense	41 0 0 0 00							17
18	Telephone Expense	3 7 0 0 00							18
19	Delivery Expense	2 8 5 0 00							19
20	Depr. Expense—Delivery Equip.	3 8 0 0 00							20
21	Depr. Expense—Office Equip.	4 1 1 0 00							21
22	Miscellaneous Expense	8 6 0 00							22
23		87 8 1 0 00		73 0 0 0 00		122 9 8 0 00		137 7 9 0 00	23
24	Net Loss			14 8 1 0 00		14 8 1 0 00			24
25		87 8 1 0 00		87 8 1 0 00		137 7 9 0 00		137 7 9 0 00	25
26									26

Required:

1. Prepare an income statement for the year ended December 31, 200X.
2. Prepare a statement of owner's equity for the year ended December 31, 200X.
3. Prepare a balance sheet as of December 31, 200X.

Module
3B

Challenge Problem

A trial balance for Sharla Knox, CPA, for the year ended December 31, 200X, is shown below:

	Sharla Knox, CPA Trial Balance December 31, 200X					
Account		**Debit**		**Credit**		
Cash		31 6 3 0 00				
Office Supplies		3 2 4 0 00				
Prepaid Insurance		5 7 0 0 00				
Automobile		38 3 0 0 00				
Accumulated Depr.—Automobile				9 6 0 0 00		
Office Equipment		36 4 0 0 00				
Accumulated Depr.—Office Equipment				12 8 0 0 00		
Accounts Payable				6 4 1 0 00		
Salaries Payable						
Sharla Knox, Capital				86 2 5 5 00		
Sharla Knox, Drawing		60 0 0 0 00				
Professional Fees				194 0 0 0 00		
Rent Expense		31 0 0 0 00				
Office Supplies Expense						
Insurance Expense						
Salary Expense		88 0 0 0 00				
Telephone Expense		4 3 6 0 00				
Automobile Expense		3 1 5 5 00				
Depr. Expense—Automobile						
Depr. Expense—Office Equipment						
Charitable Contributions Expense		3 0 0 0 00				
Reference Library Expense		3 4 0 0 00				
Miscellaneous Expense		8 8 0 00				
		309 0 6 5 00		309 0 6 5 00		

Required:

1. Transfer the above trial balance onto a work sheet and analyze and input the following adjusting entries, indicating by letter each adjusting entry:

    ✓a. The ending inventory, as of December 31, 200X, of office supplies was $985.

    ✓b. The insurance policy, effective for one year, was purchased on April 1 of this year.

c. The original purchase price of the automobile was $38,300. The estimated salvage value, after 5 years of useful life, is $9,500. Use the straight-line method of depreciation for the whole year.

d. The original purchase price of the office equipment was $36,400. The estimated salvage value, after 6 years of useful life, is $1,600. Use the straight-line method of depreciation for the whole year.

e. The weekly salary expense is $1,600. December 31 fell on a Wednesday. Salaries had been paid up through the previous Friday.

2. Complete the work sheet.
3. Prepare an income statement for the year ended December 31, 200X.
4. Prepare a statement of owner's equity for the year ended December 31, 200X. The owner invested an additional $20,000 during the year into the business. The beginning owner's capital balance was $66,255.
5. Prepare a balance sheet as of December 31, 200X.

Chapter FOUR

Adjusting, Closing, and Reversing Entries

The following modules will be covered in this chapter:

Module 4A
The Adjusting Entries
Journalizing and posting the adjusting entries to update the ledger account balances.

Module 4B
The Closing Entries
Journalizing and posting the closing entries to show accounts with balances to begin the new fiscal period; preparing a post-closing trial balance; preparing next period accounting entries to account for accruals.

Module 4C
The Reversing Entries
Journalizing and posting the reversing entries.

The Adjusting Entries

Module 4A Objectives
Careful study of this module should enable you to:
1. Journalize adjusting entries to record the adjustments as shown on the work sheet (adjustments columns).
2. Post the adjusting entries to the general ledger accounts.
3. Compute new balances in the general ledger accounts which have received the adjusting entry postings; prepare an adjusted trial balance.

In the first three chapters, you completed most of the accounting cycle—analyzing, journalizing, posting, preparing a trial balance, preparing a work sheet, and preparing financial statements. Only three steps remain: (1) journalizing and posting the adjusting entries, (2) journalizing and posting the closing entries, and (3) preparing the post-closing trial balance. These steps are covered in the first two modules of this chapter. Module 4C shows why you might wish to reverse one or more of the adjusting entries (the accruals) on the first day of the new accounting period. Because reversing entries are not required, the third module of Chapter 4 explains what happens if reversing entries are not used.

JOURNALIZING THE ADJUSTING ENTRIES

In Chapter 3, four types of adjustments were shown. Accounts were adjusted at the end of the accounting period to show their true balances:

- The Office Supplies account (to show actual supplies on hand at the end of the period);
- The Prepaid Insurance account (to show unexpired insurance);
- The Depreciation Expense (to match expired assets with the revenue they helped to produce); and
- The Salaries Payable (or Wages Payable) account (to show wages earned but not yet paid).

Each of the adjustments shown on the work sheet results in an adjusting entry that affects both the balance sheet and the income statement. An **adjusting entry** is a general journal entry to record an end-of-period adjustment to an account. **Adjustments** are increases or decreases to accounts which are indicated on the work sheet at the end of the accounting period.

After the work sheet has been completed, the adjusting entries are entered in the general journal under the heading "Adjusting Entries." They are journalized in the same order as they appear on the work sheet. The account numbers are not entered in the Posting Reference column until the posting is completed.

Explanations are not needed for adjusting entries. In Exhibit 4.1, the adjusting entries for Raynette Wray, CPA, are illustrated. The work sheet in Exhibit 4.2 is highlighted to show that the adjusting entries are taken from the Adjustments columns of the work sheet. Adjusting entries appear in the general journal immediately following the month's journal entries for transactions.

Exhibit 4.1
Adjusting Entries

	Date		Description	Post. Ref.	Debit	Credit	
1	200X		*Adjusting Entries*				1
2	Dec.	31	Office Supplies Expense	512	2 7 0 00		2
3			Office Supplies	121		2 7 0 00	3
4							4
5		31	Insurance Expense	513	1 2 0 0 00		5
6			Prepaid Insurance	123		1 2 0 0 00	6
7							7
8		31	Salary Expense	521	3 0 0 00		8
9			Salaries Payable	212		3 0 0 00	9
10							10
11		31	Depreciation Expense—Automobile	531	3 0 0 0 00		11
12			Accum. Depr.—Automobile	131.1		3 0 0 0 00	12
13							13
14		31	Depreciation Expense—Office Equip.	541	4 0 0 0 00		14
15			Accum. Depr.—Office Equip.	141.1		4 0 0 0 00	15

General Journal — Page 13

Exhibit 4.2
Work Sheet (Partial)

Account Title	Trial Balance Debit	Trial Balance Credit	Adjustments Debit	Adjustments Credit
Raynette Wray, CPA **Work Sheet** **For the Year Ended December 31, 200X**				
1 Cash	24 8 2 0 00			
2 Office Supplies	4 5 0 00			(a) 2 7 0 00
3 Prepaid Insurance	3 6 0 0 00			(b) 1 2 0 0 00
4 Automobile	14 0 0 0 00			
5 Accum. Depr.—Automobile		3 0 0 0 00		(c) 3 0 0 0 00
6 Office Equipment	20 0 0 0 00			
7 Accum. Depr.—Office Equip.		4 0 0 0 00		(d) 4 0 0 0 00
8 Accounts Payable		8 0 0 00		
9 Salaries Payable				(e) 3 0 0 00
10 Raynette Wray, Capital		42 3 2 0 00		
11 Raynette Wray, Drawing	30 0 0 0 00			
12 Income Summary				
13 Professional Fees		116 0 0 0 00		
14 Rent Expense	14 0 0 0 00			
15 Office Supplies Expense			(a) 2 7 0 00	
16 Insurance Expense			(b) 1 2 0 0 00	
17 Salary Expense	52 0 0 0 00		(e) 3 0 0 00	
18 Telephone Expense	2 3 5 0 00			
19 Automobile Expense	1 3 7 5 00			
20 Depr. Expense—Automobile			(c) 3 0 0 0 00	
21 Depr. Expense—Office Equip.			(d) 4 0 0 0 00	
22 Charitable Contributions Exp.	1 5 0 0 00			
23 Reference Library Expense	1 7 0 0 00			
24 Miscellaneous Expense	3 2 5 00			
25	166 1 2 0 00	166 1 2 0 00	8 7 7 0 00	8 7 7 0 00
26				

POSTING THE ADJUSTING ENTRIES

The adjusting entries are posted individually to the proper general ledger accounts immediately after they are recorded on the last day of the accounting period. When posted, the word *adjusting* should appear in the item column of the general ledger accounts, as shown in Exhibit 4.3.

Exhibit 4.3

Posting Adjusting Entries

Account *Office Supplies*   Account No. *121*

Date		Item	Post. Ref.	Debit	Credit	Balance Debit	Balance Credit
200X							
Dec.	1	Balance	✓			4 5 0 00	
	31	Adjusting	GJ13		2 7 0 00	1 8 0 00	

Account *Office Supplies Expense*   Account No. *512*

Date		Item	Post. Ref.	Debit	Credit	Balance Debit	Balance Credit
200X							
Dec.	31	Adjusting	GJ13	2 7 0 00		2 7 0 00	

Account *Insurance Expense*   Account No. *513*

Date		Item	Post. Ref.	Debit	Credit	Balance Debit	Balance Credit
200X							
Dec.	31	Adjusting	GJ13	1 2 0 0 00		1 2 0 0 00	

Account *Prepaid Insurance*   Account No. *123*

Date		Item	Post. Ref.	Debit	Credit	Balance Debit	Balance Credit
200X							
Dec.	1	Balance	✓			3 6 0 0 00	
	31	Adjusting	GJ13		1 2 0 0 00	2 4 0 0 00	

Account *Depreciation Expense—Automobile*   Account No. *531*

Date		Item	Post. Ref.	Debit	Credit	Balance Debit	Balance Credit
200X							
Dec.	31	Adjusting	GJ13	3 0 0 0 00		3 0 0 0 00	

Account *Accumulated Depreciation—Automobile*						Account No. *131.1*
Date	Item	Post. Ref.	Debit	Credit	Balance Debit	Balance Credit
200X						
Dec. 1	Balance	✓				3 0 0 0 00
31	Adjusting	GJ13		3 0 0 0 00		6 0 0 0 00

Account *Depreciation Expense—Office Equip.*						Account No. *541*
Date	Item	Post. Ref.	Debit	Credit	Balance Debit	Balance Credit
200X						
Dec. 31	Adjusting	GJ13	4 0 0 0 00		4 0 0 0 00	

Account *Accumulated Depreciation—Office Equip.*						Account No. *141.1*
Date	Item	Post. Ref.	Debit	Credit	Balance Debit	Balance Credit
200X						
Dec. 1	Balance	✓				4 0 0 0 00
31	Adjusting	GJ13		4 0 0 0 00		8 0 0 0 00

After adjusting entries are posted to general ledger accounts, a new balance is computed for each account. For an account with a debit balance, such as Office Supplies, the credit entry reduces the debit balance in the account. As with any other posting, a new balance is computed at the same time the debit or credit entry is made.

As you can see, the new balances in these general ledger accounts are now the same as shown in the Adjusted Trial Balance columns of the work sheet.

Concept Questions

1. What are the steps in the accounting cycle?
2. List the four major types of adjustments.
3. What is an adjusting entry? What is an adjustment?
4. Are explanations required for adjusting entries that are recorded in the general journal?
5. When posting adjusting entries, what word appears in the item column of the general ledger accounts?

MODULE SUMMARY

Adjusting and closing entries are the last two required steps in the accounting cycle. Adjustments prepared for the work sheet are journalized as adjusting entries in the general journal, and then posted to general ledger accounts. Adjustments show increases or decreases to accounts, and are made at the end of the accounting period to show actual balances and to match expenses with revenues. Each adjusting entry affects the balance sheet and the income statement. The four adjustments studied so far include supplies expense, insurance expense, depreciation expense, and salary expense. After adjusting entries are posted to general ledger accounts, new balances are computed for each account.

Key Terms

adjusting entry, *102*   adjustments, *102*

Exercises

EXERCISE 4A-1

The Adjustments columns of the work sheet show that Office Supplies has a credit of $400, and Office Supplies Expense has a debit of $400. The balance of Office Supplies in the Trial Balance columns was $900, and there was no balance for Office Supplies Expense.

    a.   What is the balance in the Office Supplies account after the adjusting entry?

    b.   Prepare the adjusting entry (in general journal format) to record this adjustment.

EXERCISE 4A-2

The Adjustments columns of the work sheet show the following debits:

Depreciation Expense—Automobile, $1,500
Depreciation Expense—Office Equipment, $800

    Prior to the above adjustments, the book values for these two assets were as follows:

Automobile	$9,000
Less Accumulated Depreciation	4,500
Book Value	$4,500
Office Equipment	$4,800
Less Accumulated Depreciation	1,600
Book Value	$3,200

a. After recording the depreciation for the period, what is the book value for the automobile?

b. What is the book value for the office equipment (after this period's depreciation)?

c. Prepare adjusting entries in general journal format to record depreciation expense for these two assets as shown on the work sheet Adjustments columns.

EXERCISE 4A-3

The Adjustments columns of the work sheet show that Prepaid Insurance is credited for $380, and Insurance Expense is debited for the same amount. The balance of Prepaid Insurance in the Trial Balance columns was $1,140, and there was no balance for Insurance Expense.

a. What is the balance in the Prepaid Insurance account following the adjusting entry?

b. Prepare the adjusting entry in general journal format to record this adjustment.

EXERCISE 4A-4

The Adjustments columns of the work sheet show that Wages Payable is credited for $625 and Wages Expense is debited for the same amount.

a. Explain why this adjustment is necessary.

b. Prepare the adjusting entry in general journal format to record this adjustment.

Module
4A

Problems

PROBLEM 4A-5 ADJUSTING ENTRIES

The partial work sheet below shows the Trial Balance and Adjustments columns for R&R Software Associates.

R & R Software Associates
Work Sheet (Partial)
For the Year Ended December 31, 200X

Account Title	Trial Balance Debit	Trial Balance Credit	Adjustments Debit	Adjustments Credit	
3	Office Supplies	1 2 0 0 00			(a) 1 8 0 00	3
4	Prepaid Insurance	2 4 0 0 00			(b) 4 0 0 00	4
5	Office Equipment	12 0 0 0 00				5
6	Accum. Depr.—Office Equip.		2 6 0 0 00		(c) 8 0 0 00	6
7	Truck	24 0 0 0 00				7
8	Accum. Depr.—Truck		11 0 0 0 00		(d) 3 0 0 0 00	8
12	Wages Payable				(e) 3 0 0 00	12
15	Office Supplies Expense			(a) 1 8 0 00		15
16	Insurance Expense			(b) 4 0 0 00		16
17	Depr. Exp.—Office Equip.			(c) 8 0 0 00		17
18	Depr. Exp.—Truck			(d) 3 0 0 0 00		18
19	Wages Expense	30 0 0 0 00		(e) 3 0 0 00		19
20						20

Required:

1. Prepare the adjusting entries in the general journal for R&R Software Associates on December 31, 200X.
2. Post the adjusting entries to the general ledger accounts.
3. Compute new balances in the general ledger accounts.

PROBLEM 4A-6 ADJUSTING ENTRIES

The partial work sheet below shows selected trial balance amounts for H.B. Jones Bookkeeping Services.

H. B. Jones Bookkeeping Services
Work Sheet (Partial)
For the Year Ended December 31, 200X

	Account Title	Trial Balance Debit	Trial Balance Credit	Adjustments Debit	Adjustments Credit	
3	Office Supplies	1 8 0 0 00				3
4	Prepaid Insurance	3 1 0 0 00				4
5	Office Equipment	10 2 0 0 00				5
6	Accum. Depr.—Office Equip.		3 8 0 0 00			6
7	Automobile	14 0 0 0 00				7
8	Accum. Depr.—Automobile		6 0 0 0 00			8
12	Wages Payable					12
15	Office Supplies Expense					15
16	Insurance Expense					16
17	Depr. Exp.—Office Equip.					17
18	Depr. Exp.—Automobile					18
19	Wages Expense	25 0 0 0 00				19
20						20

Year-end records show the following information which will require adjustments on the work sheet:

Office supplies on hand, December 31, $800
Insurance expired during the year, $1,100
Depreciation expense for office equipment, $900
Depreciation expense for the automobile, $2,000
Wages earned but not yet paid, $660

Required:

1. Prepare the adjustments as they would appear on the work sheet for H.B. Jones Bookkeeping Services, and extend those balances to the Adjusted Trial Balance columns for the work sheet.
2. Journalize the adjusting entries for H.B. Jones Bookkeeping Services on December 31, 200X.
3. Post the adjusting entries to the general ledger accounts.
4. Compute new balances in the general ledger accounts.

PROBLEM 4A-7 ADJUSTING ENTRIES

The partial work sheet below shows the Trial Balance and Adjustments columns for L&K Dance Studio.

L&K Dance Studio
Work Sheet (Partial)
For the Year Ended December 31, 200X

	Account Title	Trial Balance Debit	Trial Balance Credit	Adjustments Debit	Adjustments Credit	
3	Office Supplies	8 0 0 00			(a) 1 4 0 00	3
4	Prepaid Insurance	1 1 0 0 00			(b) 3 0 0 00	4
5	Office Equipment	7 0 0 0 00				5
6	Accum. Depr.—Office Equip.		1 6 0 0 00		(c) 8 0 0 00	6
7	Truck	11 0 0 0 00				7
8	Accum. Depr.—Truck		4 0 0 0 00		(d) 1 3 0 0 00	8
12	Wages Payable				(e) 4 0 0 00	12
15	Office Supplies Expense			(a) 1 4 0 00		15
16	Insurance Expense			(b) 3 0 0 00		16
17	Depr. Exp.—Office Equip.			(c) 8 0 0 00		17
18	Depr. Exp.—Truck			(d)1 3 0 0 00		18
19	Wages Expense	24 0 0 0 00		(e) 4 0 0 00		19
20						20

Required:

1. Journalize and post the adjusting entries for L&K Dance Studio on December 31, 200X.
2. Post the adjusting entries to the general ledger accounts.
3. Compute new balances in the general ledger accounts.

PROBLEM 4A-8 ADJUSTING ENTRIES

The partial work sheet below shows selected trial balance amounts for C.T. Albers Towing Services.

C. T. Albers Towing Services
Work Sheet (Partial)
For the Year Ended December 31, 200X

	Account Title	Trial Balance Debit	Trial Balance Credit	Adjustments Debit	Adjustments Credit	
3	Office Supplies	2 8 0 0 00				3
4	Prepaid Insurance	4 1 0 0 00				4
5	Office Equipment	8 2 0 0 00				5
6	Accum. Depr.—Office Equip.		2 4 0 0 00			6
7	Tow Truck	84 0 0 0 00				7
8	Accum. Depr.—Tow Truck		28 0 0 0 00			8
12	Wages Payable					12
15	Office Supplies Expense					15
16	Insurance Expense					16
17	Depr. Exp.—Office Equip.					17
18	Depr. Exp.—Tow Truck					18
19	Wages Expense	62 0 0 0 00				19
20						20

Year-end records show the following information which will require adjustments on the work sheet:

Office supplies on hand, December 31, $1,400
Insurance expired during the year, $2,100
Depreciation expense for office equipment, $1,000
Depreciation expense for the tow truck, $8,000
Wages earned but not yet paid, $960

Required:

1. Prepare the adjustments as they would appear on the work sheet for C.T. Albers Towing Services, and extend those balances to the Adjusted Trial Balance columns of the work sheet.
2. Journalize the adjusting entries for C.T. Albers Towing Services on December 31, 200X.
3. Post the adjusting entries to the general ledger accounts.
4. Compute new balances in the general ledger accounts.

The Closing Entries

Module 4B Objectives

Careful study of this module should enable you to:

1. Journalize closing entries to close temporary owner's equity accounts in the general ledger.
2. Post the closing entries to the general ledger accounts and update the general ledger account balances.
3. Prepare a post-closing trial balance.

JOURNALIZING THE CLOSING ENTRIES

Immediately after journalizing and posting the adjusting entries, all the temporary owner's equity accounts are closed. Each account listed on the income statement is a **temporary owner's equity account**. Temporary accounts are used to accumulate balances to list income and expenses for the period. They are "temporary" because they are open only for the accounting period, and their balances begin with zero each new accounting period. The process of reducing temporary accounts to zero balances is called the **closing procedure**.

The closing procedure consists of closing all of the temporary accounts: revenue, expense, and drawing. To close out, or remove balances from, these accounts, a new owner's equity account called Income Summary is created. **Income Summary** is also a temporary account, and it is used only for the closing procedure. This account is often called Expense and Revenue Summary, Profit and Loss Summary, or Profit and Loss.

The four steps in closing all temporary accounts are illustrated in Exhibit 4.4.

Exhibit 4.4
Closing Temporary Accounts

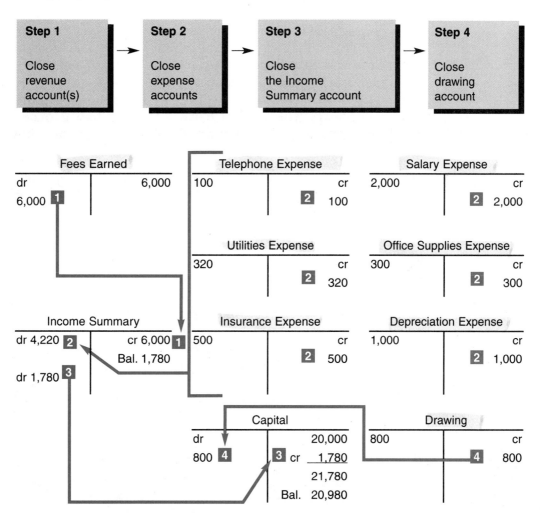

Step 1	Step 2	Step 3	Step 4
Close revenue account(s)	Close expense accounts	Close the Income Summary account	Close drawing account

Step 1.   Close the revenue account(s). Because the revenue account has a credit balance, it is closed (reduced to zero balance) by debiting it for its balance, and crediting the income account.

Step 2.   Close the expense accounts. The expense accounts have debit balances. They are closed (reduced to zero) by crediting each of them; the total of these accounts is debited to the Income Summary account.

Step 3.   Close the Income Summary account. After the above postings, there will be a debit balance or a credit balance in the
Income Summary account. A credit balance shows that revenues exceed expenses (credits exceed debits). The balance
in this account is closed to the capital account. Therefore, to
close a credit balance, the Income Summary account is debited, and the Capital account is credited.

Step 4.   Close the drawing account. The owner's drawing account
will always have a debit balance for withdrawals made
during the accounting period. To close, credit the drawing
account and debit capital.

To illustrate, let's look again at the work sheet for Raynette Wray,
CPA (as shown in Exhibit 4.5). Note that the Income Statement columns
and drawing account of the work sheet have been highlighted to show
the income and expense accounts which will be closed.

Closing entries are general journal entries which close out (zero
out) the balances of all temporary owner's equity accounts. These
entries are prepared at the end of the accounting cycle. With the closing
entries, all revenue and expense accounts (as well as the drawing
account) are reduced to zero to begin the new period.

Closing entries are entered in the general journal immediately
below the adjusting entries under the heading "Closing Entries." In
each closing entry, the account being debited is recorded first. The
account numbers are not entered in the Posting Reference column until
the posting is completed. Explanations are not needed for individual
closing entries, as shown in Exhibit 4.6.

KEY POINT

The closing procedure is the process whereby the net income or
net loss is posted to the capital account. The work sheet shows
correct ending balances, but posting the closing entries makes it
happen in the general ledger accounts.

The first closing entry closes the revenue account. The second closing entry closes all expense accounts. Even those expense accounts
which received balances due to adjusting entries are closed.

The third closing entry closes the Income Summary account, which has a credit balance of $33,980 after the revenue and expense accounts are closed. A credit balance in the Income Summary account means that revenue exceeds expense. In other words, there is a net income rather than a net loss. The Income Summary account is closed to the Capital account by debiting it and crediting capital.

Exhibit 4.6
Closing Entries

	Date	Description	Post. Ref.	Debit	Credit	
17	200X	Closing Entries				17
18	Dec. 31	Professional Fees		116 0 0 0 00		18
19		Income Summary			116 0 0 0 00	19
20						20
21	31	Income Summary		82 0 2 0 00		21
22		Rent Expense			14 0 0 0 00	22
23		Office Supplies Expense			2 7 0 00	23
24		Insurance Expense			1 2 0 0 00	24
25		Salary Expense			52 3 0 0 00	25
26		Telephone Expense			2 3 5 0 00	26
27		Automobile Expense			1 3 7 5 00	27
28		Deprec. Expense—Automobile			3 0 0 0 00	28
29		Deprec. Expense—Office Equip.			4 0 0 0 00	29
30		Charitable Contributions Expense			1 5 0 0 00	30
31		Reference Library Expense			1 7 0 0 00	31
32		Miscellaneous Expense			3 2 5 00	32
33						33
34	31	Income Summary		33 9 8 0 00		34
35		Raynette Wray, Capital			33 9 8 0 00	35
36						36
37	31	Raynette Wray, Capital		30 0 0 0 00		37
38		Raynette Wray, Drawing			30 0 0 0 00	38
39						39

General Journal — Page 13

The fourth closing entry closes the drawing account. It is credited because it has a debit balance; the Capital account is debited.

Exhibit 4.5
Work Sheet

Raynette Wray, CPA
Work Sheet
For the Year Ended December 31, 200X

	Account Title	Trial Balance Debit	Trial Balance Credit	Adjustments Debit	Adjustments Credit
1	Cash	24 8 2 0 00			
2	Office Supplies	4 5 0 00			(a) 2 7 0 00
3	Prepaid Insurance	3 6 0 0 00			(b) 1 2 0 0 00
4	Automobile	14 0 0 0 00			
5	Accum. Depr.—Automobile		3 0 0 0 00		(c) 3 0 0 0 00
6	Office Equipment	20 0 0 0 00			
7	Accum. Depr.—Office Equip.		4 0 0 0 00		(d) 4 0 0 0 00
8	Accounts Payable		8 0 0 00		
9	Salaries Payable				(e) 3 0 0 00
10	Raynette Wray, Capital		42 3 2 0 00		
11	Raynette Wray, Drawing	30 0 0 0 00			
12	Income Summary				
13	Professional Fees		116 0 0 0 00		
14	Rent Expense	14 0 0 0 00			
15	Office Supplies Expense			(a) 2 7 0 00	
16	Insurance Expense			(b) 1 2 0 0 00	
17	Salary Expense	52 0 0 0 00		(e) 3 0 0 00	
18	Telephone Expense	2 3 5 0 00			
19	Automobile Expense	1 3 7 5 00			
20	Depr. Expense—Automobile			(c) 3 0 0 0 00	
21	Depr. Expense—Office Equip.			(d) 4 0 0 0 00	
22	Charitable Contributions Exp.	1 5 0 0 00			
23	Reference Library Expense	1 7 0 0 00			
24	Miscellaneous Expense	3 2 5 00			
25		166 1 2 0 00	166 1 2 0 00	8 7 7 0 00	8 7 7 0 00
26	Net Income				
27					
28					
29					
30					
31					
32					

| Adjusted Trial Balance | | Income Statement | | Balance | | |
Debit	Credit	Debit	Credit	Debit	Credit	
24 8 2 0 00				24 8 2 0 00		1
1 8 0 00				1 8 0 00		2
2 4 0 0 00				2 4 0 0 00		3
14 0 0 0 00				14 0 0 0 00		4
	6 0 0 0 00				6 0 0 0 00	5
20 0 0 0 00				20 0 0 0 00		6
	8 0 0 0 00				8 0 0 0 00	7
	8 0 0 00				8 0 0 00	8
	3 0 0 00				3 0 0 00	9
	42 3 2 0 00				42 3 2 0 00	10
30 0 0 0 00				30 0 0 0 00		11
						12
	116 0 0 0 00		116 0 0 0 00			13
14 0 0 0 00		14 0 0 0 00				14
2 7 0 00		2 7 0 00				15
1 2 0 0 00		1 2 0 0 00				16
52 3 0 0 00		52 3 0 0 00				17
2 3 5 0 00		2 3 5 0 00				18
1 3 7 5 00		1 3 7 5 00				19
3 0 0 0 00		3 0 0 0 00				20
4 0 0 0 00		4 0 0 0 00				21
1 5 0 0 00		1 5 0 0 00				22
1 7 0 0 00		1 7 0 0 00				23
3 2 5 00		3 2 5 00				24
173 4 2 0 00	173 4 2 0 00	82 0 2 0 00	116 0 0 0 00	91 4 0 0 00	57 4 2 0 00	25
		33 9 8 0 00			33 9 8 0 00	26
		116 0 0 0 00	116 0 0 0 00	91 4 0 0 00	91 4 0 0 00	27
						28
						29
						30
						31
						32

POSTING THE CLOSING ENTRIES

Immediately after they are journalized, closing entries are posted and new balances are computed in the general ledger accounts. All new account balances will be zero, except the Capital account. One of the purposes of closing entries is to post the net income or net loss to the Capital account. Proper cross-references are provided in the Posting Reference columns of the general journal and the ledger accounts as shown in Exhibits 4.7 and 4.8.

Exhibit 4.7

Closing Entries in the General Journal

	Date	Description	Post. Ref.	Debit	Credit	
17	200X	*Closing Entries*				17
18	Dec. 31	*Professional Fees*	411	116 0 0 0 00		18
19		*Income Summary*	331		116 0 0 0 00	19
20						20
21	31	*Income Summary*	331	82 0 2 0 00		21
22		*Rent Expense*	511		14 0 0 0 00	22
23		*Office Supplies Expense*	512		2 7 0 00	23
24		*Insurance Expense*	513		1 2 0 0 00	24
25		*Salary Expense*	521		52 3 0 0 00	25
26		*Telephone Expense*	522		2 3 5 0 00	26
27		*Automobile Expense*	523		1 3 7 5 00	27
28		*Deprec. Expense—Automobile*	531		3 0 0 0 00	28
29		*Deprec. Expense—Office Equip.*	541		4 0 0 0 00	29
30		*Charitable Contributions Expense*	551		1 5 0 0 00	30
31		*Reference Library Expense*	561		1 7 0 0 00	31
32		*Miscellaneous Expense*	580		3 2 5 00	32
33						33
34	31	*Income Summary*	331	33 9 8 0 00		34
35		*Raynette Wray, Capital*	311		33 9 8 0 00	35
36						36
37	31	*Raynette Wray, Capital*	311	30 0 0 0 00		37
38		*Raynette Wray, Drawing*	312		30 0 0 0 00	38
39						39

General Journal — Page 13

Exhibit 4.8
Closing Entries in the General Ledger

Account *Raynette Wray, Capital* — **Account No.** *311*

Date	Item	Post. Ref.	Debit	Credit	Balance Debit	Balance Credit
200X						
Dec. 31	Balance					42 3 2 0 00
31	Closing	GJ13		33 9 8 0 00		76 3 0 0 00
31	Closing	GJ13	30 0 0 0 00			46 3 0 0 00

Account *Raynette Wray, Drawing* — **Account No.** *312*

Date	Item	Post. Ref.	Debit	Credit	Balance Debit	Balance Credit
200X					30 0 0 0 00	
Dec. 31	Closing	GJ13		30 0 0 0 00	-0-	

Account *Income Summary* — **Account No.** *331*

Date	Item	Post. Ref.	Debit	Credit	Balance Debit	Balance Credit
200X						
Dec. 31	Closing	GJ13		116 0 0 0 00		116 0 0 0 00
31	Closing	GJ13	82 0 2 0 00			33 9 8 0 00
31	Closing	GJ13	33 9 8 0 00			-0-

Account *Professional Fees* — **Account No.** *411*

Date	Item	Post. Ref.	Debit	Credit	Balance Debit	Balance Credit
200X						116 0 0 0 00
Dec. 31	Closing	GJ13	116 0 0 0 00			-0-

Account *Rent Expense* — **Account No.** *511*

Date	Item	Post. Ref.	Debit	Credit	Balance Debit	Balance Credit
200X					14 0 0 0 00	
Dec. 31	Closing	GJ13		14 0 0 0 00	-0-	

Account *Office Supplies Expense*   **Account No.** *512*

Date		Item	Post. Ref.	Debit	Credit	Balance Debit	Balance Credit
200X							
Dec.	1	Adjusting	GJ13	2 70 00		2 70 00	
	31	Closing	GJ13		2 70 00	- 0 -	

Account *Insurance Expense*   **Account No.** *513*

Date		Item	Post. Ref.	Debit	Credit	Balance Debit	Balance Credit
200X							
Dec.	31	Adjusting	GJ13	1 2 0 0 00		1 2 0 0 00	
	31	Closing	GJ13		1 2 0 0 00	- 0 -	

Account *Salary Expense*   **Account No.** *521*

Date		Item	Post. Ref.	Debit	Credit	Balance Debit	Balance Credit
200X						52 0 0 0 00	
Dec.	31	Adjusting	GJ13	3 0 0 00		53 3 0 0 00	
	31	Closing	GJ13		52 3 0 0 00	- 0 -	

Account *Telephone Expense*   **Account No.** *522*

Date		Item	Post. Ref.	Debit	Credit	Balance Debit	Balance Credit
200X						2 3 5 0 00	
Dec.	31	Closing	GJ13		2 3 5 0 00	- 0 -	

Account *Automobile Expense*   **Account No.** *523*

Date		Item	Post. Ref.	Debit	Credit	Balance Debit	Balance Credit
200X						1 3 7 5 00	
Dec.	31	Closing	GJ13		1 3 7 5 00	- 0 -	

Account	Depreciation Expense—Automobile							Account No. 531	
							Balance		
Date	Item	Post. Ref.	Debit	Credit		Debit		Credit	
200X									
Dec. 31	Adjusting	GJ13	3 0 0 0 00			3 0 0 0 00			
31	Closing	GJ13		3 0 0 0 00		- 0 -			

Account	Depreciation Expense—Office Equipment							Account No. 541	
							Balance		
Date	Item	Post. Ref.	Debit	Credit		Debit		Credit	
200X									
Dec. 31	Adjusting	GJ13	4 0 0 0 00			4 0 0 0 00			
31	Closing	GJ13		4 0 0 0 00		- 0 -			

Account	Charitable Contributions Expense							Account No. 551	
							Balance		
Date	Item	Post. Ref.	Debit	Credit		Debit		Credit	
200X						1 5 0 0 00			
Dec. 31	Closing	GJ13		1 5 0 0 00		- 0 -			

Account	Reference Library Expense							Account No. 561	
							Balance		
Date	Item	Post. Ref.	Debit	Credit		Debit		Credit	
200X						1 7 0 0 00			
Dec. 31	Closing	GJ13		1 7 0 0 00		- 0 -			

Account	Miscellaneous Expense							Account No. 580	
							Balance		
Date	Item	Post. Ref.	Debit	Credit		Debit		Credit	
200X						3 2 5 00			
Dec. 31	Closing	GJ13		3 2 5 00		- 0 -			

After the closing entries are journalized and posted, the only general ledger accounts with balances remaining are the **permanent accounts**. These balance sheet accounts are assets, liabilities, and the owner's equity (capital) account. When the income, expense, and drawing accounts are closed out (zero balances), the new accounting period can begin. This way, each period's revenue and expenses are matched. Only one last check is needed to be certain that the accounting equation is still in balance. This is done by preparing a post-closing trial balance.

THE POST-CLOSING TRIAL BALANCE

The **post-closing trial balance** contains a listing of all general ledger accounts that remain open (permanent accounts) after the closing process is complete (journalized and posted). Only assets, liabilities, and the owner's capital accounts remain open. The purpose of the post-closing trial balance is to prove that the general ledger is in balance at the beginning of the new accounting period. It is important to know that the accounting equation (Assets = Liabilities + Owner's Equity) is still in balance before any new transactions are recorded for the new accounting period.

The post-closing trial balance is dated as of the last day of the accounting period. It lists the accounts remaining open in numerical order. Double underlines show that the general ledger is in balance. The Raynette Wray, CPA, Post-Closing Trial Balance is shown in Exhibit 4.9.

Exhibit 4.9
Post-Closing Trial Balance

<table>
<tr><td colspan="11" align="center">Raynette Wray, CPA
Post-Closing Trial Balance
December 31, 200X</td></tr>
<tr><td>Account</td><td colspan="5" align="center">Balance</td><td colspan="5" align="center">Balance</td></tr>
<tr><td>Cash</td><td>24</td><td>8</td><td>2</td><td>0</td><td>00</td><td></td><td></td><td></td><td></td><td></td></tr>
<tr><td>Office Supplies</td><td></td><td>1</td><td>8</td><td>0</td><td>00</td><td></td><td></td><td></td><td></td><td></td></tr>
<tr><td>Prepaid Insurance</td><td>2</td><td>4</td><td>0</td><td>0</td><td>00</td><td></td><td></td><td></td><td></td><td></td></tr>
<tr><td>Automobile</td><td>14</td><td>0</td><td>0</td><td>0</td><td>00</td><td></td><td></td><td></td><td></td><td></td></tr>
<tr><td>Accum. Depreciation—Automobile</td><td></td><td></td><td></td><td></td><td></td><td>6</td><td>0</td><td>0</td><td>0</td><td>00</td></tr>
<tr><td>Office Equipment</td><td>20</td><td>0</td><td>0</td><td>0</td><td>00</td><td></td><td></td><td></td><td></td><td></td></tr>
<tr><td>Accum. Depreciation—Office Equip.</td><td></td><td></td><td></td><td></td><td></td><td>8</td><td>0</td><td>0</td><td>0</td><td>00</td></tr>
<tr><td></td><td></td><td></td><td></td><td></td><td></td><td></td><td></td><td></td><td></td><td></td></tr>
</table>

Accounts Payable									8	0	0	00		
Salaries Payable									3	0	0	00		
Raynette Wray, Capital								46	3	0	0	00		
	61	4	0	0	00		61	4	0	0	00		

The post-closing trial balance is prepared as an internal tool; it is not a financial statement such as the income statement, the statement of owner's equity, and the balance sheet. Nevertheless, it is an important statement because it ensures that the accounting equation is in balance at the beginning of the new accounting period.

What to Do with Accruals

In Module 4A, we learned about salaries that were earned but won't be paid until the next accounting period. The adjusting entry was to debit Salary Expense and to credit Salaries Payable. In Module 4B, we learned that all temporary accounts are closed. In closing entries, the Salary Expense would be closed. Salaries Payable, however, is a permanent account and would carry its balance forward.

Now consider what happens when the salaries earned in the previous accounting period are paid in the current period. In order to avoid double counting, you must be careful to debit Salaries Payable for the amount previously recognized as Salaries Expense. Otherwise, the books will show a continuing liability for Salaries Payable, and will overstate Salaries Expense.

Concept Questions

1. List the three types of temporary owner's equity accounts.
2. A new owner's equity account called _____ is created to facilitate the closing process.
3. What are the four steps of the closing process (in order)?
4. What is meant by "permanent" accounts?
5. When are closing entries prepared?
6. When are closing entries posted?
7. What is the purpose of the post-closing trial balance?

MODULE SUMMARY

Closing entries are prepared immediately after the adjusting entries are journalized and posted. All temporary owner's equity accounts are closed; that is, the revenue, expense, and drawing accounts. Income Summary, a new owner's equity account, is used to facilitate the closing process. First, revenue accounts are closed to the Income Summary account. Second, expense accounts are closed to the Income Summary account. Third, the Income Summary account is closed to the owner's capital account. Finally, the owner's drawing account is closed to the owner's capital account. Closing entries create zero balances in the temporary accounts; the only accounts remaining open are permanent accounts. Permanent accounts are assets, liabilities, and the capital account. A listing of accounts remaining open is found in the post-closing trial balance, which is prepared to prove that the general ledger and the accounting equation are still in balance. Finally, when accruals are recognized, the accountant must be careful not to count them twice. In other words, the liability account left open (Salaries Payable) contains salaries previously earned, and that balance should be removed (with a debit) rather than recognizing the same expense twice.

Module 4B

Key Terms

closing entries, *114*	permanent accounts, *122*
closing procedure, *112*	post-closing trial balance, *122*
income summary, *112*	temporary owner's equity account, *112*

Module 4B

Exercises

EXERCISE 4B-9

After the revenue and expense accounts of Jake's Barber Shop were closed December 31, 200X, the Income Summary account had a credit balance of $21,330. On December 31 (before closing entries), the Capital account of J. Adams, the owner, had a credit balance of $42,000, and the Drawing account had a debit balance of $18,420.

    a.   What is the balance in the Capital account after the closing entries are completed?

    b.   Using the journal paper provided in the Study Guide/Working Papers supplement, prepare the general journal entries to complete the closing process for Jake's Barber Shop.

EXERCISE 4B-10

After the revenue and expense accounts of Jane's Catering Service were closed on December 31, 200X, the Income Summary account had a debit balance of $6,210. On December 31 (before closing entries), the Capital account of Jane Clark, the owner, had a credit balance of $51,000, and the Drawing account had a debit balance of $22,400.

    a. What is the balance of the Capital account after the closing entries are completed?

    b. Using the journal paper provided in the Study Guide/Working Papers supplement, prepare the general journal entries to complete the closing process for Jane's Catering Service.

EXERCISE 4B-11

Jim's Repair Shop has these balances on December 31 after closing entries are completed:

Cash		$15,000
Office Supplies		3,000
Prepaid Insurance		4,500
Office Equipment	$22,000	
Less Accumulated Depreciation	8,000	14,000
Delivery Van	$18,000	
Less Accumulated Depreciation	11,000	7,000
Accounts Payable		7,500
Wages Payable		800
Jim Adkison, Capital		35,200

Required: Prepare a post-closing trial balance to verify that the general ledger is in balance.

Problems

PROBLEM 4B-12 CLOSING ENTRIES

Alice's Dry Cleaning Service has the following balances in the Adjusted Trial Balance columns of the work sheet for the period ended December 31, 200X:

	Debit	Credit
Cash	$ 18,000	
Office Supplies	4,000	
Prepaid Insurance	2,500	
Office Equipment	12,000	
Accumulated Depreciation—Office Equip.		$ 6,000
Dry Cleaning Equipment	99,000	

Accumulated Depreciation—Dry Clean. Equip.		81,000
Accounts Payable		12,000
Wages Payable		260
Alice Crane, Capital		47,830
X Alice Crane, Drawing	21,000	
X Dry Cleaning Revenue		46,000
X Rent Expense	22,000	
X Salary Expense	260	
X Insurance Expense	400	
X Supplies Expense	380	
X Depreciation Expense—Office Equip.	1,200	
X Depreciation Expense—Dry Clean. Equip.	10,000	
X Repair Expense	800	
X Telephone Expense	950	
X Miscellaneous Expense	600	
	$193,090	$193,090

Required:

1. Journalize the closing entries for Alice's Dry Cleaning Services on December 31, 200X.
2. Post the closing entries to the general ledger accounts.
3. Compute new balances in the general ledger accounts.
4. Prepare a post-closing trial balance for Alice's Dry Cleaning Services on December 31, 200X.

PROBLEM 4B-13 CLOSING ENTRIES

Problem 3B-18, on page 94, contains the work sheet for Edgar Hoover, Consulting, as of December 31, 200X. Based on that work sheet:

1. Journalize the closing entries.
2. Post the closing entries to the general ledger accounts.
3. Compute new balances in the general ledger accounts.
4. Prepare a post-closing trial balance for Edgar Hoover, Consulting, as of December 31, 200X.

PROBLEM 4B-14 CLOSING ENTRIES

Jamie's Consulting Service has the following balances in the Adjusted Trial Balance columns of the work sheet for the period ended December 31, 200X:

	Debit	Credit
Cash	$16,000	
Office Supplies	6,000	
Prepaid Insurance	4,500	

Office Equipment	6,000	
Accumulated Depreciation—Office Equip.		$ 2,800
Automobile	14,000	
Accumulated Depreciation—Automobile		6,000
Accounts Payable		1,500
Wages Payable		220
Jamie Blake, Capital		37,430
Jamie Blake, Drawing	11,000	
Consulting Fee Revenue		26,000
Rent Expense	12,000	
Salary Expense	160	
Insurance Expense	600	
Supplies Expense	440	
Depreciation Expense—Office Equipment	900	
Depreciation Expense—Automobile	1,000	
Repair Expense	500	
Telephone Expense	250	
Miscellaneous Expense	600	
	$73,950	$73,950

Required:

12/14/99

1. Journalize and post the closing entries in the general journal for Jamie's Consulting Services on December 31, 200X.
2. Post the closing entries to the general ledger accounts.
3. Compute new balances in the general ledger accounts.
4. Prepare a post-closing trial balance for Jamie's Consulting Services on December 31, 200X.

PROBLEM 4B-15 CLOSING ENTRIES

Problem 3B-20, on page 96, contains the work sheet for Eric Klobas, Consulting, as of December 31, 200X. Based on that work sheet:

1. Journalize the closing entries.
2. Post the closing entries to the general ledger accounts.
3. Compute new balances in the general ledger accounts.
4. Prepare a post-closing trial balance for Eric Klobas, Consulting, as of December 31, 200X.

Module 4C

The Reversing Entries

Module 4C Objectives
Careful study of this module should enable you to:
1. Prepare reversing entries and post them to the general ledger accounts.
2. Understand the procedure required if you do not use reversing entries.

PREPARING REVERSING ENTRIES

In Modules 4A and 4B, you learned how to journalize and post the adjusting and closing entries. Temporary accounts are closed (zero balances) and permanent accounts remain open. The accounting equation is in balance, as evidenced by the post-closing trial balance. You are now ready to begin the next accounting period.

But before you begin recording the new month's transactions, there is one more point to consider. When you prepared adjusting entries, you may have created new balances in asset or liability accounts for which there was previously a zero balance. (The adjusting entry created a new balance in a permanent account, and closing entries did not zero out the balance.)

For example, in Chapter 3 we debited Salary Expense and credited Salaries Payable (a liability account) for the amount of wages earned but not yet paid ($300). If salaries were earned and paid in the same accounting period, no adjusting or reversing entries would be needed. In the second module of Chapter 4, we closed all temporary accounts. After the adjusting and closing entries were posted, the general ledger accounts showed these balances:

Account *Salary Expense*							Account No. *521*	
Date	Item	Post. Ref.	Debit	Credit	Balance			
					Debit		Credit	
200X								
Dec. 31	Balance				52 000 00			
31	Adjusting	GJ13	3 00 00		52 300 00			
31	Closing	GJ13		52 300 00	- 0 -			

Account *Salaries Payable*							Account No. *212*	
Date	Item	Post. Ref.	Debit	Credit	Balance			
					Debit		Credit	
200X								
Dec. 31	Adjusting	GJ13		3 00 00			3 00 00	

The Salaries Payable account was listed on the post-closing trial balance, as it should be, because the amount was owed from the previous accounting period. But now let's think about what happens when the next payroll is made. For example, let's say that on January 15, payroll of $2,000 is paid, which includes the $300 of **accrued** wages (those earned but not yet paid). To make this entry correctly, the $300 amount must not be entered a second time, since it has already been reported as a salary expense on the previous year's income statement. Therefore, the following entry would be necessary:

	General Journal				Page *14*	
	Date	Description	Post. Ref.	Debit	Credit	
1	200X					1
2	Jan. 15	Salary Expense		1 700 00		2
3		Salaries Payable		3 00 00		3
4		Cash			2 000 00	4
5						5

This entry recognizes that $300 was an expense of the previous accounting period, so for this pay period the $300 is deducted as a debit from the Salaries Payable account. It would not be appropriate to debit Salary Expense for $2,000 and credit Cash for the same amount.

Because you must remember to follow this procedure for all adjusting entries which created new balances in asset or liability accounts, many accountants prefer to use reversing entries. **Reversing entries are used to eliminate balances in asset or liability accounts so that entries made in subsequent accounting periods will be correct without considering balances caused by adjusting entries.**

If a reversing entry is used, the adjusting entry would be "reversed" on the first day of the new accounting period as follows:

	Date		Description	Post. Ref.	Debit	Credit	
1	200X		*Reversing Entry*				1
2	*Jan.*	*1*	*Salaries Payable*	212	3 0 0 00		2
3			*Salary Expense*	521		3 0 0 00	3
4							4

General Journal   Page *14*

When posted to the general ledger, the accounts now look like this:

Account *Salary Expense*   Account No. *521*

Date		Item	Post. Ref.	Debit	Credit	Balance Debit	Balance Credit
200X							
Dec.	31	*Balance*				52 0 0 0 00	
	31	*Adjusting*	GJ13	3 0 0 00		52 3 0 0 00	
	31	*Closing*	GJ13		52 3 0 0 00	- 0 -	
200X							
Jan.	1	*Reversing*	GJ14		3 0 0 00		3 0 0 00

Account *Salaries Payable*   Account No. *212*

Date		Item	Post. Ref.	Debit	Credit	Balance Debit	Balance Credit
200X							
Dec.	31	*Balance*	GJ13		3 0 0 00		3 0 0 00
200X							
Jan.	1	*Reversing*	GJ14	3 0 0 00			- 0 -

You will note that the liability account, Salaries Payable, now has a zero balance, but the Salary Expense account has a $300 *credit* balance. This will enable you to make the entry for the January 15 payroll without considering the balances in other accounts:

	Date	Description	Post. Ref.	Debit	Credit	
5	200X					5
6	Jan. 15	Salary Expense		2 0 0 0 00		6
7		Cash			2 0 0 0 00	7
8						8

General Journal — Page 14

Thus, when this journal entry is posted, Salary Expense for this period will be correct ($1,700):

Account *Salary Expense*   Account No. 521

Date	Item	Post. Ref.	Debit	Credit	Balance Debit	Balance Credit
200X						
Dec. 31	Balance				52 0 0 0 00	
31	Adjusting	GJ13	3 0 0 00		52 3 0 0 00	
31	Closing	GJ13		52 3 0 0 00	- 0 -	
200X						
Jan. 1	Reversing	GJ14		3 0 0 00		3 0 0 00
15		GJ14	2 0 0 0 00		1 7 0 0 00	

As you can see, you do not have to use reversing entries. But if you choose to omit them, you must carefully examine all adjusting entries to see whether new balances were created in asset or liability accounts. If so, special consideration must be given in the next accounting period to be sure that expenses are not reported twice (once in the previous period when adjusting entries were posted and again in the current period when the expenses are actually paid). The chart in Exhibit 4.10 summarizes the reversing (or not reversing) process as related to the payment of salaries.

Exhibit 4.10

Reversing Process (as Related to Payment of Salary)

Adjusting Entry:

			General Journal	Post. Ref.	Debit	Credit	
						Page 20	
	Date		Description				
12	Dec.	31	Salary Expense		3 0 0 00		12
13			Salaries Payable			3 0 0 00	13
14							14

Closing Entry:

20	Dec	31	Income Summary		3 0 0 00		20
21			Salary Expense			3 0 0 00	21
22							22

Note: Salaries Payable (liability account) is open and will appear on the post-closing trial balance.

Without Reversing Entry:

18	Jan.	15	Salary Expense		1 7 0 0 00		18
19			Salaries Payable		3 0 0 00		19
20			Cash			2 0 0 0 00	20
21							21

Reversing Entry:

			General Journal	Post. Ref.	Debit	Credit	
						Page 21	
	Date		Description				
1			*Reversing Entries*				1
2	Jan.	1	Salaries Payable		3 0 0 00		2
3			Salary Expense			3 0 0 00	3
4							4

Note: Salaries Payable is closed; a credit balance is created in the expense account.

5	Jan.	15	Salary Expense		2 0 0 0 00		5
6			Cash			2 0 0 0 00	6
7							7

Concept Questions:

1. What is meant by "accrued" wages?
2. What entry does a reversing entry reverse?
3. If reversing entries are not used, what must you be careful to watch?

MODULE SUMMARY

Reversing entries are not required. But they do facilitate the journal entries for the next accounting period. One advantage of using reversing entries is that you do not have to recheck adjusting entries to ensure that an expense has not been recorded twice. A reversing entry merely "reverses" the adjusting entry. Because the expense account was closed to zero in the closing process, the effect of the reversing entry is to create a credit balance in an expense account and to close the liability account. This procedure allows for proper recognition of expenses in the new accounting period (when they are actually paid).

Key Terms

accrued, *129*   reversing entries, *130*

Exercises

EXERCISE 4C-16

Check which of the following adjusting entries would be a candidate for using a reversing entry:

_____ Depreciation Expense debit, Accumulated Depreciation credit
_____ Insurance Expense debit, Prepaid Insurance credit
_____ Wages Expense debit, Wages Payable credit
_____ Supplies Expense debit, Supplies credit

EXERCISE 4C-17

Put these steps of the accounting cycle in order:

_____ Journalize transactions.
_____ Post transactions.
_____ Analyze source documents.
_____ Prepare the work sheet.

_____ Journalize and post the closing entries.
_____ Prepare the financial statements.
_____ Journalize and post reversing entries.
_____ Journalize and post adjusting entries.
_____ Prepare the Post-Closing Trial Balance.

Problems

PROBLEM 4C-18 REVERSING ENTRY

During the year, $25,000 of wages were earned and paid. As of December 31, 200X, Roberts' Gift Wrap owed an additional $500 of wages that were earned but not yet paid. These wages will be paid January 13 in the bi-weekly payroll of $3,000.

Required:

1. Journalize the adjusting entry for wages earned but not yet paid.
2. Journalize the closing entry.
3. Journalize the reversing entry.
4. Post the adjusting, closing, and reversing entries to the Wages Expense and Wages Payable general ledger accounts.
5. Journalize and post payment of the $3,000 payroll on January 13.

PROBLEM 4C-19 NO REVERSING ENTRY

Using the same information supplied in Problem 4C-18, prepare needed general journal entries without using a reversing entry.

PROBLEM 4C-20 REVERSING ENTRY

During the year, $38,000 of wages were earned and paid. As of December 31, 200X, Betty's Dry Cleaning owed an additional $1,100 of wages that were earned but not yet paid. These wages will be paid January 13, 200X, in the bi-weekly payroll of $4,000.

Required:

1. Journalize the adjusting entry for wages earned but not yet paid.
2. Journalize the closing entry.
3. Journalize the reversing entry.
4. Post the adjusting, closing, and reversing entries to the Wages Expense and Wages Payable general ledger accounts.
5. Journalize and post payment of the $4,000 wages on January 13.

PROBLEM 4C-21 NO REVERSING ENTRY

Using the same information supplied in Problem 4C-20, prepare needed general journal entries without using a reversing entry.

Challenge Problem

Jill Benson, Architect, has accounts and balances at the end of December, 200X, as shown on the Trial Balance columns of the work sheet below. The following adjustments need to be made:

a.   An inventory of office supplies on hand shows a balance of $450.
b.   The amount of prepaid insurance which has expired or was used during the year amounted to $800.
c.   Depreciation expense for the year on the automobile totaled $3,000.
d.   Depreciation for the year for office equipment was $1,500.
e.   Accrued wages (owed but not yet paid) for the last three days of December total $950.

Jill Benson, Architect
Work Sheet (Partial)
For Year Ended December 31, 200X

	Account Title	Trial Balance Debit	Trial Balance Credit	Adjustments Debit	Adjustments Credit
1	Cash	11 2 0 0 00			
2	Office Supplies	8 0 0 00			
3	Prepaid Insurance	2 8 0 0 00			
4	Automobile	15 0 0 0 00			
5	Accum. Depr.—Automobile		3 0 0 0 00		
6	Office Equipment	12 0 0 0 00			
7	Accum. Depr.—Office Equip.		4 0 0 0 00		
8	Accounts Payable		2 1 0 0 00		
9	Wages Payable				
10	Jill Benson, Capital		22 0 0 0 00		
11	Jill Benson, Drawing	9 0 0 0 00			
12	Professional Fees		58 0 0 0 00		
13	Rent Expense	9 2 0 0 00			
14	Wages Expense	22 0 0 0 00			
15	Office Supplies Expense				
16	Insurance Expense				
17	Telephone Expense	1 8 0 0 00			
18	Automobile Repair Expense	9 0 0 00			
19	Depreciation Exp.—Automobile				
20	Depr. Exp.—Office Equipment				
21	Charitable Contributions Exp.	1 1 0 0 00			
22	Professional Development Exp.	3 0 0 0 00			
23	Miscellaneous Expense	3 0 0 00			
24		89 1 0 0 00	89 1 0 0 00		
25					

Required:

1. Complete the work sheet. Enter the adjustments described above into the Adjustments columns. Extend the balances to the Adjusted Trial Balance columns, the Income Statement columns, and the Balance columns.
2. Prepare the journal entries to record the adjusting entries.
3. Prepare the journal entries to record the closing entries.
4. Prepare the journal entry to record the reversing entry on January 1 of the next year.

Comprehensive Review Problem 2

Matlin Repair Service has the following balances on January 1, 200X.

		Debit	Credit
Cash	111	$ 8,500	
Office Supplies	121	3,000	
Prepaid Insurance	131	4,000	
Office Equipment	141	12,000	
Accumulated Depreciation—Equip.	141.1		$ 2,000
Truck	151	20,000	
Accumulated Depreciation—Truck	151.1		8,000
Accounts Payable	211		9,000
Notes Payable	221		4,000
M. Matlin, Capital	311		24,500

An examination of the chart of accounts reveals the following temporary accounts:

M. Matlin, Drawing	312
Repair Fees	411
Wages Expense	511
Rent Expense	521
Insurance Expense	522
Office Supplies Expense	531
Depreciation Expense—Equip.	541
Depreciation Expense—Truck	545
Repairs Expense	551
Telephone Expense	555
Utilities Expense	565
Advertising Expense	575
Miscellaneous Expense	599

The following transactions occurred during the month of January, 200X.

January 1 Paid monthly rent, $700.
2 Performed services on account, $1,500.
3 Paid for ads in newspaper, $100.
5 Paid $200 on existing note for $4,000.
7 Paid one week's wages to part-time workers, $500.
9 Performed services for cash, $1,700.
11 Paid telephone bill, $92.
12 Paid utilities bill, $128.
13 Received $800 for services previously performed.
14 Paid the week's wages to part-time workers, $500.
18 Paid $300 on account to creditors.
20 Performed services for cash, $1,600.
21 Paid the week's wages to part-time workers, $500.
22 Owner withdrew $400 for personal use.
24 Paid $280 for truck repairs.
26 Paid $40 for stamps and postage. (Misc. expense)
27 Performed services on account, $1,100.
28 Paid the week's wages to part-time workers, $500.
30 Gave $100 to the high school athletic program (advertising).

At the end of the month, records reveal the following information:

1. Office supplies on hand, $2,200.
2. Insurance expired during the month, $400.
3. Depreciation expense on the office equipment for the month, $200.
4. Depreciation expense on the truck for the month, $250.
5. Wages earned but not yet paid for December 29 and 30, $200.

Required:

1. Record the account balances in the general ledger accounts as of January 1, 200X.
2. Record the transactions in a general journal. Number the general journal pages beginning with page 22.
3. Post the journal to four-column accounts in the general ledger; keep running balances in all accounts.
4. Prepare a work sheet for the month ending January 31, 200X.
5. Prepare the financial statements (the income statement, the statement of owner's equity, and the balance sheet).
6. Journalize and post the adjusting entries.
7. Journalize and post the closing entries.
8. Prepare a port-closing trial balance.

Chapter FIVE

Accounting for Cash

The following modules will be covered in this chapter:

Module 5A
Accounting for Cash

Accounting for cash receipts and cash payments, setting up a change fund, and using a petty cash fund.

Module 5B
Banking Procedures

Banking procedures relating to a checking account, reconciling a bank statement, and journalizing entries from the bank reconciliation.

Accounting for Cash

Module 5A Objectives
Careful study of this module should enable you to:
1. Define the term "Cash" and understand how the cash account is affected by cash receipts and cash payments.
2. Define internal control and detail the accounting and control responsibilities for processing cash receipts.
3. Journalize the daily cash deposit, using the account "Cash Short and Over" for any shortage or overage in the count of cash.
4. Understand the nature of a change fund, including how one is established.
5. Understand the nature of a "Petty Cash Fund," including how it is established and replenished.

Now that you have covered the accounting cycle, let's look more closely at the cash account. The account title Cash includes currency (dollar bills) and coins, cash items on hand, and cash on deposit in one or more bank accounts. **Cash items on hand** includes checks, drafts, credit card receipts, and money orders that have not yet been deposited in the bank.

Where cash is involved, it is a good management policy to adopt a system of internal control. **Internal control** involves the methods designed to safeguard assets. An internal policy relating to cash requires that all cash and cash items be deposited daily in a bank. Notice in Exhibit 5.1 the assignment of key accounting and control responsibilities for processing cash receipts.

Exhibit 5.1

Key Accounting and Control Responsibilities

Responsibility 1   On a daily basis, a mail clerk opens customer remittances and prepares a list of the checks for deposit. Three copies of this list are made, one of which is retained by the mail clerk. One copy of the list, along with the checks, is sent to the cashier, while the remaining copy is forwarded to the accounting department.

Responsibility 2   The cashier prepares a daily deposit slip listing the checks received from customers, makes the deposit, and then sends a duplicate copy of the deposit ticket to the accounting department.

Responsibility 3   An accounting clerk determines that the listing of receipts prepared by the mail clerk and the receipts reflected by the duplicate copy of the deposit ticket agree. Then, the clerk makes the appropriate entries to record the receipts.

As you can see in Exhibit 5.1, there should be a separation of duties involving the handling of cash.

Cash Receipts

Cash and cash items received by a business are known as **cash receipts**. A cash register is a useful device to record receipts of currency and coins.

Many business transactions involve credit sales. Part of the bill or statement may include a detachable form showing the remitter's (customer or client) name, address, and the amount of payment. An example of such a form, which is the top part of a monthly statement that a patient would receive, is shown in Exhibit 5.2.

Exhibit 5.2

Patient's Monthly Statement

Dr. Dale Jenkins
2715 Creekbend Dr.
Houston, TX 77089-4825

MAKE CHECKS PAYABLE TO THE ABOVE.
TO INSURE PROPER CREDIT
PLEASE RETURN THIS PORTION IN THE ENCLOSED ENVELOPE.

PHONE NUMBER	DATE
555-1822	10/31/0X

ACCOUNT NUMBER	PATIENT	PLEASE PAY THIS AMOUNT
231505	Melvin Bowers	172.00

RETAIN BOTTOM PORTION FOR INCOME TAX PURPOSES.
IT WILL BE THE ONLY RECORD WHICH YOU WILL RECEIVE.
(SEE REVERSE SIDE FOR INSTRUCTIONS)

TEAR HERE   **TEAR HERE**

ACCOUNT NUMBER	PATIENT NAME & RESPONSIBLE PARTY	PHONE NUMBER	DATE
231505	Melvin Bowers Elsie Bowers	555-1501	10/31/0X

MO	DAY	YR	DESCRIPTION	AMOUNT
09	15	0X	INITIAL OFFICE VISIT, EXAM	65.00
09	25	0X	Oral Surgery	795.00
09	29	0X	Post-op office visit	
09	30	0X	Medical insurance filed, $860	
10	25	0X	Received insurance check	688.00 CR

Jenkins Medical Clinic, Inc.	BALANCE DUE
	172.00

DISREGARD THIS STATEMENT IF IT HAS BEEN PAID WITHIN THE LAST 10 DAYS

This form provides the source document for journalizing the cash received. The initial record of cash received should be prepared by someone other than the accountant. The cash is then given to the person authorized to handle bank deposits. The accountant uses the initial records in preparing journal entries for cash receipts. As mentioned earlier in discussing internal control over cash, the procedure of using two or more persons to handle cash reduces the danger of theft. For example, a two-person system of handling cash involves one person counting, and the other person preparing the deposit slip.

Cash Payments

Cash and cash items paid by a business are known as cash payments. Payment may be made in cash or by check. When payments are made in cash, a receipt should be obtained as evidence of the payment. When payments are made by check, the canceled check serves this purpose.

The bank account, sometimes called Cash in Bank, is debited for cash deposits and credited for checks written. If a business has more than one bank account, a separate ledger account may be kept for each bank. Examples such as Cash—Mercantile Bank, or Cash—Pacific Federal could be used. Sometimes, cash is transferred between bank accounts. For example, the journal entry to show a $2,500 cash transfer on March 1, from Pacific Federal to Mercantile Bank, would be as follows:

General Journal

	Date	Description	Post. Ref.	Debit	Credit	
1	Mar. 1	Cash—Mercantile Bank		2 5 0 0 00		1
2		Cash—Pacific Federal			2 5 0 0 00	2
3		Transfer of cash between banks				3
4						4

Cash Short and Over

(handwritten: debit/exp. credit/rev.)

Sometimes there is a difference between the cash count and the daily deposit. This usually results from human error in making change. Most businesses have a special ledger account entitled Cash Short and Over, which is used to keep track of daily shortages and overages of cash.

A journal entry should be entered daily to record the amount of cash sales for the day. At the end of the day, the cash count is compared to the cash register tape. Any shortages or overages are recognized in the journal entry. For example, assume that the cash register tape on March 15 indicates cash sales for the day are $2,450.00 The cash count indicates $2,447.00. The journal entry to record the cash deposit would be as follows:

	Date		Description	Post. Ref.	Debit	Credit	
General Journal							
20	Mar.	15	Cash		2 4 4 7 00		20
21			Cash Short and Over		3 00		21
22			Income from Services			2 4 5 0 00	22
23			To record cash sales				23
24							24

Notice that the amount shown on the cash register tape is credited to Income from Services. The actual cash count is debited to Cash. The difference between the debit to Cash and the credit to Income from Services represents a shortage or overage. For illustrative purposes, assume the cash register tape on March 16 indicates cash sales for the day are $1,983.00. The cash count indicates $1,992.00. The journal entry to record the cash deposit would be as follows:

	Date		Description	Post. Ref.	Debit	Credit	
General Journal							
25	Mar.	16	Cash		1 9 9 2 00		25
26			Cash Short and Over			9 00	26
27			Income from Services			1 9 8 3 00	27
28			To record cash sales				28
29							29

KEY POINT

Always credit the appropriate revenue account such as Income from Services, or Service Revenue, for the amount that appears on the cash register tape. Always debit Cash for the actual cash count. When there is a difference, the account Cash Short and Over is used to balance the debits and credits.

At the end of the accounting period, the Cash Short and Over account will contain either a debit or credit balance. A debit balance represents an expense and is included with Miscellaneous Expense on the income statement. A credit balance represents revenue and is included with Miscellaneous Revenue on the income statement.

Change Fund

Many businesses like to start off the day with a **change fund** for those customers or clients who do not have the exact amount of change. A change fund is classified as an asset and appears in the balance sheet as a current asset. For illustrative purposes, assume a change fund of $200 is needed. The journal entry to establish a change fund on June 1 would appear as follows:

	Date	Description	Post. Ref.	Debit	Credit	
1	June 1	Change Fund		2 0 0 00		1
2		Cash			2 0 0 00	2
3		To establish a change fund				3
4						4

General Journal

When a business has a change fund, the method of determining the cash deposit will vary slightly. For illustrative purposes, assume the cash register tape on August 5 indicates cash sales of $1,755.00. The cash count including the change fund is $1,950.00. The amount of cash to deposit is $1,750.00, after deducting the $200 change fund.

KEY POINT

Always deduct the amount in the change fund from cash before making the cash deposit.

The journal entry would appear as follows:

	Date	Description	Post. Ref.	Debit	Credit	
5	Aug. 5	Cash		1 7 5 0 00		5
6		Cash Short and Over		5 00		6
7		Income from Services			1 7 5 5 00	7
8		To record cash sales				8
9						9

General Journal

Petty Cash Fund

Sometimes it is convenient to pay for small items using an office fund known as a **petty cash fund** (petty means small or little). Such a fund eliminates the necessity of writing business checks for small dollar amounts. To establish a petty cash fund, a check is written to Petty Cash for the desired amount. The journal entry establishing a petty cash fund on September 27 would appear as follows:

General Journal

	Date	Description	Post. Ref.	Debit	Credit	
26	Sep. 27	Petty Cash		1 0 0 00		26
27		Cash			1 0 0 00	27
28		To establish a petty cash fund				28
29						29

Petty cash is an asset that can be listed immediately below Cash on the balance sheet. Most accountants, however, combine petty cash with cash and show one total in the cash account.

To maintain good internal control, one individual should be assigned responsibility for the petty cash fund. This responsibility would include making sure that a petty cash voucher is filled out each time the fund is used. These vouchers should be numbered consecutively and signed by the petty cash fund custodian and the person receiving the cash. An example of a petty cash voucher is shown in Exhibit 5.3.

Exhibit 5.3
Petty Cash Voucher

Petty Cash Voucher		
No. _____ 16 _____	**Date**	*January 15, 200X*
Paid to _ *Barbara Nolting* _	**Amount**	
For _ *American Cancer Society* _		35 | 00
Charge to _ *Charitable Contribution Expense* _		
Remittance received		
_ *Barbara Nolting* _	**Approved by**	*Delwin Harris*

Petty Cash Payments Record

When a petty cash fund is maintained, it is good practice to keep a formal record of all payments from the fund. A special multi-column form, known as a **petty cash payments record**, is used. Its primary use is to provide, in summary form, the information needed to journalize the replenishment of the petty cash fund.

In a petty cash payments record, the headings of the Distribution columns may vary depending upon the types of expenditures. In accounting practice, the preferred sequence of headings is alphabetical, with Miscellaneous Expenses last. The voucher number (Vou. No.) column is used to record the voucher number assigned to the petty cash voucher. These headings represent accounts that will be charged for the payments.

The petty cash payments record of Melissa Vowell, a business consultant, is shown on pages 148 and 149 in Exhibit 5.4. A narrative of the petty cash transactions follows.

Jan. 1   Vowell issued a check for $200 payable to Lisa Roehrl, Petty Cash Fund Custodian, to establish the petty cash fund. Roehrl cashed the check and placed the money in a secure cash box.

source document for journal

A notation of the amount received is made in the Description column of the petty cash payments record. In addition, this transaction is entered in the journal as follows:

	Date		Description	Post. Ref.	Debit	Credit	
1	200X						1
2	Jan.	1	Petty Cash		2 0 0 00		2
3			Cash			2 0 0 00	3
4			To establish petty cash fund				4
5							5

General Journal

During the month of January, the following payments were made from the petty cash fund.

Jan.   3 Paid $15.00 to Wilkerson's Auto Repair for repairing the company automobile. Voucher no. 1.

  5 Reimbursed Vowell $18.90 for the amount spent on entertaining a client at lunch. Voucher no. 2.

  9 Gave Vowell $15.00 for personal use. Voucher no. 3.

There is no special Distribution column for entering amounts withdrawn by the owner for personal use. Therefore, this $15 payment is entered in the Amount column at the extreme right of the petty cash payments record.

  10 Gave the American Cancer Society a $20.00 donation. Voucher no. 4.

  11 Paid $23.50 for typewriter repairs. Voucher no. 5.

  15 Reimbursed Vowell $20.85 for travel expenses. Voucher no. 6.

  17 Paid $25.00 to Expert Detail Shop for cleaning the company automobile. Voucher no. 7.

  19 Paid $10.75 for mailing a package. Voucher no. 8.

  24 Donated $10.00 for Community Child Care, Inc. Voucher no. 9.

  26 Paid $25.00 for postage stamps. Voucher no. 10.

  31 Reimbursed Vowell $5.30 for a long-distance telephone call made from a public telephone. Voucher no. 11.

Exhibit 5.4

Petty Cash Payments Record

	Day	Description	Vou. No.	Total Amount	Distribution of Debits	
					Auto Expense	Charit. Contr. Exp.
1	1	AMOUNTS FORWARDED				
2	1	Received in fund $200.00				
3	3	Automobile repairs	1	15 00	15 00	
4	5	Client luncheon	2	18 90		
5	9	Melissa Vowell, personal use	3	15 00		
6	10	American Cancer Society	4	20 00		20 00
7	11	Typewriter repairs	5	23 50		
8	15	Travel expense	6	20 85		
9	17	Cleaning automobile	7	25 00	25 00	
10	19	Postage expense	8	10 75		
11	24	Community Child Care, Inc.	9	10 00		10 00
12	26	Postage stamps	10	25 00		
13	31	Long-distance call	11	5 30		
14				189 30	40 00	30 00
15	31	Balance $ 10.70				
16	31	Replenished fund 189.30				
17		Total $200.00				
18						

Page 1   **PETTY CASH PAYMENTS**

Replenishing the Petty Cash Fund

The petty cash fund should be replenished whenever the fund runs low and at the end of each accounting period so that the accounts are brought up to date. The sum of the Distribution columns of the petty cash payments record must equal the sum of the Total Amount column. After proving the petty cash payments record, the totals are entered and the record is ruled as shown above and on page 149.

The information in the petty cash payments record is then used to replenish the petty cash fund. On January 31, a check for $189.30 is issued to the petty cash custodian. The check may be written to "Petty Cash," but the account Petty Cash is never debited when replenishing it. The journal entry to record the replenishment of the fund is as follows.

FOR THE MONTH OF January, 200X

	Distribution of Debits						
Postage Exp.	Telephone Exp.	Travel & Ent. Exp.	Misc. Exp.	Account	Amount	
						1
						2
						3
		1 8 90				4
				M. Vowell, Drawing	1 5 00	5
						6
			2 3 50			7
		2 0 85				8
						9
1 0 75						10
						11
2 5 00						12
	5 30					13
3 5 75	5 30	3 9 75	2 3 50		1 5 00	14
						15
						16
						17
						18

General Journal

	Date		Description	Post. Ref.	Debit	Credit	
1	200X						1
2	Jan.	31	Automobile Expense		4 0 00		2
3			Charitable Contributions Expense		3 0 00		3
4			Postage Expense		3 5 75		4
5			Telephone Expense		5 30		5
6			Travel and Entertainment Expense		3 9 75		6
7			Miscellaneous Expense		2 3 50		7
8			Melissa Vowell, Drawing		1 5 00		8
9			Cash			1 8 9 30	9
10			To replenish petty cash fund				10
11							11

KEY POINT

When replenishing the petty cash fund, debit each account affected and credit Cash. Do not debit or credit Petty Cash unless the
fund is to be increased or decreased.

Concept Questions

1. What is included in the account titled Cash?
2. What account title is used to record shortages and overages of cash?
3. What is the purpose of a petty cash fund?
4. When a petty cash fund is replenished, what account title(s) are debited and credited?

If you cannot answer the above concept questions, go back and review the module material before continuing to the next module.

MODULE SUMMARY

The account title Cash includes cash, cash items on hand, and cash on deposit in a bank. It is good management to have internal control over the receipt and payment of cash. A cash register tape is an effective internal control device to record cash receipts. Cash receipts should be deposited daily. The cash count should be compared with the cash register tape. The account title Cash Short and Over is used to record daily shortages and overages. A change fund is used to begin the day for those customers who do not have the exact amount of change. A petty cash fund is used to pay for small items. A petty cash payments record is used to keep track of petty cash disbursements. A summary of this record is used to record the journal entry to replenish the petty cash fund.

Key Terms

Cash in Bank, *142*
cash items on hand, *139*
cash payments, *142*
cash receipts, *140*
Cash Short and Over, *142*

change fund, *144*
internal control, *139*
petty cash fund, *145*
petty cash payments record, *146*

Exercises

EXERCISE 5A-1

Betty Astin is a financial consultant. She keeps three cash accounts in her ledger: (1) Cash on Hand, (2) Cash—First City National Bank, and (3) Cash—Columbia Federal Bank. Cash on Hand is used for all incoming fees; deposits are transferred to and checks are written from the other two accounts. Prepare journal entries to enter the following transactions in the general journal.

Feb. 2 Received $3,600 in professional fees from clients.
    13 Deposited $4,900 in First City National Bank.
    15 Deposited $2,500 in Columbia Federal Bank.
    19 Paid $720 on account to Henderson Supply Company by check on Columbia Federal Bank.
    23 Paid $600 on account to Stanton Equipment Company by check on First City National Bank.
    28 Recorded bank service charges (Miscellaneous Expense) as follows: First City National Bank, $17.80, and Columbia Federal Bank, $12.70.
    28 Transferred $5,000 from First City National Bank to Columbia Federal Bank.

EXERCISE 5A-2   HW 10/18/99

Based on the following information, prepare the daily cash deposits, in general journal form, using the account title "Cash Short and Over" for any cash shortages or overages. A change fund was established for $200. Determine the balance in the Cash Short and Over account and identify the type of account the balance represents—income or expense. Hint: Remember to deduct the $200 change fund from the actual cash count.

Date	Cash Register Tape Amount	Actual Cash Count
Aug. 5	$1,430.65	$1,632.56
6	941.52	1,140.93
7	683.39	882.25
8	683.60	882.45
9	1,356.30	1,552.25

EXERCISE 5A-3

On September 1, 200X, Rachel's Accounting Services established a petty cash fund in the amount of $150. The following payments were made from the fund in September:

Automobile Expense	$ 28.35
Miscellaneous Expense	19.25
Postage Expense	70.00
Supplies Expense	24.16
Telephone Expense	6.27
Total	$148.03

Required:

1. Prepare the journal entry to establish the petty cash fund on September 1. A cash balance of $1.65 remained in the petty cash fund on September 30.
2. Prepare the journal entry to replenish the fund on September 30. Use the Cash Short and Over account for any shortage or overage in the petty cash fund.

EXERCISE 5A-4

Jewell Ramariz, a computer consultant, completed the following petty cash transactions during the month of August, 200X.

Aug. 2 Issued check for $200 payable to Jim Graves, who serves as petty cash custodian.

4 Reimbursed Ramariz $23.80 for entertaining a client at lunch. Voucher No. 1.

7 Paid Lopez Car Wash $8.25 for washing the company automobile. Voucher No. 2.

11 Gave Ramariz $20 for personal use. Voucher No. 3.

14 Gave the American Heart Association a $50 donation. Voucher No. 4.

16 Paid Johnson Office Machines $7.90 for typewriter repairs. Voucher No. 5.

17 Paid $9.40 for mailing a package. Voucher No. 6.

22 Reimbursed Ramariz $5.45 for a long distance call. Voucher No. 7.

25 Paid $35 for postage stamps. Voucher No. 8.

28 Donated $10 to Girl Scouts of America. Voucher No. 9.

31 Paid Ron Tonkin Auto $19.95 for servicing the company automobile. Voucher No. 10.

Required:

1. Open a petty cash payments record for the month of August, 200X, with the following column headings:

   Day   Description   Voucher No.   Total Amount   Auto Expense
   Charitable Contributions Expense   Postage Expense
   Telephone Expense   Travel and Entertainment Expense
   Miscellaneous Expense   Account   Amount

2. Record the preceding petty cash transactions in the petty cash pay-
    ments record. Then foot all the amount columns, determine the total
    needed to replenish the fund. Complete the record assuming the
    petty cash fund was replenished on August 31.

Problems

PROBLEM 5A-5

On September 1, 200X, a change fund was established for Sheffield
Communications for $300. Listed below are the daily cash register tape
amounts for sales and the related cash counts during the first week of
September.

	Cash Register Tape	Cash in Drawer
Sept. 1	$635.25	$936.50
2	547.80	841.60
3	498.50	795.50
4	510.90	812.65
5	673.40	971.95

Required:

1. Prepare the journal entry to record the establishment of the change
    fund on September 1.
2. Prepare the journal entries to record the cash sales and cash short and
    over for each of the five days.
3. Post to the Cash Short and Over account.
4. Determine the ending balance of the Cash Short and Over account.
    Does it represent an expense or revenue?

PROBLEM 5A-6

On May 1, 200X, a petty cash fund was established for $175. The following
vouchers were issued during May:

Date	Voucher No.	Purpose	Amount
May 1	1	Typewriter ribbons	$12.65
5	2	Postage stamps	32.00
10	3	Gas & oil for company car	12.45
12	4	Telephone call	4.15
13	5	Donation (Salvation Army)	20.00
17	6	Newspaper (Misc.)	10.25
20	7	Cleaning & washing car	16.00
24	8	Drawing (M. Carson)	12.00
28	9	Window washing (Misc.)	18.00
31	10	Car servicing	19.95

Required:

1. Prepare the journal entry to establish the petty cash fund.
2. Enter the petty cash payments for May on page 1 of the petty cash payments record using the following columns:

   Day   Description   Voucher No.   Total Amount
   Automobile Expense   Charitable Contributions Expense
   Office Supplies Expense   Postage Expense   Telephone Expense
   Miscellaneous Expense   Account   Amount

3. Total and rule the petty cash record.
4. A balance of $16.45 remained in the petty cash fund. Prepare the journal entry to replenish the petty cash fund. Make the appropriate entry in the petty cash record.

PROBLEM 5A-7

On October 1, 200X, a change fund was established for the Stennet Company for $200. Listed below are the daily cash register tape amounts for sales and the related cash counts during the first week of October.

	Cash Register Tape	Cash in Drawer
Oct. 1	$325.70	$520.20
2	397.42	559.92
3	265.00	467.35
4	345.85	544.70
5	287.65	492.10

Required:

1. Prepare the journal entry to record the establishment of the change fund on October 1.
2. Prepare the journal entries to record the cash sales and cash short and over for each of the five days.
3. Post to the Cash Short and Over account.
4. Determine the ending balance of the Cash Short and Over account. Does it represent an expense or revenue?

PROBLEM 5A-8

On June 1, 200X, a petty cash fund was established for $250. The following vouchers were issued during June:

Date	Voucher No.	Purpose	Amount
June 1	1	Typewriter ribbons	$19.85
5	2	Postage stamps	35.00
10	3	Gas & oil for company car	19.45
12	4	Telephone call	8.65
13	5	Donation (United Way)	60.00
17	6	Newspaper (Misc.)	16.25
20	7	Cleaning & washing car	18.25
24	8	Drawing (J. Eary)	18.00
28	9	Window washing (Misc.)	14.50
30	10	Car servicing	19.95

Required:

1. Prepare the journal entry to establish the petty cash fund.
2. Enter the petty cash payments for June on page 1 of the petty cash payments record using the following columns:

   Day   Description   Voucher No.   Total Amount
   Automobile Expense   Charitable Contributions Expense
   Office Supplies Expense   Postage Expense   Telephone Expense
   Miscellaneous Expense   Account   Amount

3. Total and rule the petty cash record.
4. A cash balance of $22.35 remained in the petty cash fund. Prepare the journal entry to replenish the petty cash fund. Use the Cash Short and Over for any shortage or overage. Make the appropriate entry in the petty cash record.

Banking Procedures

Module 5B Objectives

Careful study of this module should enable you to:

1. Open a checking account, make deposits, endorse and write checks.
2. Reconcile a bank statement.
3. Journalize entries affecting the cash account from the bank reconciliation.

In the first module of this chapter, we discussed how a business accounts for its cash receipts. We also looked at how a business uses a petty cash fund for small cash payments. Let's continue our discussion of cash by examining how a business accounts for larger cash payments with the aid of a checking account.

CHECKING ACCOUNT

The forms involved with opening and using a checking account are the signature card, deposit tickets, checks, and bank statements. See Exhibits 5.5 and 5.6 for examples of a signature card and deposit ticket.

Opening a Checking Account

To open a checking account, proper approval is needed from the bank, along with an initial cash deposit. A signature card, shown in Exhibit 5.5, must be completed and signed by each person authorized to sign checks. This card is kept on record for the bank to verify the depositor's signature. To aid in identification, the depositor's social security number or business identification number is shown on the card.

Exhibit 5.5
Signature Card

LAST NAME, FIRST NAME, MIDDLE INITIAL	ACCT #	
	TYPE	
	DATE	INIT.
STREET ADDRESS TOWN	STATE ZIP	

I CERTIFY THAT THE NUMBER SHOWN ON THIS FORM IS MY CORRECT TAXPAYER
IDENTIFICATION NUMBER AND THAT I AM NOT SUBJECT TO BACKUP WITHHOLDING.

SIGNATURE 1	DATE OF BIRTH	SOCIAL SECURITY NO.
	/ /	
SIGNATURE 2		
SIGNATURE 3		

Making Deposits

A deposit ticket, shown in Exhibit 5.6, is a form used by the bank. It summarizes the count of coins, currency and checks being deposited. Each check should be identified by its ABA (American Bankers Association) Number. This number is the small fraction printed in the upper right hand corner of each check. Only the numerator (the top number) of this fraction is used.

The deposit ticket is totaled and all cash items (including checks) are given to the bank teller. The teller processes the deposit and provides a machine-printed receipt.

Endorsements

Each check that is to be deposited must be endorsed by the depositor. The endorsement consists of stamping or writing the depositor's name on the back of the check. There are two basic endorsements.

1. Blank endorsement. The depositor simply signs his or her name on the back of the check. The check is payable to any bearer.

Exhibit 5.6
Deposit Ticket

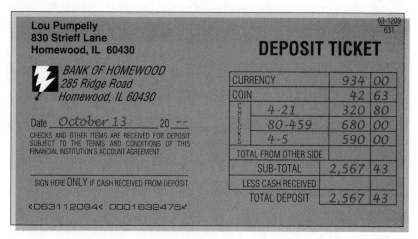

2. Restrictive endorsement. The depositor adds words such as "For Deposit Only" or "Pay to Karen Douglas Only." This restricts the payment of the check.

A widely used business practice when endorsing checks for deposit is to use a rubber stamp to print the endorsement. A check that has been stamped with a restrictive endorsement is shown in Exhibit 5.7.

Exhibit 5.7
Restrictive Endorsement

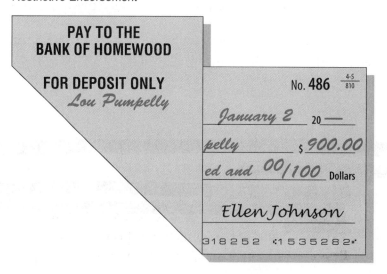

Deposits by Mail and Night Deposits

Deposits by mail should consist only of checks. It is extremely risky to send cash through the mail. A machine-printed receipt for the deposit is returned through the mail. A night deposit involves putting the deposit in a secured bag and placing the bag in a designated slot at the bank. A bank employee will later verify the deposit. The machine-printed receipt for the deposit is returned with the bag.

Automated Teller Machines

Many banks now make automated teller machines available at all times for use by depositors. Each depositor has a plastic card (see Exhibit 5.8) and a code number. The depositor inserts the card into the machine, keys in his or her personal identification (pin) number, indicates whether the transaction is a withdrawal or a deposit, and keys in the amount. The machine has a drawer or slot for the withdrawal or deposit. A machine-printed receipt is given at the time of the transaction.

Exhibit 5.8
Automated Teller

Writing Checks

A check is a document that orders a bank to pay cash from a depositor's account. There are three parties to every check.

1. Drawer—the depositor who orders the bank to pay cash.
2. Drawee—the bank on which the check is drawn.
3. Payee—the person being paid the cash.

Business checks usually come bound in the form of a book. Each check may be attached to a check stub that contains space to record all relevant information about the check. See example of checks and check stubs below. Three steps should be followed in preparing a check.

Step 1   Complete the check stub.
Step 2   Enter the date, payee name, and amount on the check.
Step 3   Sign the check.

It is very important for the drawer to complete the check stub first. The check stub provides the information to later enter the proper journal entry. On the check stub (see Exhibit 5.9), record the date, who the check is written to, and for what purpose. Also, the account to be debited should be written on the line beginning with ACCT. The amount of the check should be subtracted from the balance brought forward, then the ending balance of cash should be written in the balance carried forward line.

Exhibit 5.9
Checks and Check Stubs

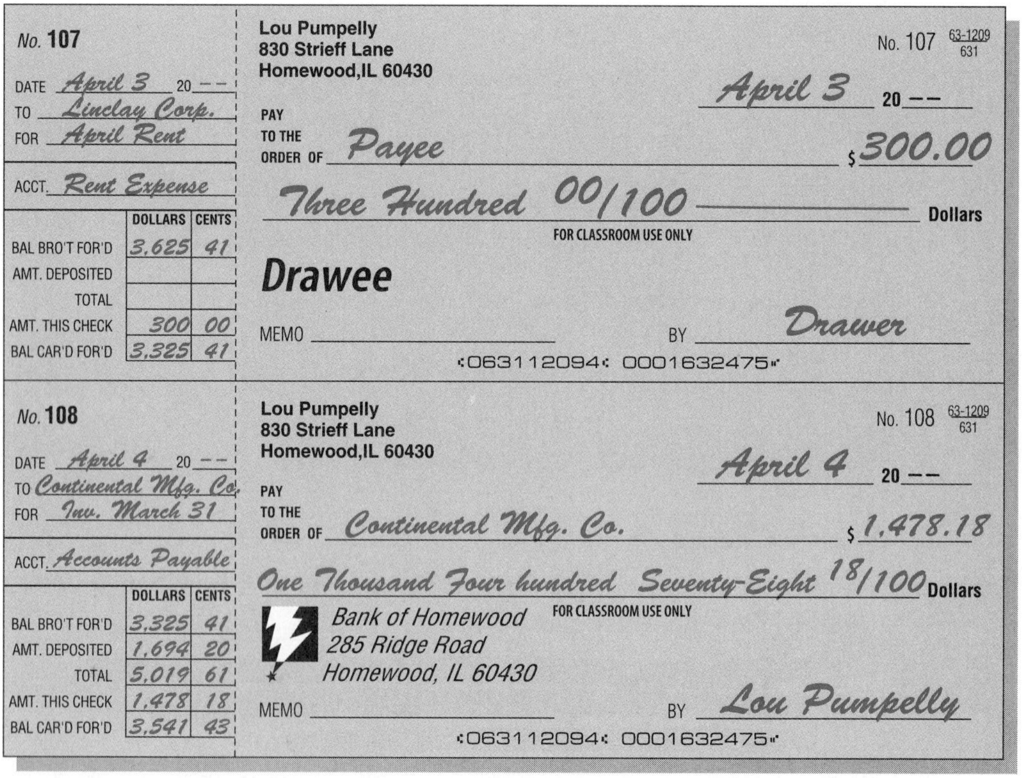

Bank Statement

Once a month, the bank mails a statement of account, called a bank statement, to each depositor. Exhibit 5.10 on page 162 is an example of a bank statement. The statement includes the following:

1. The beginning balance for the period
2. Deposits and other amounts (such as a bank collection of a note receivable) added during the period
3. Checks and other amounts (such as an NSF check, which stands for non-sufficient funds, and represents a check that was attempted to be deposited to our account but the customer/client did not have enough funds to back up the check) subtracted during the period
4. The ending balance for the period

Included with the bank statement are canceled checks (the depositor's checks paid by the bank during the period) and any other items that increased or decreased the account balance. Note: Not all banks return canceled checks. In this case, a request is made for a copy of the canceled check.

Reconciling the Bank Statement.   When the bank statement is received, the depositor should compare the ending checkbook balance to the ending bank statement balance. This process of bringing the book and bank balances into agreement is called a bank reconciliation. The most common reasons for differences between the checkbook and bank balances are the following:

1. **Outstanding checks**—Checks written by the depositor that have not yet cleared the bank for payment.
2. **Deposits in transit**—Deposits recorded on the depositor's books but have not yet been received or recorded on the bank records.
3. **Service charges**—Bank charges for services such as check processing and printing.
4. **Collections**—Collections of promissory notes or charge accounts made by the bank on behalf of the depositor. In addition, interest may have been earned on a promissory note left for collection.
5. **Deductions**—Deductions for the payment of authorized bills, such as rent or mortgage payments.

6. **Not sufficient funds (NSF) checks**—These checks were rejected by the bank because the customer (drawer) did not have sufficient funds to cover the amount.
7. **Errors**—Errors made by the bank or the depositor.

Exhibit 5.10
Bank Statement

STATEMENT	⚡ BANK OF HOMEWOOD		

LOU PUMPELLY
830 STRIEFF LANE
HOMEWOOD, IL 60430

Reference Number: 16 3247 5
Statement Date: Nov. 21, 20—
Statement Instructions:
Page Number: 1

Beginning Balance	No. of Deposits and Credits	We Have Added these Deposits and Credits Totaling	No. of Withdrawals and Charges	We Have Subtracted these Withdrawals and Charges Totaling	Resulting in a Statement Balance of
$2,721.51	2	$2,599.31	17	$3,572.73	$1,748.09

Document Count	Average Daily Balance this Statement Period	Minimum Balance this Statement Period	Date	Amount

If Your Account does not Balance, Please See Reverse Side and Report any Discrepancies to our Customer Service Department.

DATE	DESCRIPTION	AMOUNT	BALANCE
10/20	Beginning Balance		2,721.51
10/27	Check No. 207	−242.00	2,479.51
10/28	Check No. 212	−68.93	2,410.58
10/28	Check No. 213	−58.00	2,352.58
10/29	Deposit	867.00	3,219.58
11/3	Deposit	1,732.31	4,951.89
11/3	Check No. 214	−18.98	4,932.91
11/3	Check No. 215	−229.01	4,703.90
11/3	Check No. 216	−452.13	4,251.77
11/3	Check No. 217	−94.60	4,157.17
11/10	Check No. 218	−1,800.00	2,357.17
11/10	DM: NSF	−200.00	2,157.17
11/10	Check No. 220	−32.42	2,124.75
11/10	Check No. 221	−64.08	2,060.67
11/10	Check No. 222	−210.87	1,849.80
11/18	Check No. 223	−18.00	1,831.80
11/18	Check No. 225	−23.31	1,808.49
11/18	Check No. 226	−58.60	1,749.89
11/19	DM: Service Charge	−1.80	1,748.09

EC – Error Correction
CM – Credit Memo
DM – Debit Memo
NSF – Not Sufficient Funds
ATM – Automated Teller Machine
TR – Wire Transfer

Steps in Preparing the Bank Reconciliation.   Use the following three steps in preparing the bank reconciliation.

Step 1   Identify deposits in transit and any related errors.
Step 2   Identify outstanding checks and any related errors.
Step 3   Identify additional reconciling items.

Deposits in Transit and Related Errors.   Follow these steps.

1. Compare deposits listed on the bank statement with deposits in transit on last month's bank reconciliation. All of last month's deposits in transit should appear on this month's bank statement.
2. Compare the remaining deposits on the bank statement with deposits listed in the accounting records. Any deposits listed in the accounting records but not on the bank statement are deposits in transit on the current bank reconciliation.
3. If there are differences between the deposits listed on the bank statement and those listed in the accounting records, the error needs to be corrected.

Outstanding Checks and Related Errors.   Follow these steps.

1. Compare canceled checks with the bank statement and the accounting records. If the amounts differ, the error needs to be corrected.
2. As each canceled check is compared with the accounting records, place a check mark on the check stub to indicate that the check has cleared.
3. The checks without check marks represent outstanding checks and should be listed on the bank reconciliation form.

Additional Reconciling Items.   Such things as service charges, NSF checks, and collections represent additional reconciling items. The bank notifies the depositor of service charges and NSF checks by issuing **debit memos**. The bank notifies the depositor of collections by issuing **credit memos**.

Format of a Bank Reconciliation.   A general format for the bank reconciliation is shown in Exhibit 5.11. Not all of the reconciling items shown in this format would appear in every bank reconciliation.

Exhibit 5.11

Bank Reconciliation Form

Ending bank statement balance		$ _____
Add: Deposits in transit	$ _____	
Bank errors that understate		
bank statement balance	_____	_____
Subtotal		$ _____
Deduct: Outstanding checks	$ _____	
Bank errors that overstate		
bank statement balance	_____	_____
Adjusted bank balance		$ _____
Ending checkbook balance		$ _____
* Add: Bank credit memos	$ _____	
Recording errors that		
understate checkbook balance	_____	_____
Subtotal		$ _____
* Deduct: Bank debit memos	$ _____	
Recording errors that		
overstate checkbook balance	_____	_____
Adjusted checkbook balance		$ _____

* Note: All additions and deductions to the book balance must be journalized and posted to the general ledger cash account.

To illustrate the preparation of a bank reconciliation, we will use the Lou Pumpelly bank statement shown on page 162. That statement shows an ending balance of $1,748.09. The balance in Pumpelly's general ledger cash account is $2,293.23. The three steps described on page 163 were used to identify the reconciling items. The completed bank reconciliation is shown in Exhibit 5.12 on page 165.

1. A deposit of $637.02 on November 21 on the books had not been received by the bank. The deposit in transit is added to the bank statement balance.
2. Check number 219 for $200, number 224 for $25, and number 227 for $67.78, are outstanding. These outstanding checks are subtracted from the bank statement balance.
3. Check number 214 was written for $18.98, but was entered on the check stub and on the books as $19.88. This $.90 error is added to the checkbook balance because an extra $.90 has been deducted from the checkbook balance. This check was written in payment of an account payable.

4. The bank returned an NSF check for $200. This amount is deducted from the book balance. The check was from a customer who made a payment on account.
5. The bank service charge was $1.80. This amount is deducted from the book balance.

Exhibit 5.12
Bank Reconciliation

Lou Pumpelly Bank Reconciliation November 21, 200X													
Bank statement balance, November 21									1	7	4	8	09
Add deposit in transit										6	3	7	02
									2	3	8	5	11
Deduct outstanding checks:													
No. 219	2	0	0	00									
No. 224		2	5	00									
No. 227		6	7	78			2	9	2	78			
Adjusted bank balance									2	0	9	2	33
Checkbook balance, November 21									2	2	9	3	23
*Add error on stub for Check No. 214													90
									2	2	9	4	13
*Deduct NSF check	2	0	0	00									
*Bank service charge			1	80			2	0	1	80			
Adjusted checkbook balance									2	0	9	2	33

Journal Entries. All additions and deductions to the book balance must be journalized and posted to the Cash account. Note the three items in the lower portion of the Lou Pumpelly bank reconciliation. These are items the bank knew about, but the company did not. A journal entry is required for each item.

The $.90 item is an error that occurred when the check amount was incorrectly entered in the books. Cash was credited for $.90 too much and Accounts Payable was debited for $.90 too much. The following journal entry will correct the error:

General Journal

	Date		Description	Post. Ref.	Debit	Credit	
22	Nov	21	Cash		90		22
23			Accounts Payable			90	23
24							24

The $200 NSF check represents a debit memo from the bank. The check received from a customer for a payment on account is worthless. The following journal entry is required:

	Date		Description	Post. Ref.	Debit	Credit	
25	Nov.	21	Accounts Receivable		2 0 0 00		25
26			Cash			2 0 0 00	26
27							27

The $1.80 bank service charge represents another debit memo from the bank. Bank service charges are usually small and are charged to Miscellaneous Expense.

	Date		Description	Post. Ref.	Debit	Credit	
28	Nov.	21	Miscellaneous Expense		1 80		28
29			Cash			1 80	29
30							30

As an alternative, the last two entries could be journalized in one compound journal entry as follows:

	Date		Description	Post. Ref.	Debit	Credit	
31	Nov.	21	Accounts Receivable		2 0 0 00		31
32			Miscellaneous Expense		1 80		32
33			Cash			2 0 1 80	33
34							34

The above journal entries complete our example for the Lou Pumpelly bank reconciliation. However, our example did not include a bank collection. For illustrative purposes, assume that the bank collected a note for $3,030. The principle was $3,000 and interest earned was $30. The bank would have included a credit memo for $3,030 with the bank statement. The journal entry would appear as follows:

	Date		Description	Post. Ref.	Debit	Credit	
12	Dec.	1	Cash		3 0 3 0 00		12
13			Note Receivable			3 0 0 0 00	13
14			Interest Income			3 0 00	14
15							15

General Journal

Electronic Funds Transfer (EFT) uses a computer rather than money or checks to complete transactions with the bank. These computer applications include payrolls, social security payments, and retail purchases. The use of EFT can present a challenge to preparing bank reconciliations. Many of the source documents disappear under an EFT environment because the data is transmitted electronically and a paper copy does not exist.

Concept Questions

1. For checks to be deposited, what are the two basic endorsements?
2. Define the following three parties to a check: drawer, drawee, payee.
3. In a bank reconciliation, how are outstanding checks and deposits in transit handled?
4. Define and give an example of a debit memo and a credit memo.
5. How is an NSF check, received from a client, journalized?

If you cannot answer the above concept questions, review the module material.

MODULE SUMMARY

The forms involved with opening and using a checking account include a signature card, deposit tickets, checks, and bank statements. When depositing checks, either a blank endorsement or restrictive endorsement can be used. The three parties to any check are the drawer, the drawee, and the payee. The drawer is the depositor who orders the bank to pay cash. The drawee is the bank on which the check is drawn. The payee is the person being paid the cash.

Once a month the bank mails a statement of account, called a bank statement. This statement should be reconciled to the general ledger cash account. The following three steps should be used to prepare the bank reconciliation: Step 1, identify deposits in transit and any related errors; Step 2, identify outstanding checks and any related errors; Step 3, identify additional reconciling items including bank debit and credit memos. Upon completing the bank reconciliation, all additions and deductions to the book balance must be journalized and posted to the general ledger cash account.

Module 5B

Key Terms

bank statement, *161*	drawer, *159*
blank endorsement, *157*	endorsement, *157*
canceled checks, *161*	errors, *162*
collections, *161*	NSF checks, *162*
credit memos, *163*	outstanding checks, *161*
debit memos, *163*	payee, *159*
deductions, *161*	restrictive endorsement, *158*
deposit ticket, *157*	service charges, *161*
deposits in transit, *161*	signature card, *156*
drawee, *159*	

Exercises

EXERCISE 5B-9 √

Match the following words with their definitions.

C 1. An endorsement where the depositor simply signs on the back of the check

E 2. An endorsement which contains words like "For Deposit Only" together with the signature

A 3. A card filled out and signed by each person authorized to sign checks on an account

D 4. The depositor who orders the bank to pay cash from the depositor's account

F 5. The bank on which the check is drawn

G 6. The person being paid the cash

B 7. A check which has been paid by the bank and is being returned to the depositor

a. signature card
b. canceled check
c. blank endorsement
d. drawer
e. restrictive endorsement
f. drawee
g. payee

EXERCISE 5B-10 ✓

Denise Brown is preparing a daily deposit for her checking account in the Jefferson National Bank at the close of business on May 15, 200X.

$20 bills—18 *360*   quarters—42 *10.50*
$10 bills—26 *260*   dimes—23 *2.30*
$ 5 bills—33 *165*   nickels—62 *3.10*
$ 1 bills—47 *47*   pennies—39 *.34*
                       half dollars—4 *2.00*

Checks from customers were in the following amounts:

$224.50 $315.80 $129.00

Required: Complete the following information for Brown's deposit ticket:

Date   *May 15, 200X*
Currency $ *832.00*
Coins $ *18.29*
Checks $ *699.30*

Total Deposit   *$1,519.59*

EXERCISE 5B-11

Based on the following information, prepare a check and stub.

Date: October 19, 200X
Check to: Union Supply Depot
Amount: $810.75
For: Office Equipment
Balance forward: $5,934.95
Signature: Sign your name

EXERCISE 5B-12

Indicate whether the action at the left will result in an addition to (+) or subtraction from (–) the ending bank balance or the ending checkbook balance.

	Ending Bank Balance	Ending Checkbook Balance
a. Deposits in transit to the bank	*+*	
b. Error in checkbook, check was recorded as $84 but was actually $48		*+*
c. Debit memo for bank service charges		*–*
d. Outstanding checks	*–*	

e. NSF check received from client   _____   _____

f. Error in bank deposit, appeared as $400
    on the statement but was actually $4,000   +   _____

g. Credit memo from bank advising they
    collected a note for us   _____   +

EXERCISE 5B-13

In reconciling the December bank statement for Hansen Electronics Company on December 31, 200X, the following was determined:

1. Received a debit memo for a bank service charge of $16.25.
2. Comparison of the canceled checks with the check stubs revealed that check No. 913 was correctly written for $175.18, but recorded in the accounting records as $157.18. The check was used to pay accounts payable.
3. Received a credit memo for $3,598.50 for collecting a note receivable. The principal was $3,200. Interest earned, $398.50.
4. A debit memo for an NSF check. The check was for $225 and was received from a client.

Required: Prepare the required journal entries.

Module 5B

Problems

PROBLEM 5B-14

The following information relates to the bank account of Judy Eary's Financial Consulting Service on July 31:

Balance per check stub, July 31			$ 9,567.97
Balance per bank statement, July 31			10,274.45
Deposits in transit:	7/29	$365.00	
	7/30	429.00	
Outstanding checks:	No. 2932	187.00	
	No. 2941	823.45	
	No. 2946	735.68	
Bank service charge:		15.65	
NSF check:		221.00	

Error on check no. 2899:   Check was written correctly for $98. Check was incorrectly recorded as $89. Accounts Payable was debited.

Required:

1. Prepare a bank reconciliation as of July 31, 200X.
2. Prepare the required journal entries.

PROBLEM 5B-15

The balance in the checking account as of November 30 is $4,478.08. The bank statement shows an ending balance of $7,410.85. The following information is discovered by comparing checks deposited and written, and noting service fees, and other debit and credit memos shown on the bank statement.

Deposits in transit:	11/29	$735.20
	11/30	225.91
Outstanding checks:	No. 1823	318.65
	No. 1829	234.80
	No. 1836	692.37
Debit memos:		
Bank service charge:		17.35
NSF check:		328.49
Credit memo:	Note receivable collected by bank	
	Principal	$2,700.00
	Interest earned	275.90

Error on check no. 1811:   Check was written correctly for $124 for Office Supplies. Check was incorrectly recorded as $142.

Required:

1. Prepare a bank reconciliation as of November 30, 200X.
2. Prepare the required journal entries.

PROBLEM 5B-16

The following information relates to the bank account of Andy Anderson's Athletic Foot Ware on May 20:

Balance per check stub, May 20			$8,774.47
Balance per bank statement, May 20			9,175.36
Deposits in transit:	5/18	$221.73	
	5/19	76.28	
Outstanding checks:	No. 2732	232.71	
	No. 2741	84.52	
	No. 2746	681.66	
Bank service charge:		12.74	
NSF check:		341.25	

Error on check no. 2796:   Check was written correctly for $17. Check was incorrectly recorded as $71. Accounts Payable was debited.

Required:

1. Prepare a bank reconciliation as of May 20, 200X.
2. Prepare the required journal entries.

PROBLEM 5B-17

The balance in the checking account as of November 25 is $8,916.80. The bank statement shows an ending balance of $11,735.61. The following information is discovered by comparing checks deposited and written, and noting service fees, and other debit and credit memos shown on the bank statement.

Deposits in transit:	11/23	$359.73
	11/24	422.88
Outstanding checks:	No. 1923	48.66
	No. 1929	395.99
	No. 1936	517.20
Debit memos:		
Bank service charge:		13.33
NSF check:		419.87
Credit memo:	Note receivable collected by bank	
	Principal	$2,750.00
	Interest earned	295.77

Error on check no. 1911: Check was written correctly for $269 for Utilities Expense. Check was incorrectly recorded as $296.

Required:

1. Prepare a bank reconciliation as of November 25, 200X.
2. Prepare the required journal entries.

Module
5B

Challenge Problem

Vicki Hehr opened a new business on June 1, 200X called Vicki's Bath and Body Shop. The following selected transactions were completed during the month.

June 1 Established a $100 change fund
    1 Established a $200 petty cash fund
    8 Recorded cash sales for the day: Cash register tape indicates an amount of $2,154.79. The cash count, including the $100 change fund, is $2,252.63.
   15 Replenished the petty cash fund. The following summarizes the information from the petty cash payments record.

Automobile Expense	$ 29.38
Vicki Hehr, Drawing	48.25
Charitable Contributions Expense	70.00
Postage Expense	35.00
Telephone Expense	5.29
Miscellaneous Expense	6.17
Total	$194.09

The amount of cash remaining in the fund is $5.26.

15 Recorded cash sales for the day: Cash register tape indicates an amount of $1,993.94. The cash count, including the $100 change fund, is $2,094.19.

20 Increased the size of the petty cash fund, $50, to a total of $250.

22 Recorded cash sales for the day: Cash register tape indicates an amount of $2,377.22. The cash count, including the $100 change fund, is $2,474.57.

25 Received the monthly bank statement. The following information pertains to the bank reconciliation:

Ending bank statement balance	$5,191.44
Ending Cash account balance	3,523.96
Deposit in transit: 6/24	299.66
Outstanding checks (total):	715.58
Debit memos:	
Bank service charge:	12.36
NSF check:	255.82
Credit memo: Collection of note receivable:	
Principal	$2,380.00
Interest earned	66.74

Error on check no. 1660:   Check was written correctly for $96. Check was incorrectly recorded as $69. Accounts Payable was debited.
Error on bank statement: A deposit on June 10 was for $1,000. The bank statement incorrectly shows a deposit of $100.

29 Recorded cash sales for the day: Cash register tape indicates an amount of $1,773.43. The cash count, including the $100 change fund, is $1,875.68.

Required: Prepare all necessary journal entries for the above transactions.

Chapter SIX

Payroll Accounting

The following modules will be covered in this chapter:

Module 6A

Employee Earnings and Deductions

Calculating earnings and deductions, using a payroll register and earnings record, and preparing journal entries to record the payroll.

Module 6B

Employer Payroll Taxes

Compute employer's payroll taxes (FICA, FUTA, and SUTA), and prepare journal entries to record the employer's payroll taxes.

Employee Earnings and Deductions

Module 6A Objectives
Careful study of this module should enable you to:
1. Calculate employee earnings and deductions.
2. Maintain a payroll register and employee earnings record which list gross pay, deductions, and net pay.
3. Prepare journal entries needed to record the payroll.

In Chapter 5, we learned more in-depth information about the cash account and its many important applications. In this chapter, we will expand upon another important concept—that of wages and salaries earned by employees. In previous chapters, we recorded wages paid during the month and accounted for wages earned but not yet paid at the end of the month. Here we will fully discuss what happens each time the payroll is met during the month. This includes new forms and registers, tax tables, and journal entries. Payroll accounting is important because employers are required by federal, state, and local laws to keep payroll accounting records—for the business as a whole and for each employee.

EMPLOYEE EARNINGS AND DEDUCTIONS

The first step in payroll accounting is to compute the total amount of pay that has been earned. A monthly **salary** is paid to workers who receive regular and equal paychecks for services performed. Salary is usually expressed as an annual figure, such as $18,000 per year, and a monthly amount, such as $1,500 per month. **Wages** are earnings which are based on the number of hours worked or units produced. The term salaries and wages are often used interchangeably.

An **employee** earns a salary or wages and is under the control and direction of an employer. But not every individual who performs services for a business is considered an employee. An **independent**

contractor is one who performs a service for a fee but is not subject to the control of those for whom the service is performed. The difference between an employee and an independent contractor is an important legal distinction. For accounting purposes, it is important to know that a business must keep records of employee deductions and pay employee payroll taxes only for employees. Independent contractors are paid a fee without deductions for taxes or other benefits, and they must maintain their own records.

Computing Gross Wages

Unless an employee works for a fixed monthly or biweekly amount, the first step in preparing payroll is determining the total or gross wage earned. For example, time clocks and time cards are often used to record employee arrival and departure times. Hours worked are multiplied by appropriate rates to determine total amounts earned. **Regular wages** are computed by multiplying hours worked by the hourly wage rate.

The **Fair Labor Standards Act**, commonly called the Federal Wage Hours Law, provides that employers must pay one and one-half times the regular rate for **overtime**, which is defined as hours worked over 40 hours per week. Generally, a premium or extra rate is also paid for hours worked on Saturdays, Sundays, holidays, or other special days.

Deductions from Earnings

There are two types of deductions subtracted from gross pay: (1) mandatory and (2) voluntary. The first and largest category is mandatory, and it includes federal income taxes withheld, state and local taxes withheld, and FICA (social security taxes) withheld. Voluntary deductions include items such as savings, car payments, insurance, and charitable contributions.

Income Taxes. Under federal law, employers are required to withhold income tax from each employee's earnings. The amount withheld is based on four factors: (1) total earnings of the employee; (2) marital status of the employee; (3) the number of withholding allowances claimed by the employee; and (4) the length of the employee's pay period. Each employee completes an Employee's Withholding Allowance Certificate (*Form W-4*) showing marital status and number of allowances claimed. A **withholding allowance** is an amount on which no federal income tax will be withheld. Each taxpayer is permitted one withholding allowance for him or herself, plus additional allowances for spouse and dependents. In addition, a special withholding allowance may be appropriate depending on marital status, number of jobs held, whether the taxpayer's spouse works, and amounts earned on jobs held. Additional withholding allowances are permitted for employees who will have large itemized deductions or tax credits.

The Form W-4 shown below is for a married taxpayer with six withholding allowances.

<u>Exhibit 6.1</u>
Withholding Allowance Certificate

Form **W-4** Department of the Treasury Internal Revenue Service	**Employee's Withholding Allowance Certificate** ▶ For Privacy Act and Paperwork Reduction Act Notice, see page 2.	OMB No. 1545-0010 **200X**
1 Type or print your first name and middle initial Ken M.	Last name Stone	2 Your social security number 393 58 8194

Home address (number and street or rural route) 1546 Swallow Drive	3 ☐ Single ☒ Married ☐ Married, but withhold at higher Single rate. Note: *If married, but legally separated, or spouse is a nonresident alien, check the Single box.*
City or town, state, and Zip code St. Louis, MO 63144-4752	4 If your last name differs from that on your social security card, check here and call 1-800-772-1213 for a new card . . . . . ▶ ☐

5	Total number of allowances you are claiming (from line H above or from the worksheets on page 2 if they apply) . .	5 6
6	Additional amount, if any, you want withheld from each paycheck	6 $
7	I claim exemption from withholding for 1998, and I certify that I meet **BOTH** of the following conditions for exemption:	
	• Last year I had a right to a refund of **ALL** Federal income tax withheld because I had **NO** tax liability **AND**	
	• This year I expect a refund of **ALL** Federal income tax withheld because I expect to have **NO** tax liability.	
	If you meet both conditions, enter "EXEMPT" here . . . . ▶ 7	

Under penalties of perjury, I certify that I am entitled to the number of withholding allowances claimed on this certificate or entitled to claim exempt status.

Employee's signature ▶ *Ken M. Stone*	Date ▶ *January 3* , 20--

8 Employer's name and address (Employer: Complete 8 and 10 only if sending to IRS)	9 Office code (optional)	10 Employer identification number

Cat. No. 10220Q

Employers who do not have automated payroll accounting use the **wage-bracket method** of determining income tax to be withheld. The withholding tax tables are provided by the Internal Revenue Service. To use the tables, you must know the amount of gross earnings, the marital status of the employee, and the number of withholding allowances being claimed. As shown in Exhibit 6.2, for a married person who has three withholding allowances and $310 in weekly earnings, the amount of tax withheld would be $5. (Note: You must be on the line which reads "At least … $310 But less than $320.")

Exhibit 6.2

Portion of Federal Withholding Tax Tables

MARRIED Persons—WEEKLY Payroll Period

(For Wages Paid in 1998)

If the wages are—		And the number of withholding allowances claimed is—										
At least	But less than	0	1	2	3	4	5	6	7	8	9	10
		The amount of income tax to be withheld is—										
$290	$300	26	18	10	2	0	0	0	0	0	0	0
300	310	27	19	12	4	0	0	0	0	0	0	0
310	320	29	21	13	5	0	0	0	0	0	0	0
320	330	30	22	15	7	0	0	0	0	0	0	0
330	340	32	24	16	8	0	0	0	0	0	0	0
340	350	33	25	18	10	2	0	0	0	0	0	0
350	360	35	27	19	11	3	0	0	0	0	0	0
360	370	36	28	21	13	5	0	0	0	0	0	0
370	380	38	30	22	14	6	0	0	0	0	0	0
380	390	39	31	24	16	8	0	0	0	0	0	0
390	400	41	33	25	17	9	2	0	0	0	0	0
400	410	42	34	27	19	11	3	0	0	0	0	0
410	420	44	36	28	20	12	5	0	0	0	0	0
420	430	45	37	30	22	14	6	0	0	0	0	0
430	440	47	39	31	23	15	8	0	0	0	0	0
440	450	48	40	33	25	17	9	1	0	0	0	0
450	460	50	42	34	26	18	11	3	0	0	0	0
460	470	51	43	36	28	20	12	4	0	0	0	0
470	480	53	45	37	29	21	14	6	0	0	0	0
480	490	54	46	39	31	23	15	7	0	0	0	0
490	500	56	48	40	32	24	17	9	1	0	0	0
500	510	57	49	42	34	26	18	10	3	0	0	0
510	520	59	51	43	35	27	20	12	4	0	0	0
520	530	60	52	45	37	29	21	13	6	0	0	0
530	540	62	54	46	38	30	23	15	7	0	0	0
540	550	63	55	48	40	32	24	16	9	1	0	0
550	560	65	57	49	41	33	26	18	10	2	0	0
560	570	66	58	51	43	35	27	19	12	4	0	0
570	580	68	60	52	44	36	29	21	13	5	0	0
580	590	69	61	54	46	38	30	22	15	7	0	0

State and local taxes also may be withheld, if the employee works in a state that has an income tax. Also, some cities and counties may require the deduction of a tax on the income of the employee. If so, these deductions require the use of a tax withholding table similar to the one used for federal taxes.

Social Security (FICA) Taxes. The Federal Insurance Contributions Act (FICA) of 1938 requires most employers to withhold **FICA taxes** from all employees' earnings. The amount withheld for these taxes is the employee's contribution to federal programs for old-age, survivors, and disability insurance (**OASDI**) and health insurance (**HI**), or Medicare.

Employers collect the FICA taxes from employees and pay the taxes to the U.S. Treasury. The employee's portion of each tax is collected by deducting it from the gross earnings each pay period. The amount of tax withheld is computed by multiplying the taxable wages by the tax rate in effect at the time the wages are received. For 1998, the OASDI tax is 6.2% of each employee's wages for the first $68,400 earned, and the HI tax is 1.45% of each employee's entire wages earned. For the sake of convenience in this chapter, we will use an OASDI rate of 6.5% on the first $60,000, and an HI rate of 1.5% on all wages earned.

The social security and Medicare tax rates change frequently. In addition, the maximum earnings subject to social security change frequently. There are annual rates and amounts, and when an employee exceeds a cap such as $68,400 for OASDI tax during the year, he or she is no longer subject to the tax. If an employee has more than one employer, and thereby has more tax withheld than required, a refund for excess withholdings is given when the employee files his or her income tax return the following year. The rates and amounts begin anew each year; when Congress changes rates or maximum amounts, those changes begin with the new calendar year or at some designated point in the future. For example, a law enacted in June of 1999 would take effect January 1, 2000.

As shown in Exhibit 6.3, a total of $26 OASDI tax ($400 × 6.5%) is deducted from Ken Stone's paycheck. A total of $6 HI tax ($400 × 1.5%) is deducted as well.

Exhibit 6.3
Payroll Check Deductions

		December 19, 200X	PAYROLL CHECK NO. **505**
Pay To:	**Ken Stone** **44 Gladstone Drive** **Minneapolis, MN 32044**		

Exactly: *THREE HUNDRED THIRTY AND 00/100THS DOLLARS****$330.00*

B. Crane Edwards

Gross Paycheck	Inc. Tax	OASDI	Deductions HI	Opt. 1	Opt. 2	Total	Net Paycheck
$400.00	38.00	26.00	6.00			70.00	$330.00

Other Deductions. Voluntary deductions from employee earnings are authorized by the individual employee. For example, an employee may choose to have a sum deducted each month for the purchase of U.S. savings bonds, health insurance, savings deposits, pension plans, or charitable contributions. These deductions may vary widely and depend on specific agreements between the employee and employer.

Employer Records

Employers keep a **payroll register** which is a multi-column form used to collect and compute payroll data for employees. The register lists the following for each employee and is used to record payroll in the journal:

1. Name, address, and social security number
2. Gross earnings, date of paycheck, and pay period of employment covered by each paycheck
3. The gross amount of earnings accumulated since the first of the year
4. The amounts of any taxes or other items withheld

In Exhibit 6.4, a computerized payroll register, also known as a payroll earnings record, is shown for a company with five employees.

Employers also maintain an individual **employee's earnings record** for each employee, as required by federal law. This record provides cumulative information with each new pay period. Exhibit 6.5 on pages 182–183 presents a computerized employee's earnings record which shows current and total wages paid to date, current and total deductions, net pay, and check number issued.

Exhibit 6.4
Payroll Register

| Name | Emp. No. | # of Allw. | M/S | Earnings | | | | Taxable |
				Regular	Overtime	Total	Cum. Total	Unempl. Comp.
December 19, 200X								
Collins, Pamela	1	4	M	520.00		520.00	26,320.00	
Gunther, James	2	1	S	360.00	40.00	400.00	20,400.00	
Stone, Ken	3	6	M	400.00		400.00	6,200.00	400.00
Raines, Russell	4	3	M	440.00		440.00	11,600.00	
Wilson, Randy	5	1	S	300.00	30.00	330.00	7,100.00	

The payroll register is a summary of the earnings of all employees for each pay period, while the earnings record is a summary of the annual earnings to date of each employee. Earnings records may show quarterly earnings as well as annual earnings. This information is needed so that the employer can prepare the annual Wage and Tax Statement (*Form W-2*) which must be mailed to each employee by January 31 of the following year.

The Form W-2 is supplied to the IRS, and copies are given to the employee to file with federal and state income tax returns. A Form W-2 for Ken Stone appears in Exhibit 6.6 on page 184.

Journalizing Employee Earnings and Deductions

The process of recording gross earnings of employees and their withholdings is called **recording the payroll**. To record the wages and salaries of employees, an expense account is needed. It may be called Salaries Expense or Wages Expense.

KEY POINT

The Salaries Expense or Wages Expense account is debited for the total amount of *gross earnings* of all employees for each pay period.

To account for amounts which have been withheld, we will use some liability accounts. Liability accounts are credited for the amounts withheld because these amounts will be paid in cash quickly. For example, the FICA tax and Federal Income tax withheld will be paid to a bank depository for the Internal Revenue Service.

Taxable	Taxable Earnings and Deductions								
FICA—OASDI	Tax 6.5%	FICA—HI	Tax 1.5%	Federal Inc. Tax	Health Ins.	Credit Union	Total Deduc.	Net Payck.	Ck. #
520.00	33.80	520.00	7.80	47.00	10.00	15.00	113.60	406.40	503
400.00	26.00	400.00	6.00	51.00		10.00	93.00	307.00	504
400.00	26.00	400.00	6.00	38.00			70.00	330.00	505
440.00	28.60	440.00	6.60	56.00	8.00		99.20	340.80	506
330.00	21.45	330.00	4.95	37.00			63.40	266.60	507

Exhibit 6.5

Employee's Earnings Record

Name: Richard Adams   **Sex:** Male
Address: 1546 Swallow Drive   **Marital Status:** Married
City: St. Louis, MO 63144-4752   **Allowances:** 4

Earnings			Taxable Earnings				
Regular	Overtime	Total	[7,000] Unemploy. Comp.	[60,000] FICA— OASDI	Tax 6.5%	FICA—HI	Tax 1.5%
1,800.00		1,800.00	1,800.00	1,800.00	117.00	1,800.00	27.00
1,800.00		1,800.00	1,800.00	1,800.00	117.00	1,800.00	27.00
1,800.00		1,800.00	1,800.00	1,800.00	117.00	1,800.00	27.00
First Quarter:							
5,400.00		5,400.00	5,400.00	5,400.00	351.00	5,400.00	81.00
1,800.00		1,800.00	1,600.00	1,800.00	117.00	1,800.00	27.00
1,800.00		1,800.00		1,800.00	117.00	1,800.00	27.00
1,800.00		1,800.00		1,800.00	117.00	1,800.00	27.00
Second Quarter:							
5,400.00		5,400.00	1,600.00	5,400.00	351.00	5,400.00	81.00
1,800.00		1,800.00		1,800.00	117.00	1,800.00	27.00
1,800.00		1,800.00		1,800.00	117.00	1,800.00	27.00
1,800.00		1,800.00		1,800.00	117.00	1,800.00	27.00
Third Quarter:							
5,400.00		5,400.00		5,400.00	351.00	5,400.00	81.00
1,800.00		1,800.00		1,800.00	117.00	1,800.00	27.00
1,800.00		1,800.00		1,800.00	117.00	1,800.00	27.00
1,800.00		1,800.00		1,800.00	117.00	1,800.00	27.00
Fourth Quarter:							
5,400.00		5,400.00		5,400.00	351.00	5,400.00	81.00
Yearly Total:							
21,600.00		21,600.00	7,000.00	21,600.00	1,404.00	21,600.00	324.00

Department: Maintenance   **Social Security Number:** 393-58-8914
Occupation: Service   **Date of Birth:** August 17, 1964
Pay Rate: $1,800/month   **Date Employed:** January 1, 200X

and Deductions

Federal Inc. Tax	Health Ins.	Credit Union	Total	Net Paycheck	Date	Check No.
190.00	25.00	10.00	369.00	1,431.00	January 31, 200X	111
190.00	25.00	10.00	369.00	1,431.00	February 28, 200X	203
190.00	25.00	10.00	369.00	1,431.00	March 31, 200X	289
570.00	75.00	30.00	1,107.00	4,293.00		
190.00	25.00	10.00	369.00	1,431.00	April 30, 200X	346
190.00	25.00	10.00	369.00	1,431.00	May 31, 200X	408
190.00	25.00	10.00	369.00	1,431.00	June 30, 200X	489
570.00	75.00	30.00	1,107.00	4,293.00		
190.00	25.00	10.00	369.00	1,431.00	July 31, 200X	551
190.00	25.00	10.00	369.00	1,431.00	August 31, 200X	622
190.00	25.00	10.00	369.00	1,431.00	September 30, 200X	700
570.00	75.00	30.00	1,107.00	4,293.00		
190.00	25.00	10.00	369.00	1,431.00	October 31, 200X	782
190.00	25.00	10.00	369.00	1,431.00	November 30, 200X	801
190.00	25.00	10.00	369.00	1,431.00	December 31, 200X	888
570.00	75.00	30.00	1,107.00	4,293.00		
2,280.00	300.00	120.00	4,428.00	17,172.00		

Exhibit 6.6

Wage and Tax Statement

a Control number	2222	OMB No. 1545-0008		

b Employer's identification number 43-0211630		**1** Wages, tips, other compensation 22,450.00	**2** Federal income tax withheld 1,159.00

c Employer's name, address, and ZIP code Westly, Inc. 5221 Natural Bridge St. Louis, MO 63115-8230	**3** Social security wages 22,450.00	**4** Social security tax withheld 1,459.25

5 Medicare wages and tips 22,450.00   **6** Medicare tax withheld 336.75

7 Social security tips   **8** Allocated tips

d Employee's social security number 393-58-8194

9 Advance EIC payment   **10** Dependent care benefits

e Employee's name, address, and ZIP code

Ken M. Stone
1546 Swallow Drive
St. Louis, MO   63144-4752

11 Nonqualified plans   **12** Benefits included in box 1

13 See Instrs. for Form W-2   **14** Other

15 Statutory employee / Deceased / Pension plan / Legal rep. / Hshld. emp. / Subtotal / Deferred compensation

16 State	Employer's state I.D. No.	**17** State wages, tips, etc.	**18** State income tax	**19** Locality name St. Louis County	**20** Local wages, tips, etc. $22,450.00	**21** Local income tax $231.80

Department of the Treasury—Internal Revenue Service

Form **W-2** Wage and Tax Statement **2000**

Copy D For Employer

For Paperwork Reduction Act Notice, see separate instructions.

The following T accounts will help you visualize the journal entry to record the payroll:

Salaries (Wages) Expense	
Debit to enter gross earnings for employees of the pay period.	

Employees' Income Tax Payable	
Debit to enter payment of income tax previously withheld.	Credit to enter income taxes withheld from employees' earnings.

FICA Tax Payable—OASDI	
Debit to enter payment of FICA tax previously withheld.	Credit to enter FICA taxes withheld (OASDI).

FICA Tax Payable—HI	
Debit to enter payment of FICA tax previously withheld.	Credit to enter FICA taxes withheld (HI).

The liability accounts, for FICA and Federal Income tax withheld, are credited when the payroll is recorded. When the amounts withheld are paid to a bank depository, the liability accounts are debited (and Cash is credited).

Similarly, voluntary deductions from employees' wages are also liability accounts which are credited for amounts withheld. These liability accounts are debited for subsequent payments, such as to a savings plan. The journal entry to record payment would be as follows:

	Date	Description	Post Ref.	Debit	Credit	
		General Journal			Page 20	
1		Employee Savings Plans Payable		2 5 0 00		1
2		Health Insurance Premiums Payable		3 0 0 00		2
3		Employee Charitable Contributions				3
4		Payable		1 0 0 00		4
5		Cash			6 5 0 00	5

The journal entries to record a payroll which includes both mandatory and voluntary deductions and to pay the payroll would be as follows:

	Date	Description	Debit	Credit	
22	Dec. 17	Wages Expense	3 8 0 0 00		22
23		Employees' Income Tax Payable		3 9 0 00	23
24		FICA Tax Payable—OASDI		2 3 5 60	24
24		FICA Tax Payable—HI		5 5 10	25
26		Health Insurance Premiums			26
27		Payable		7 8 00	27
28		United Way Contributions			28
29		Payable		4 2 00	29
30		Wages Payable		2 9 9 9 30	30
31		Payroll for week ended			31
32		December 19			32
33	17	Wages Payable	2 9 9 9 30		33
		Cash		2 9 9 9 30	

When the withheld taxes are paid to the bank depository for the IRS, the liability accounts are debited and Cash is credited, as follows:

	Date	Description	Debit	Credit	
37	Dec. 24	Employees' Income Tax Payable	3 9 0 00		37
38		FICA Tax Payable—OASDI	2 3 5 60		38
39		FICA Tax Payable—HI	5 5 10		39
40		Cash		6 8 0 70	40

Concept Questions

1. How are wages different from salaries?
2. How is an employee different from an independent contractor?
3. Explain how regular wages are computed.
4. Overtime, weekend, and holiday pay often pay higher rates. How is this type of pay computed?
5. What is a withholding allowance?
6. What does social security tax provide for workers? Define and explain the initials OASDI and HI.
7. How is a payroll register different from an employee's earnings record?
8. To record the payroll, what account is debited for gross earnings?
9. When taxes (income taxes and FICA taxes) withheld are paid, what accounts are debited?

MODULE SUMMARY

The payment of wages and salaries is more than a debit to an expense account and a credit to Cash. Employers must compute gross earnings, withhold mandatory and voluntary deductions, keep required records of payroll and earnings, and pay required deposits of withholdings to a bank depository for the IRS.

First, gross earnings are computed. The regular wage rate is multiplied by the number of hours worked (for the first 40 hours in a week). Overtime hours are multiplied by one and one-half times the regular rate; weekend and holiday pay are also paid at some premium rate, often twice the regular rate. Gross earnings is the total of regular, overtime, and other premium wages.

Next, deductions are computed. Mandatory deductions include federal income tax, state and local tax (if applicable), and social security taxes. Social security taxes (FICA) are in two parts: (1) old age, survivors, and disability insurance (OASDI); and (2) health insurance (HI), which is commonly know as Medicare. The 1998-99 rates are 6.2% of the first $68,400 earned for OASDI (social security) and 1.45% of all wages earned for HI (Medicare). When a worker exceeds the OASDI maximum, there is no further deduction for that year. Because these rates and maximum amounts change often, we are using a standard 6.5% of the first $60,000 for OASDI and 1.5% of all wages earned for Medicare.

Employers keep a payroll register, which lists all employees, their earnings, withholdings, and net pay. In addition, the individual employee's earnings record is required by federal law. It keeps a complete itemization of each employee's earnings, withholdings, and net pay during the year.

To journalize gross employee earnings and deductions is called recording the payroll. The expense account (usually Salaries or Wages Expense) is debited for gross wages and the liability accounts are credited for the amount withheld. The difference between the expense account and the liability accounts is net wages. This amount is eventually debited to Wages Payable and credited to Cash because it represents the total of the paychecks issued.

Module 6A	*Key Terms*

employee, *175*	overtime, *176*
employee's earnings record, *180*	payroll register, *179*
Fair Labor and Standards	recording the payroll, *181*
Act, *176*	regular wages, *176*
FICA taxes, *178*	salary, *175*
HI, *178*	wage-bracket method, *177*
independent contractor, *175*	wages, *175*
OASDI, *178*	withholding allowance, *176*

Module 6A	*Exercises*

EXERCISE 6A-1

Compute gross earnings based on the following information:

   a. Jenny Anderson worked 40 hours last week, and her hourly rate is $9.10. Compute her total weekly gross pay.

   b. John Miller works for an hourly wage of $7.25. Last month he worked an additional 25 hours and was told he would be paid overtime. Compute his overtime rate and total wages plus overtime earnings.

   c. Betty Adams worked 52 hours last week, which included 8 hours overtime and 4 hours on Sunday. She gets double time for Sunday work. Her regular rate of pay is $7.12 per hour. Compute her total earnings.

   d. Kerry Richardson worked 49 hours last week, which included 6 hours overtime and 3 hours on a holiday. He gets double time for holiday work. His regular rate of pay is $8.00 per hour. Compute his total earnings.

EXERCISE 6A-2   HW 11/2/99

Based on the following information, compute the amounts which will be with-held for (a) FICA—OASDI (social security) insurance and (b) FICA—HI (Medicare) insurance. (Assume OASDI is 6.5% of the first $60,000 and Medicare is 1.5% of all wages earned.)

- a.   Michael Rankin's gross pay is $1,560. His earnings prior to this pay-check were $25,600.
- b.   Michelle Howell's gross pay is $2,580. Her earnings prior to this pay-check were $58,500.
- c.   Peggy Buck's gross pay is $892. Her earnings prior to this paycheck were $13,420.
- d.   Richard Heiser's gross pay is $1,850. His earnings prior to this pay-check were $62,000.

EXERCISE 6A-3

Based on the following information, compute net pay for each of the employ-ees listed below.

- a.   Andrea Hadley had regular wages of $345, overtime wages of $28.10, income tax withheld of $44.10, FICA—OASDI withheld of $24.25, and FICA—HI of $5.18.
- b.   Richard Kreitz had regular wages of $620, overtime wages of $44, income tax withheld of $70, FICA—OASDI withheld of $43.16, FICA—HI withheld of $9.96, savings bonds of $50, and health insurance of $13.
- c.   Emily Noll had regular wages of $580, overtime wages of $68, income tax withheld of $90, FICA—OASDI withheld of $42.12, FICA—HI withheld of $9.72, and charitable contributions of $20.
- d.   Brian Ford had regular wages of $390, overtime wages of $48, and holiday pay of $80. He had income tax withheld of $80, FICA—OASDI of $33.67, FICA—HI withheld of $7.77, savings to credit union of $40, and health insurance of $25.

Module
6A

Problems   11/3/99

PROBLEM 6A-4 PAYROLL REGISTER

Marley's Accounting Services has four employees who are paid weekly. All employees are married. Using the federal withholding tax table in Exhibit 6.2 on page 178, and social security tax rates of 6.5% on the first $60,000 (OASDI), and 1.5% on all wages earned (Medicare), prepare the payroll register for the following employees:

Name	With. Allow.	Prior Earnings	Regular Pay	Overtime	Cum. Total
Margaret Smith	3	3,000.00	500.00	0.00	3,500.00
Ronald Johnson	4	8,000.00	360.00	30.00	8,390.00
Mark Atkeson	1	3,000.00	420.00	0.00	3,420.00
Ryan Kellerman	2	8,000.00	350.00	30.00	8,380.00

In addition to mandatory deductions, Margaret Smith had $25 withheld for health insurance and $40 withheld for the pension plan; Ronald Johnson had $18 withheld for health insurance and $15 for the credit union (savings); Mark Atkeson had $22 withheld for health insurance and $20 for the pension plan; and Ryan Kellerman had $25 withheld for the pension plan and $10 for the credit union.

PROBLEM 6A-5 EMPLOYEE'S EARNINGS RECORD

Prepare an individual employee earnings record for Kate Beyerly for one quarter. She is married, claims one withholding allowance, and receives a weekly salary of $400. In addition to mandatory deductions, she has $10 withheld from each paycheck for health insurance, $15 for savings, and $5 for United Way. She had no overtime earnings last quarter (13 weeks).

PROBLEM 6A-6 JOURNALIZING EMPLOYEE EARNINGS AND DEDUCTIONS

11/4

According to the payroll register of Johnson Janitorial Services, this week's gross earnings were $25,000, with the following amounts withheld from employees' paychecks:

Federal income tax withheld	$2,928
FICA—OASDI tax withheld	1,625
FICA—HI tax withheld	375
Health insurance withheld	300
Charitable contributions withheld	250

Required: Prepare the journal entry to record the payroll.

PROBLEM 6A-7 PAYROLL REGISTER

11/3/99

Archie's Bookkeeping Company has four employees who are paid weekly. All employees are married. Using the federal withholding tax table in Exhibit 6.2 on page 178, and social security tax rates of 6.5% on the first $60,000 (OASDI) and 1.5% on all wages earned (Medicare), prepare the payroll register for the following employees:

Name	With. Allow.	Prior Earnings	Regular Pay	Overtime	Cum. Total
Francis Clark	3	2,000.00	300.00	0.00	2,300.00
Willard Jennings	2	8,000.00	510.00	20.00	8,530.00
Jack Bailey	4	9,000.00	500.00	0.00	9,500.00
Chris Ellerman	1	7,000.00	400.00	100.00	7,500.00

In addition to mandatory deductions, Francis Clark had $22 withheld for health insurance and $30 withheld for the pension plan; Willard Jennings had $28 withheld for health insurance and $25 for the credit union; Jack Bailey had $21 withheld for health insurance and $10 for savings; and Chris Ellerman had $32 withheld for the pension plan and $10 for the credit union.

PROBLEM 6A-8 EMPLOYEE'S EARNINGS RECORD

Prepare an individual employee earnings record for Kyle Jackson for one quarter. He is married, claims one withholding allowance, and receives a weekly salary of $500. In addition to mandatory deductions, he has $15 withheld from each paycheck for health insurance, $10 for savings, and $10 for United Way. He had no overtime earnings last quarter (13 weeks).

PROBLEM 6A-9 JOURNALIZING EMPLOYEE EARNINGS AND DEDUCTIONS

According to the payroll register of Alicia's Maid Services, this week's gross earnings were $19,000, with the following amounts withheld from employees' paychecks:

Federal income tax withheld	$1,900
FICA—OASDI tax withheld	1,235
FICA—HI tax withheld	285
Health insurance withheld	200
Charitable contributions withheld	150

Required: Prepare the journal entry to record the payroll.

Employer Payroll Taxes

Module 6B Objectives
Careful study of this module should enable you to:
1. Compute payroll taxes imposed on the employer, including matching FICA taxes, Federal Unemployment Taxes (FUTA), and State Unemployment Taxes (SUTA).
2. Explain employer's payroll tax payments for FICA and federal income taxes withheld, and explain tax payments for FUTA and SUTA taxes levied against the employer.
3. Prepare journal entries to record employer's payroll taxes.

Payroll Taxes Imposed On The Employer

Social Security Taxes. Social security (FICA) taxes are levied on employers at the same rate and on the same earnings base as employees. As previously mentioned, the rate and earnings base change frequently, at the discretion of Congress. We are using a standard rate in this chapter of 6.5% of the first $60,000 for the OASDI portion of social security, and 1.5% of all wages earned for the Medicare portion of social security. Thus, the employer is required to match whatever is withheld from employees' wages. The employer's share, together with the amounts withheld from employees' paychecks, must be paid periodically to a bank depository for the IRS.

Federal Unemployment Tax (FUTA). A payroll tax called **Federal Unemployment Tax** (FUTA) is levied on employers for the purpose of financing the cost of federal oversight of the state unemployment compensation program. The money collected from employers is used to assist workers who are laid off from their jobs. This tax is levied on employers and is not deducted from employees' earnings. Employers who employ one or more persons for at least one day in each of 20 or more weeks in a calendar year, or who pay wages of $1,500 or more in any calendar quarter, are subject to this tax.

Like the FICA tax, Congress can change both the rate and the taxable base of the FUTA tax. For 1998, the FUTA rate was 6.2% of the first $7,000 of each employee's wages. From this, a credit of 5.4% is allowed for payments to state unemployment programs, leaving a federal rate of 0.8% (6.2 – 5.4) which is the effective FUTA rate. This means a total of 6.2% will be levied.

State Unemployment Tax (SUTA). All states have unemployment compensation laws which provide for payment of benefits to qualified unemployed workers. The funds for these benefits are provided by a payroll tax imposed on employers called the **State Unemployment Tax** (SUTA).

Under the laws of most states, there is a **merit rating system** which provides a tax-saving incentive to employers to stabilize employment. This system allows an employer's rate to be less than the maximum rate of 5.4%, but with full credit being given for the 5.4% when figuring the amount of FUTA due (0.8%). For purposes of this chapter, we will assume a standard rate of 5.4% even though in some states employers pay less than this rate if a merit system is used.

The employer's rate for SUTA is set by the state—it is based on the number of claims for unemployment compensation filed against that employer, and upon the total amount of unemployment compensation benefits paid by the state as a result of those claims. In other words, if a company lays off many workers, that company's SUTA rate will be high. But if a company rarely lets workers go, the rate can be lower (to give employers incentive to retain workers). The SUTA rate is affected only when employers discharge employees without cause. That is, when an employee is fired for just cause, he/she is not entitled to unemployment benefits.

In the case of both FUTA and SUTA, the tax rate and maximum amount per employee are set annually. When an employee's earnings exceed the maximum amount ($7,000), the employer no longer pays a tax based on that employee's earnings. Each year, the maximum amount per employee starts over. Should the Congress raise the rate or the amount for FUTA, the increase would take effect the following tax year. Should an employee have more than one job, each employer would be required to pay the tax on the base amount of the employee's wages. In other words, unlike OASDI, there's no maximum amount per employee; each employer would pay FUTA based on the first $7,000 earned by each employee from that employer.

Accounting for Employer Payroll Taxes

You will recall from Module 6A that gross earnings of employees are entered in an expense account called Wages Expense or Salaries Expense, and that the process is called *recording the payroll*. The next step is called **recording employer payroll taxes**. We will debit an account called Payroll Tax Expense for the total payroll taxes imposed on the employer. We will credit liability accounts for the individual payroll tax amounts which must be deposited with the U.S. Treasury—matching FICA, FUTA, and SUTA.

Payroll Tax Expense	
Debit to enter total FICA, FUTA, and SUTA taxes imposed on the employer.	

FICA Tax Payable—OASDI		FICA Tax Payable—HI	
Debit to enter payment of OASDI tax previously withheld and matched.	Credit to enter OASDI taxes withheld and matched.	Debit to enter payment of HI tax previously withheld and matched.	Credit to enter HI taxes withheld and HI taxes matched.

FUTA Tax Payable		SUTA Tax Payable	
Debit to enter payment of FUTA tax.	Credit to enter FUTA tax imposed on the employer.	Debit to enter payment of SUTA tax.	Credit to enter SUTA tax imposed on the employer.

FICA Tax Payable—OASDI and FICA Tax Payable—HI are the same liability accounts illustrated previously in this chapter. The accounts are now credited for an identical amount, which is the employer's *matching* of FICA taxes. When the tax is paid, the accounts are debited and Cash is credited.

FUTA Tax Payable and SUTA Tax Payable are two separate liability accounts. When monies are remitted to the federal government and state government, respectively, these liability accounts are debited and Cash is credited.

The payroll register lists employee earnings and amounts subject to FUTA and SUTA taxes. For each employee, when earnings exceed $7,000, there is no further tax levied against the employer.

For example, consider the following portion of a payroll register:

				Taxable Earnings	
Name	Prior Earnings	Gross Earnings	Cumulative Total	Unemployment Compensation	FICA
Alexander, Pam	5,500	500.00	6,000.00	500.00	500.00
Bailey, Timothy	6,680	420.00	7,100.00	320.00	420.00
Crowley, Barb	10,510	650.00	11,160.00	0.00	650.00
Dawson, Ansel	59,500	2,500.00	62,000.00	0.00	500.00

For Pam Alexander, her cumulative earnings of $6,000 means that all $500 of this paycheck is subject to both unemployment tax and FICA tax. Timothy Bailey's earnings of $420 take him over the $7,000 FUTA/SUTA cap; therefore, only $320 (which takes him to the $7,000 mark) is subject to unemployment tax. Hereafter, no more FUTA or SUTA are due based on Timothy Bailey's earnings. Both Barb Crowley and Ansel Dawson have surpassed the $7,000 mark, so no further unemployment tax is due. Ansel Dawson has exceeded the social security maximum with this paycheck, and only $500 of his paycheck was subject to this tax.

Journalizing the Employer's Payroll Taxes

The payroll taxes imposed on employers are entered at the same time wages are paid. Typically, the accountant would record the payroll, as presented in the first half of this chapter, then immediately record the employer's payroll taxes.

The information needed to properly enter employer payroll taxes is contained in the payroll register. The easiest way to get the information is to look at the total of the column headed Unemployment Compensation. It lists all income subject to the unemployment compensation tax. The total of this line can be multiplied by the state tax rate (assumed to be 5.4% of the first $7,000 of each employee's wages) and by the federal rate of 0.8% to determine the employer's unemployment taxes due. (Since both FUTA and SUTA are based on the first $7,000 of each employee's wages, only one column is needed to determine whether the threshold of $7,000 has been met.) In the payroll register shown in Module 6A (Exhibit 6.4), only Ken Stone has not reached the $7,000 FUTA/SUTA cap. Therefore, his entire $400 paycheck is subject to unemployment taxes of $400 × 5.4% (SUTA) and $400 × 0.8% (FUTA).

Similarly, the amount of FICA tax withheld from employees' paychecks must be matched by employers. To double-check accuracy of the computations, you can multiply the total of the FICA column of the payroll register by double the FICA rate (half for withholding, and half for matching by the employer).

To record the employer's payroll taxes, each liability account (FICA Tax Payable—OASDI, FICA Tax Payable—HI, FUTA Tax Payable, and SUTA Tax Payable) is credited for its respective amount, and Payroll Tax Expense is debited for the total. For example, a January payroll totals $5,000. When the payroll was made, $500 was withheld for federal income taxes, $325 was withheld for FICA—OASDI, and $75 was withheld for FICA—HI (Medicare). (These amounts were previously credited to the liability accounts when the payroll was recorded.)

To record the employer's payroll tax, you would make the following general journal entry:

Recording matching tax

	Date		Description	Post Ref.	Debit	Credit	
22	Jan.	19	Payroll Tax Expense		7 1 0 00		22
23			FICA Tax Payable—OASDI			3 2 5 00	23
24			FICA Tax Payable—HI			7 5 00	24
25			FUTA Tax Payable (5,000 × 0.8%)			4 0 00	25
26			SUTA Tax Payable (5,000 × 5.4%)			2 7 0 00	26
27			To record employer payroll				27

General Journal — Page 1

KEY POINT

The FICA portions are matching what was previously withheld from employees' gross earnings.

When the amounts withheld are paid to the appropriate bank depository, the following journal entries would be made.

	Date		Description	Post Ref.	Debit	Credit	
1	Feb.	1	Employees' Income Tax Payable		5 0 0 00		1
2			FICA Tax Payable—OASDI		6 5 0 00		2
3			FICA Tax Payable—HI		1 5 0 00		3
4			Cash			1 3 0 0 00	4
5			Paid balance due for taxes				5
6			withheld and matching FICA				6
7							7
8		1	Federal Unemployment Tax Payable		4 0 00		8
9			Cash			4 0 00	9
10			Paid federal unemployment tax				10
11							11
12		1	State Unemployment Tax Payable		2 7 0 00		12
13			Cash			2 7 0 00	13
14			Paid state unemployment tax				14
15							15

General Journal — Page 1

Other withholdings, such as health insurance, savings, or charitable contributions which were recorded as liabilities, are also debited and Cash is credited when they are paid.

Concept Questions

1. What are the three payroll taxes imposed on the employer?
2. What is the FUTA rate, and what is the base amount of each employee's wages?
3. What is the SUTA rate, and what is the base amount of each employee's wages?
4. The information needed to properly enter employer payroll taxes is contained in what record?

MODULE SUMMARY

At the same time you record the payroll, you should also record the payroll taxes imposed on the employer. There are three taxes imposed: (1) a matching FICA tax, (2) Federal Unemployment Tax (FUTA), and (3) State Unemployment Tax (SUTA).

For all social security taxes withheld from employees' paychecks, the employer must match or pay an equal amount. FUTA is levied against all (and only) employers; the tax rate used is 0.8% of the first $7,000 of each employee's earnings. SUTA is levied by all states. The maximum SUTA rate used here is 5.4% of the first $7,000 of each employee's earnings, although a merit rating system may allow some employers to receive credit for 5.4% while actually paying less.

Like FICA Tax Payable—OASDI and FICA Tax Payable—HI, FUTA Tax Payable and SUTA Tax Payable are separate liability accounts. These accounts are credited for the amount owing; they are debited when the amounts are paid to federal and state government. ·

The journal entry to record the employer's payroll taxes consists of crediting the liability accounts (matching FICA withheld, FUTA Tax Payable, and SUTA Tax Payable), and debiting Payroll Tax Expense for the total. The liability accounts are debited and Cash is credited when taxes are paid.

Key Terms

Federal Unemployment Tax (FUTA), *191*
merit rating system, *192*
recording employer payroll taxes, *193*
State Unemployment Tax (SUTA), *192*

Exercises   11/5

EXERCISE 6B-10

Based on the following information, compute (a) the amount of FUTA Tax Payable, and (b) the amount of SUTA Tax Payable.

a. Total wages for the first quarter:

James Brown	$5,600
Millie Hanson	3,800
George Anderson	4,200
Ardys Johnson	5,900

156.00

b. Total wages for the second quarter:

James Brown	$1,400
Millie Hanson	3,200
George Anderson	2,800
Ardys Johnson	1,000

EXERCISE 6B-11

Below is a partial payroll register. From the information provided, compute (a) matching FICA taxes, (b) FUTA Tax Payable, and (c) SUTA Tax Payable.

Name	Prior Earnings	Gross Earnings.	Cumulative Total	FICA Withheld*	
				OASDI	HI
Andy Howard	2,000	1,000.00	3,000.00	65.00	15.00
Rachel Edwards	1,800	900.00	2,700.00	58.50	13.50
Myrna Hamilton	5,000	2,500.00	7,500.00	162.50	37.50
Patricia Hankins	2,600	1,100.00	3,700.00	71.50	16.50

*year 2000 is subject to FUTA and SUTA

EXERCISE 6B-12   11/5

Based on the following information, prepare the journal entry to (a) record the payroll, and (b) record the employer's payroll taxes. Assume all gross earnings are subject to FUTA and SUTA tax.

Gross Earnings	$6,800
Federal income tax withheld	780
FICA—OASDI withheld	442
FICA—HI withheld	102
Health insurance premium withheld	250

Module
6B

Problems   HW 11/5

PROBLEM 6B-13 PAYROLL REGISTER WITH FUTA AND SUTA

Fredrick's Financial Planners has four employees who are paid weekly. Using social security tax rates of 6.5 % on the first $60,000 (OASDI) and 1.5% on wages earned (Medicare), and FUTA and SUTA rates of 0.8% of the first $7,000 for each employee and 5.4% on the first $7,000 for each employee, respectively, prepare the payroll register for the following employees on June 30, 200X. Assume a 10% federal income tax withholding rate (rather than using tax tables).

Name	With. Allow.	Prior Earnings	Regular Pay	Overtime	Cum. Total
Christie Akins	2	6,000.00	450.00	0.00	6,450.00
Marilyn McArthur	3	9,000.00	950.00	50.00	10,000.00
Henry Olsen	1	12,000.00	1,000.00	100.00	13,100.00
Michael Webster	4	5,200.00	750.00	0.00	5,950.00

PROBLEM 6B-14 JOURNALIZING THE PAYROLL AND JOURNALIZING THE EMPLOYER'S PAYROLL TAXES

Based on Problem 6B-13 on the previous page, prepare the following:

a.   Journalize the payroll.
b.   Journalize payment of the payroll.
c.   Journalize the employer's payroll taxes.
d.   Journalize payment of the employer's payroll taxes (FICA, FUTA, and SUTA), including matching FICA and income taxes withheld.

PROBLEM 6B-15 JOURNALIZING THE PAYROLL AND THE EMPLOYER'S PAYROLL TAXES

Wendy Roberts Catering Services had the following payroll information for its March 31, 200X payroll:

Gross employee earnings	$18,000
Federal income tax withheld	2,000
FICA—OASDI withheld	1,170
FICA—HI withheld	270
Health insurance withheld	500
Charitable contributions withheld	300

None of the employees has exceeded the $7,000 limit for FUTA and SUTA. Assume FUTA and SUTA rates of 0.8% and 5.4%, respectively.

Required:

a.   Journalize the payroll.
b.   Journalize payment of the payroll.
c.   Journalize the employer's payroll taxes.
d.   Journalize payment of the employer's payroll taxes (FICA, FUTA, and SUTA), including matching FICA and income taxes withheld.

PROBLEM 6B-16 PAYROLL REGISTER WITH FUTA AND SUTA

Marjorie's Travel Professionals has four employees who are paid weekly. Using social security tax rates of 6.5 % on the first $60,000 (OASDI) and 1.5% on all wages earned (Medicare), and FUTA and SUTA rates of 0.8% of the first $7,000 for each employee and 5.4% on the first $7,000 for each employee, respectively, prepare the payroll register for the following employees on June 30, 200X. Assume a 10% federal income tax withholding rate (rather than using tax tables).

Name	With. Allow.	Prior Earnings	Regular Pay	Overtime	Cum. Total
Virginia Adams	2	5,000.00	1,000.00	0.00	6,000.00
Kenneth Williams	3	8,500.00	900.00	50.00	9,450.00
Richard Anderson	1	11,000.00	1,200.00	100.00	14,000.00
Ryan Webber	4	5,100.00	650.00	0.00	5,750.00

PROBLEM 6B-17 JOURNALIZING THE PAYROLL AND JOURNALIZING THE EMPLOYER'S PAYROLL TAXES

Based on Problem 6B-16 above, prepare the following:

a. Journalize the payroll.
b. Journalize payment of the payroll.
c. Journalize the employer's payroll taxes.
d. Journalize payment of the employer's payroll taxes (FICA, FUTA, and SUTA), including matching FICA and income taxes withheld.

PROBLEM 6B-18 JOURNALIZING THE PAYROLL AND THE EMPLOYER'S PAYROLL TAXES

Mike Burke Golf Lessons had the following payroll information for its March 31, 200X payroll:

Gross employee earnings	$22,000
Federal income tax withheld	3,000
FICA—OASDI withheld	1,430
FICA—HI withheld	330
Health insurance withheld	300
Charitable contributions withheld	250

None of the employees has exceeded the $7,000 limit for FUTA and SUTA. Assume FUTA and SUTA rates of 0.8% and 5.4%, respectively.

Required:

a. Journalize the payroll.
b. Journalize payment of the payroll.
c. Journalize the employer's payroll taxes.
d. Journalize payment of the employer's payroll taxes (FICA, FUTA, and SUTA), including matching FICA and income taxes withheld.

Module
6B

Challenge Problem

Merlin Enterprises maintains a payroll for six workers. Four earn hourly wages and two are on salary. Overtime is paid at one and one-half times the regular rate. Required payroll deductions include income tax and social security tax. FUTA and SUTA tax rates are 0.8% and 5.4%, respectively. The following payroll data is provided for the week ended January 8, 200X:

Name	Pay Rate	Data
Mike Smith	$7.50/hour	Worked 44 hours last week Married, 1 exemption $24 health insurance
Bill Johnson	$8.20/hour	Worked 48 hours last week Married, 2 exemptions $22.50 health insurance
Alice Krauss	$9.50/hour	Worked 42 hours last week Married, 0 exemptions $10 health insurance
Barbara Krane	$480/week	Married, 1 exemption $25 health insurance

Required:

1. Complete the payroll register for the week of ended January 8, 200X.
2. Prepare journal entries to record the payroll.
3. Prepare journal entries to record the employer's payroll taxes on this week's payroll.
4. Prepare journal entries to (a) pay the payroll on January 8, (b) pay social security tax withholdings and income tax withholdings to the federal government on January 10, (c) pay FUTA to the federal government on February 15, and (d) pay SUTA to the state government on February 15.

Chapter SEVEN

Accounting for Personal Services (Attorneys)

The following will be covered in this chapter

Accounting for Attorneys
Understanding the cash basis and the modified cash basis of accounting.
Understanding the special characteristics of accounting for attorneys.
Performing the tasks involved in accounting for attorneys.

Accounting for Attorneys

Chapter 7 Objectives
Careful study of this chapter should enable you to:
1. Understand the cash basis, and the modified cash basis of accounting.
2. Understand the special characteristics of accounting for attorneys.
3. Perform the tasks involved in accounting for attorneys.

The basis of accounting you have learned up to this point is called the accrual basis of accounting. Under the **accrual basis**, revenue and expenses are recognized when earned or incurred, regardless of when cash is received.

Under a pure **cash basis** of accounting, revenue is recognized only when cash is received. Expenses are recognized only when paid in cash. There are no adjustments for depreciation of long-term assets or for the usage of supplies or other prepaid items. This accounting method violates the matching principle. The cash basis of accounting is acceptable for federal and state income tax purposes. However, very few (if any) businesses use a pure cash basis of accounting. Most businesses who use the cash basis will adjust for the depreciation of long-term assets

and possibly adjust for the usage of supplies, insurance and other prepaid items. This method of accounting is called the modified cash basis.

Under a **modified cash basis** of accounting, revenue and expenses
are recognized only when cash is received or paid. However, assets
purchased on account are entered in the journal with a credit to
Accounts Payable. Prepaid assets such as supplies and prepaid insurance may be adjusted at the end of the accounting period to show how
much was used. Also, long-term assets, such as equipment, are depreciated over their useful life. This method of accounting is used with
personal service businesses such as attorneys, dentists, and physicians,
whose income is earned from performing personal services.

The reason that attorneys use the modified cash basis of accounting
rather than the accrual basis is because of the nature of their receivables
and how they are collected. Sometimes attorney fees are quite large and
the collection of these fees may be extended over a long period of time.
In other cases, the attorney fees may prove to be uncollectible and will
never materialize as revenue. By using the modified cash basis of
accounting, attorneys will be taxed only on the amount of cash
received.

Special Characteristics of Accounting for an Attorney. This chapter
relates to personal services performed by an attorney. An attorney may
represent either a plaintiff or a defendant. A person or company bringing a suit against someone else is called the **plaintiff**. The person or
company being sued is called the **defendant**.

To illustrate the modified cash basis of accounting for an attorney, a
chart of accounts for Wilson Simmons, Attorney at Law, is shown in
Exhibit 7.1 on the next page.

Accounts appearing for the first time in the illustrated chart of
accounts will be discussed before the records of Simmons are
presented.

**Account No. 121, Clients' Trust Account, Account No. 221, Liability
for Trust Funds, Account No. 421, Collection Fees Revenue.** Funds
received or collected by an attorney and held for a client must be
deposited in a separate bank account after deducting the attorney's collection fee. For example, suppose Rachel Hiner, Attorney at Law, was
hired to collect an outstanding debit of $900. Hiner's collection fee is

Exhibit 7.1

Chart of Accounts

Wilson Simmons, Attorney at Law
Chart of Accounts

Assets

111	Cash
112	Petty Cash Fund
121	**Clients' Trust Account**
131	**Advances on Behalf of Clients**
141	Office Supplies
185	Automobile
185.1	Accumulated Depreciation—Automobile
191	Office Equipment
191.1	Accumulated Depreciation—Office Equipment

Liabilities

221	**Liability for Trust Funds**
231	Employees' Income Tax Payable
232	FICA Tax Payable—OASDI
233	FICA Tax Payable—HI
241	FUTA Tax Payable
251	SUTA Tax Payable

Owner's Equity

311	Wilson Simmons, Capital
312	Wilson Simmons, Drawing
331	Income Summary

Revenue

411	Legal Fees Revenue
421	**Collection Fees Revenue**

Expenses

541	Rent Expense
542	Salary Expense
543	Office Supplies Expense
545	Telephone Expense
546	Automobile Expense
547	Depreciation Expense—Automobile
548	Depreciation Expense—Office Equipment
551	Law Library Expense
552	Payroll Taxes Expense
557	Charitable Contributions Expense
572	Miscellaneous Expense

33⅓%. If all $900 is collected by Hiner, $300 or 33⅓% is deposited in Hiner's cash account. Hiner will also credit the account Collection Fees Revenue, Account No. 421, for $300. The remaining $600 is debited to a special bank account called Clients' Trust Account, Account No. 121, and credited to an account called Liability for Trust Funds, Account No. 221, which represents the amount owed to Hiner's client. The balance in the Client's Trust Account and Liability for Trust Funds will always be equal.

To further illustrate, assume Simmons collects an account for Kingston Department Store for $800 on a commission basis of 25%. The following journal entry is made:

	Date		Description	Post Ref.	Debit	Credit	
20	May	14	Cash		2 0 0 00		20
21			Clients' Trust Account		6 0 0 00		21
22			Liability for Trust Funds			6 0 0 00	22
23			Collection Fees Revenue			2 0 0 00	23
24			Collected an account on behalf				24
25			of Kingston Department				25
26			Store and recorded fee earned.				26
27							27

General Journal — Page 1

When the amount collected is paid to the client, the following journal entry is made:

	Date		Description	Post Ref.	Debit	Credit	
28	May	15	Liability for Trust Funds		6 0 0 00		28
29			Clients' Trust Account			6 0 0 00	29
30			Payment to Kingston Dept.				30
31			Store of Collection made				31
32			for them.				32
33							33

General Journal — Page 1

Advances on Behalf of Clients, Account No. 131. Payments for items such as court filing fees, fees charged by accountants for doing audits, and the cost of obtaining depositions are sometimes made for clients. These payments are debited to the account Advances on Behalf of Clients and later billed to the clients. A record of the payments made and remittances received is also made in the client's account on an office docket (an auxiliary record which provides a complete record of each legal case). A minimum amount, usually below $1, can be established below which the firm will absorb the expense to save clerical work.

BOOKS OF ACCOUNT

Simmons uses the following books of account:

1. General books
   a. Cash receipts journal
   b. Cash payments journal

          c. General journal
          d. General ledger
    2. Auxiliary records
          a. Petty cash payments record
          b. Lawyer's office docket
          c. Lawyer's collection docket
          d. Employee's earnings record
          e. Checkbook used with Account No. 111
          f. Checkbook used with Account No. 121

Cash Receipts Journal

The **cash receipts journal** is a book of original entry used to record all receipts of cash. Simmons's cash receipts journal is reproduced on pages 220-221. It contains six amount columns arranged as follows:

1. General Credit
2. Revenue
    a. Legal Fees Revenue 411 Cr.
    b. Collection Fees Revenue 421 Cr.
3. Liability for Trust Funds 221 Cr.
4. Clients' Trust Account 121 Dr.
5. Cash 111 Dr.

Posting from this journal includes posting by column totals, called "summary posting," and posting from the general credit column, called "individual posting." Refer to Simmons's cash receipts journal on pages 220-221.

Below the double lines, or totals, beginning with the post reference column and reading across to the right, the columns are numbered 1 through 7. Refer to these numbers as we review the posting process from this journal. The Post Reference column (number 1) is used for posting the individual entries appearing in the General Credit column (number 2). The General Cr. column (number 2) is used to record payments made by clients for items charged to Advances on Behalf of Clients. When posting from the General Cr. column (number 2), conclude the posting process by writing the general ledger account number in the post reference column (number 1). Notice the check mark under the total of the General Cr. column (number 2). This check mark is a reminder that the total is not posted but the individual entries in the General Cr. column are posted. Also notice the check marks appearing in the Post Reference column (number 1). These check marks are a reminder that the amounts are not posted individually but are posted

| | | | POST | | GENERAL | | | REVENUE | | | | | LIABILITY FOR TRUST FUNDS | | |
	DATE	DESCRIPTION	**1** REF.	**2**	CR.	**3**		Legal Fees 411 Cr.	**4**		Coll. Fees 421 Cr.	**5**	221 CR.		
1															
2															

CASH RECEIPTS JOURNAL

| | CLIENTS' TRUST ACCOUNT | | | CASH | | |
6	121 DR.		**7**	111 DR.		
						1
						2

in total. The next three column totals, Legal Fees Revenue 411 Cr., Collection Fees Revenue 421 Cr., and Liability for Trust Funds 221 Cr. (numbers 3, 4, and 5) are all posted in total as credits to their respective account titles. The last two column totals, Clients' Trust Account 121 Dr. and Cash 111 Dr. (numbers 6 and 7), are posted in total as debits to their respective account titles. Notice how many entries are in the Cash 111 Dr. column total (number 7). Only the total is posted. This saves much time in the posting process as compared to the general journal that you learned in an earlier chapter. Account numbers are written in parentheses below the column totals to indicate that the totals have been posted to the general ledger, (numbers 3 through 7). As a proof of the journal, the total of the four credit columns (numbers 2 through 5) must equal the total of the two debit columns (numbers 6 and 7).

Cash Payments Journal

The **cash payments journal** is a book of original entry used to record all payments of cash. Simmons's cash payments journal is reproduced on pages 222-223. It contains eight amount columns arranged as follows:

1. General Dr.
2. Liability for Trust Funds 221 Dr.
3. Salary Expense 542 Dr.
4. Employees' Income Tax Payable 231 Cr.
5. FICA Tax Payable—OASDI 232 Cr.
6. FICA Tax Payable—HI 233 Cr.
7. Clients' Trust Account 121 Cr.
8. Cash 111 Cr.

The debits to Employees' Income Tax Payable and FICA Tax Payable should be entered in the General Dr. column when these taxes are paid.

There is a check number column to the left of Cash 111 Cr. column to account for the law firm's cash account. There is also a check number column to the left of Clients' Trust Account 121 Cr. column to account for payment to the clients of their cash. Summary and individual posting from this journal is similar to that from the cash receipts journal.

General Journal

The third book of original entry is a two-column general journal. It is used for transactions that cannot be entered in the cash receipts journal or the cash payments journal. For example, the journal entry to record the employer's payroll tax expense is entered in the general journal as shown on page 224. Also, the end-of-period adjusting and closing entries are entered in the general journal.

General Ledger

Simmons uses a four-column account form for the general ledger accounts. The first pair of debit and credit columns shows the amount of the actual debit or credit from the special or general journal. The next pair of debit and credit columns shows the ending balance of the account.

Petty Cash Payments Record

Simmons maintains a petty cash fund in the amount of $150.

Lawyer's Office Docket

An office docket is a form used to maintain a memorandum record of each legal case with a client. A model filled-in office docket (reproduced for Exhibit 7.2 on page 210) shows the history of the case of Warehouse Sales Co., plaintiff, vs. Jean Keith, defendant.

When an attorney's accounts are kept on a cash basis, there is no Accounts Receivable account for the client, but the information must be kept on the office docket. The client's account, as recorded on the office docket, should be charged for:

1. Fees for services rendered.
2. Payments on behalf of the client, such as filing fees and other expenses paid for the client.

The client's account should be credited for:

1. Payments received for services.
2. Reimbursements for advances made on behalf of the client.

In the illustration below, the client is charged for the following:

Exhibit 7.2

Lawyer's Office Docket

Client	*Warehouse Sales Co.*		Address	*623 Washburn Rd., City*	No. *460*

	IN RE:	Court	*Common Pleas, Dolan County*	
		Court File No.	*11649*	20 *0X*
	Warehouse Sales Co.	Calendar No.	*826*	Attorney for *Plaintiff*
	vs.	Other Attorneys		
	Jean Keith	Nature of Matter	*Lawsuit*	
		Remarks		

Date	Services Rendered	Fees and Payments	Money Received — Purpose	Money Received — Amount	Balance Due
Apr. *18*	*Fee for preparing case*	*1 5 0 0 00*			*1 5 0 0 00*
23	*Suit fee*	*2 0 00*			*1 5 2 0 00*
May *1*			*Retainer*	*3 0 0 00*	*1 2 2 0 00*
28			*Balance due*	*1 2 2 0 00*	*- 0 -*
	Carried forward				

April

> 18   Amount of the fee agreed upon at the time the case was taken, $1,500.
>
> 23   Amount advanced in payment of suit fee, $20.

The account is credited for the following:

May

> 1   Amount received as a retainer, $300.
>
> 28   Amount received in payment of balance due on account, $1,220.

Lawyer's Collection Docket

Lawyers who collect accounts for clients may use a form known as a **collection docket**. A model filled-in copy of a collection docket is shown in Exhibit 7.3 on page 211.

Exhibit 7.3
Lawyer's Collection Docket

Debtor	Thomas A. Ludlow		Date claim rec'd	5/3/XX	No. 63
Address	808 Delaware St., City		Date Disposed of	6/22/XX	
			Total Amount	$450	
Business			Amount Collected	$450	
Creditor	Evans Plumbing Co.		Fee	$150	
Address	300 W. Center St.		Expense		
			Amount Remitted	$300	
Rec'd claim from			Check No.	67 & 74	

Attorney for debtor			Received from Creditor			
Calls on debtor			Date	For		Amount
Correspondence			5/22/XX	Fee		1 0 0 00
			6/20/XX	Fee		5 0 00

Received from Debtor				Paid to Creditor		

Date	Amount	Date	Amount	Check No.	Amount	Check No.	Amount
5 22	3 0 0 00			67	2 0 0 00		
6 20	1 5 0 00			74	1 0 0 00		

Remarks   Statement of account. Collection fee 33⅓%.
              No suit without further instructions.

The docket provides a record of the case of the Evans Plumbing Co., creditor, vs. Thomas A. Ludlow, debtor. It also furnishes a record of the amounts collected from the debtor and the amounts paid to the creditor.

Attorneys usually take most collection cases on a percentage basis. Any expenses incurred in making collections should be charged to the expense accounts of the attorney. If, however, a client has agreed to pay any expenses incident to a lawsuit, such as court costs, the amounts paid by the attorney should be charged to the client's account.

In the illustration, the following transactions were recorded on the collection docket for the Evans Plumbing Co.

May 22   Collected $300 from Thomas A. Ludlow, debtor.
May 29   Paid $200 to the Evans Plumbing Co.
June 20   Collected $150 from Thomas A. Ludlow, debtor.
June 22   Paid $100 to the Evans Plumbing Co.

The amount of the commission of $33\frac{1}{3}\%$ is deducted from the amounts collected from the debtor and is entered on the collection docket as follows:

May 22 $100 ($300 × $33\frac{1}{3}\%$)
June 20 $ 50 ($150 × $33\frac{1}{3}\%$)

Employee's Earnings Record

The employee's earnings record was discussed in Chapter 6. We will use the same format as that presented earlier.

ACCOUNTING PROCEDURE

Following is a summary of transactions completed by Simmons during the month of May. These transactions are recorded in the special journals and general journal on pages 220-235. Follow each transaction by frequently referring to the journals and auxiliary records. You will find the journal or auxiliary record listed at the end of each transaction.

Tuesday, May 1
  1. Paid May office rent, $1,000, check no. 884. *Cash Payments Journal.*

Wednesday, May 2
  2. Received $300 from Warehouse Sales Co. as a retainer in the lawsuit of Warehouse Sales Co. vs. Jean Keith, Case No. 460. *Cash Receipts Journal. See Docket No. 460,* (page 210).

3. Issued Check No. 885 for $74.20 for electric bill. *Cash Payments Journal.*
4. Received $525 from Joyce Peden for services rendered in preparation of a will. *Cash Receipts Journal.*

Thursday, May 3

5. Issued Check No. 886 for $86.21 to the Public Telephone Co. for April telephone service. *Cash Payments Journal.*
6. Received $2,200 from S.R. Sabatini in payment of the balance due on Case No. 456. *Cash Receipts Journal.*
7. Received for collection from the Evans Plumbing Company, a statement of its account with Thomas A. Ludlow. Ludlow's account is over 12 months past due. Collection fee 33⅓%; no suit without further instructions. Collection No. 63. *See Example Collection Docket No. 63, (page 211).*

Friday, May 4

8. Received $1,695 from the Stofko Manufacturing Company in full payment of Case No. 454. *Cash Receipts Journal.*
9. Issued Check No. 887 for $101.46 for gas, oil and services rendered during April. *Cash Payments Journal.*
10. Received $325 from Adam Salinas for participating in a financial planning conference with Salinas' stockbroker and insurance agent.

END-OF-WEEK WORK

a. Footed the cash receipts and cash payments journals and proved the footings. The beginning cash balance was $22,104.32. The balance on May 4 was $25,887.45 Proved the balance in the checkbook as follows:

Checkbook balance, May 1	$22,104.32
Add cash received May 1–4	5,045.00
	$27,149.32
Deduct cash payments May 1–4	1,261.87
Checkbook balance, May 4	$25,887.45

b. Completed the individual postings from the General Dr. column of the cash payments journal to the ledger accounts. When posting from the cash payments and cash receipts journals, use CP and CR (and the page number), respectively, in the Post Ref. columns of the general ledger accounts. See page 224 for an example.

Monday, May 7

11. Received $460 from Brown and Hanson, family psychologists, for drafting a partnership agreement. *Cash Receipts Journal.*

Tuesday, May 8

12. Agreed to represent a client, Janet Wray Jazzercize Studio, Inc., in the purchase of a building. Minimum fee $875. Case No. 461. Received $200 as a retainer. *Cash Receipts Journal*

13. Received an invoice for $212.89 from Hancock Stationery Co. for office supplies. Note: Since Simmons's books are kept on the cash basis, invoices for expenses are not recorded until paid. When expense invoices are received, they are filed in an unpaid invoice file until paid.

Wednesday, May 9

14. Received $680.01 from Elizabeth J. Jenkins in payment of the amount due on Collection 60. *Cash Receipts Journal.*
     Note: Cash, Account No. 111, was debited for $226.67. Clients' Trust Account, Account No. 121, was debited for $453.34. Liability for Trust Funds, Account No. 221, was credited for $453.34. Collection Fees Revenue, Account No. 421, was credited for $226.67. A memorandum entry was also made in the collection docket for the amount received from the debtor.

Thursday, May 10

15. Issued Check No. 888 for $1,368.79 for law books. *Cash Payments Journal.*

Friday, May 11

16. Issued Check No. 889 for $100 to the Handicapped Camp Fund. *Cash Payments Journal.*

17. Received $150 from Star Electric Co., Inc. for preparing and filing an electrician's lien on the property of Walter Brook. *Cash Receipts Journal.*

END-OF-WEEK WORK

a. Proved the footings of the cash receipts and cash payments journals.

b. Proved the balance in the checkbook used with Account No. 111, $25,455.33.

c.   Compared the balance in the Clients' Trust Account, Account No. 121, $453.34, with the balance of $453.34 in the checkbook used with Account No. 121.

d.   Completed the individual postings from the cash payments journal to the ledger accounts.

Monday, May 14

18. Issued check no. 890 for $100 to the State Bar Association for annual dues. *Cash Payments Journal.*

19. Received $175 from Teresa Bonita for preparing a lease on office space in a building owned by Bonita. *Cash Receipts Journal.*

20. Issued Check No. 891 for $825.30 for the following payroll taxes:

Employees' income tax withheld		$368.00
FICA Tax Payable—OASDI	$380.94	
FICA Tax Payable—HI	76.36	457.30
Amount of check		$825.30

21. Simmons telephoned the Dolan National Bank and learned that the check for $680.01 received from Elizabeth J. Jenkins had cleared. Issued Check No. 66 to Russ Jewelry Company, $453.34, which represents the full amount of Collection No. 60 ($680.01 less a collection fee of $226.67). See Transaction No. 14. *Cash Payments Journal.*

Note: The collection fee had been recorded at the time the remittance was received from the debtor. A memorandum entry was made in the collection docket showing:

a. date the case was disposed

b. total amount collected

c. total amount of the attorney's fees

d. amount sent to the client

e. check number

Tuesday, May 15

22. Issued Check No. 892 for $549.60 to part-time law clerk for salary $672, less $72 withheld for income tax and $50.40 withheld for FICA tax ($42 for FICA Tax—OASDI and $8.40 for FICA Tax—HI). *Cash Payments Journal.*

23. Issued Check No. 893 for $671.62 to office secretary for gross wages $845, less $110 withheld for income tax, and $63.38 withheld for FICA tax ($52.82 for FICA Tax—OASDI and $10.56 for FICA Tax—HI). *Cash Payments Journal.*

24. Received $3,850 from the Tuttle Engineering Company in full payment of Case No. 457.

    Note: This remittance is in payment of the balance due for legal fees $3,200, and $650 for payment for work done by an accountant paid by Simmons on April 16 and debited to Advances on Behalf of Clients. The check was recorded in the cash receipts journal by debiting Cash, $3,850, crediting Advances on Behalf of Clients, $650, and by crediting Legal Fees Revenue, $3,200.

Wednesday, May 16

25. Simmons withdrew $2,250 for personal use. Check No. 894. *Cash Payments Journal.*

26. Purchased office microwave, issued Check No. 895 for $443.37. *Cash Payments Journal.*

Thursday, May 17

27. Issued Check No. 896 to Hancock Stationery Co. for $212.89 in payment of the invoice received on May 8. See May 8 transaction. *Cash Payments Journal.*

28. Received $9,250 in payment for services rendered on the settlement of the estate of Arturo Cruz, deceased. Case No. 452. *Cash Receipts Journal.*

Friday, May 18

29. Received $125 from Cindy Troy for drawing a power of attorney to authorize her to act in her mother's behalf. *Cash Receipts Journal.*

END-OF-WEEK WORK

a. Proved the footings of the cash receipts and cash payments journals.

b. Proved the balance in the checkbook used with Account No. 111, $33,802.55.

c. Completed the individual postings from the cash receipts journal and the cash payments journal to the ledger accounts.

Monday, May 21

30. Simmons has been engaged to represent the Stalwart Manufacturing Co. in the purchase of a building at a minimum fee of $2,000. Case No. 462. Received a check for $200 as a retainer and also received a check for $5,000 as a deposit on the purchase price. *Cash Receipts Journal.*

Note: Cash was debited and Legal Fees Revenue was credited for $200. Clients' Trust Account was debited and Liability for Trust Funds was credited for $5,000.

31. Issued Check No. 897 for $728.55 for a new printer. *Cash Payments Journal.*

Tuesday, May 22

32. Received $300 from Thomas A. Ludlow to apply to his account with the Evans Plumbing Co. Collection No. 63. *Cash Receipts Journal.* This transaction is similar to Transaction No. 14.

Wednesday, May 23

33. Received $675 from the Janet Wray Jazzercize Studio, Inc. in payment of the balance due for legal work done in connection with the purchase of a building. Case No. 461. See Transaction No. 12. *Cash Receipts Journal.*

Thursday, May 24

34. Barbara Angotti has engaged Simmons to handle the incorporation of a temporary help agency. Minimum fee $850. Received $150 as a retainer. Case No. 463. *Cash Receipts Journal.*

35. Received an invoice for $146.65 from the Esquire Supply Co. for legal forms.
     Note: Invoices for expenses are recorded only when paid.

END-OF-WEEK WORK

a. Proved the footings of the cash receipts and cash payments journals.
b. Proved the balance in the checkbook used with Account No. 111, $34,199.
c. Proved the balance in the checkbook used with Account No. 121, $5,200.
d. Completed the individual postings from the cash receipts journal and the cash payments journal to the ledger accounts.

Monday, May 28

36. Received $1,225 from Warehouse Sales Co. in payment of the balance due on account. Case No. 460. See Transaction No. 24. *Cash Receipts Journal.*

37. Issued Check No. 898 for $301.56 in payment of personal expenses. *Cash Payments Journal.*

38. Received $225 from Jan Amendola for a title search of a house Amendola wishes to buy.

Tuesday, May 29

39. Issued Check No. 899 for $720 to R. W. Payne, CPA, in payment of her statement covering accounting services rendered to Simmons's client, T. J. Marco, Case No. 453. *Cash Payments Journal.*
40. Received $280 from P. T. Louden in settlement of account. Case No. 455. *Cash Receipts Journal.*
41. Issued Check No. 67 for $200 to remit a partial collection from Thomas Ludlow in the amount of $300 less a 33⅓% collection fee. Collection No. 63. This relates to Transaction No. 32. *Cash Payments Journal.*

Wednesday, May 30

42. Simmons withdrew $3,500 for personal use. Check No. 900. *Cash Payments Journal.*

Thursday, May 31

43. Issued Check No. 901 for $609.75 for part-time law clerk (salary of $750, less $84 withheld for income tax, less $46.88 withheld for FICA Tax—OASDI, and less $9.37 withheld for FICA Tax—HI). *Cash Payments Journal.*
44. Issued Check No. 902 for $719.73 for office secretary (salary of $905.56, less $118 withheld for income tax, less $56 withheld for FICA Tax—OASDI, and less $11.32 withheld for FICA Tax—HI). *Cash Payments Journal.*
45. Issued Check No. 903 for $133.21 to replenish the petty cash fund. Expenses during the month paid from the petty cash fund included: advances on behalf of clients, $25; cash withdrawal by owner, $22.54; automobile expense, $32.55; charitable contribution, $30; miscellaneous expense, $7.34; and office supplies, $15.78. *Cash Payments Journal.*
46. Recorded payroll tax expenses of $287.72 in the general journal. Payroll tax expenses are: FICA Tax Payable—OASDI, $198.30; FICA Tax Payable—HI, $39.65; FUTA Tax Payable, $11.38; and SUTA Tax Payable, $38.39. *General Journal.*

END-OF-MONTH WORK

a. Proved the footings, entered the totals, and ruled the cash receipts and cash payments journals.
b. Proved the balance in the checkbook used with Account No. 111, $29,944.75.

c.   Proved the balance in the checkbook used with Account No. 121, $5,000.

d.   Completed the individual postings from the cash receipts journal, cash payments journal, and general journal to the ledger accounts. Note: Since this was the end of the month, the summary posting was completed and the account numbers were written immediately below the totals of the columns in the cash receipts and cash payments journals. Also note the check marks in the post reference column of the cash receipts and cash payments journals. A check mark indicates that the amount will be posted in total, not individually.

KEY POINT

The auxiliary records, office docket and/or collection docket, need to be updated after each transaction.

END-OF-YEAR WORK

We have just completed the transactions for May, which is the fifth month of a calendar year. In order to demonstrate the entire accounting cycle, we are going to perform the end-of-year accounting procedures that are normally done at the end of the year. The following steps were done to complete the accounting cycle for Wilson Simmons, Attorney at Law:

1.   A trial balance was taken from the general ledger accounts and appears on the work sheet, pages 230–231.

2.   The following adjustments were entered on the work sheet:
     a.   The ending inventory of office supplies, as of May 31, was $1,415.
     b.   Depreciation for five months on the automobile was $975.
     c.   Depreciation for five months on the office equipment was $545.

3.   Completed the work sheet.

4.   Using the work sheet, financial statements were prepared. The income statement, statement of owner's equity, and balance sheet are shown on pages 233–234.

5.   The adjusting and closing entries were entered on page 13 of the general journal and are shown on page 232.

6.   The adjusting and closing entries were posted to the general ledger.

7.   A post-closing trial balance was prepared and is shown on page 235.

	Date		Description	Post Ref.	General Cr.			
			Cash Receipts Journal 1 2					
1	200X							
2	May	1	Warehouse Sales Co. Case No. 460	✓				
3		2	J. Peden—Will	✓				
4		3	S.R. Sabatini Case No. 456	✓				
5		4	Stofko Mfg. Co. Case No. 454	✓				
6		4	Salinas—Financial Planning Conf.	✓				
7								
8		7	Brown & Hanson—Partnership Agreement	✓				
9		8	J. Wray Jazzercize Studio Inc. Case No. 461	✓				
10		9	E.J. Jenkins Collection No. 60	✓				
11		11	Star Electric Co., Inc.—Electrician's Lien	✓				
12								
13		14	T. Bonita—Lease	✓				
14		15	Tuttle Engineering Co. Case No. 457					
15			Advances on Behalf of Clients	131	6	5	0	00
16		17	A. Cruz Case No. 452	✓				
17		18	C. Troy—Power of Attorney	✓				
18					6	5	0	00
19		21	Stalwart Mfg. Co. Case No. 462	✓				
20		22	T.A. Ludlow Collection No. 63	✓				
21		23	J. Wray Jazzercize Studio, Inc. Case No. 461	✓				
22		24	B. Angotti Case No. 463	✓				
23					6	5	0	00
24		28	Warehouse Sales Co. Case No. 460					
25			Advances on Behalf of Clients	131		2	5	00
26		28	J. Amendola—Title Search	✓				
27		29	P.T. Louden Case No. 455	✓				
28					6	7	5	00
29								
30					(✓)			
31								
32								
33								
34								
35								
36								

	3	4	5	6	7	Page 25
	Revenue		Liability for Trust Funds 221 Cr.	Clients' Trust Account 121 Dr.	Cash 111 Dr.	
	Legal Fees 411 Cr.	Coll. Fees 421 Cr.				
1						
2	300 00				300 00	
3	525 00				525 00	
4	2 200 00				2 200 00	
5	1 695 00				1 695 00	
6	325 00				325 00	
7	5 045 00				5 045 00	
8	460 00				460 00	
9	200 00				200 00	
10		226 67	453 34	453 34	226 67	
11	150 00				150 00	
12	5 855 00	226 67	453 34	453 34	6 081 67	
13	175 00				175 00	
14						
15	3 200 00				3 850 00	
16	9 250 00				9 250 00	
17	125 00				125 00	
18	18 605 00	226 67	453 34	453 34	19 481 67	
19	200 00		5 000 00	5 000 00	200 00	
20		100 00	200 00	200 00	100 00	
21	675 00				675 00	
22	150 00				150 00	
23	19 630 00	326 67	5 653 34	5 653 34	20 606 67	
24						
25	1 200 00				1 225 00	
26	225 00				225 00	
27	280 00				280 00	
28	21 335 00	326 67	5 653 34	5 653 34	22 336 67	
29	(411)	(421)	(221)	(121)	(111)	
30						
31						
32						
33						
34						
35						
36						

Cash Payments Journal

	Date	Description	Post Ref.	General Dr.	Liability for Trust Funds 221 Dr.	Salary Expense 542 Dr.
1	200X					
2	May 1	Rent Expense	541	1 0 0 0 00		
3	2	Miscellaneous Expense	572	7 4 20		
4	3	Telephone Expense	545	8 6 21		
5	4	Automobile Expense	546	1 0 1 46		
6				1 2 6 1 87		
7	10	Law Library Expense	551	1 3 6 8 79		
8	11	Charitable Contributions Expense	557	1 0 0 00		
9				2 7 3 0 66		
10	14	Miscellaneous Expense	572	1 0 0 00		
11	14	Employees' Income Tax Payable	231	3 6 8 00		
12		FICA Tax Payable—OASDI	232	3 8 0 94		
13		FICA Tax Payable—HI	233	7 6 36		
14	14	Collection No. 60	✓		4 5 3 34	
15	15	Ana Santos	✓			6 7 2 00
16	15	Patricia Collins	✓			8 4 5 00
17	16	Wilson Simmons, Drawing	312	2 2 5 0 00		
18	16	Office Equipment	191	4 4 3 37		
19	17	Office Supplies	141	2 1 2 89		
20				6 5 6 2 22	4 5 3 34	1 5 1 7 00
21	21	Office Equipment	191	7 2 8 55		
22				7 2 9 0 77	4 5 3 34	1 5 1 7 00
23	28	Wilson Simmons, Drawing	312	3 0 1 56		
24	29	Adv. on Behalf of Clients, Case 453	131	7 2 0 00		
25	29	Collection No. 63	✓		2 0 0 00	
26	30	Wilson Simmons, Drawing	312	3 5 0 0 00		
27	31	Ana Santos	✓			7 5 0 00
28	31	Patricia Collins	✓			9 0 5 65
29	31	Advances on Behalf of Clients	131	2 5 00		
30		Wilson Simmons, Drawing	312	2 2 54		
31		Automobile Expense	546	3 2 55		
32		Charitable Contributions Expense	557	3 0 00		
33		Miscellaneous Expense	572	7 34		
34		Office Supplies	141	1 5 78		
35				11 9 4 5 54	6 5 3 34	3 1 7 2 65
36						
37				(✓)	(221)	(542)

	Emp. Income Tax Payable 231 Cr.				FICA Tax Pay. OASDI 232 Cr.				FICA Tax Pay. HI 233 Cr.			Check No.	Clients' Trust Account 121 Cr.			Check No.	Cash 111 Cr.					
1																							
2																884	1	0	0	0	00	
3																885			7	4	20	
4																886			8	6	21	
5																887		1	0	1	46	
6																	1	2	6	1	87	
7																888	1	3	6	8	79	
8																889		1	0	0	00	
9																	2	7	3	0	66	
10																890		1	0	0	00	
11																						
12																						
13																891		8	2	5	30	
14													66		4	5	3	34					
15		7	2	00		4	2	00			8	40					892		5	4	9	60	
16	1	1	0	00		5	2	82		1	0	56					893		6	7	1	62	
17																	894	2	2	5	0	00
18																	895		4	4	3	37
19																	896		2	1	2	89
20	1	8	2	00		9	4	82		1	8	96		4	5	3	34		7	7	8	3	44
21																	897		7	2	8	55
22	1	8	2	00		9	4	82		1	8	96		4	5	3	34		8	5	1	1	99
23																	898		3	0	1	56
24																	899		7	2	0	00
25													67	2	0	0	00						
26																	900	3	5	0	0	00
27		8	4	00		4	6	88			9	37					901		6	0	9	75
28	1	1	8	00		5	6	60		1	1	32					902		7	1	9	73
29																						
30																						
31																						
32																						
33																						
34																	903		1	3	3	21
35	3	8	4	00	1	9	8	30		3	9	65		6	5	3	34	14	4	9	6	24	
36																						
37		(231)				(232)				(233)					(121)				(111)			

General Journal
Page 12

	Date		Description	Post Ref.	Debit	Credit	
1	200X						1
2	May	31	Payroll Taxes Expense	552	2 8 7 72		2
3			FICA Tax Payable—OASDI	232		1 9 8 30	3
4			FICA Tax Payable—HI	233		3 9 65	4
5			FUTA Tax Payable	241		1 1 38	5
6			SUTA Tax Payable	251		3 8 39	6
7			Employer's payroll tax for May				7
8							8
9							9
10							10
11							11
12							12
13							13
14							14

General Ledger

Account Cash — Account No. 111

Date		Item	Post Ref.	Debit	Credit	Balance Debit	Balance Credit
200X							
May	1	Balance	✓			22 1 0 4 32	
	31		CR25	22 3 3 6 67		44 4 4 0 99	
	31		CP23		14 4 9 6 24	29 9 4 4 75	

Account Petty Cash Fund — Account No. 112

Date		Item	Post Ref.	Debit	Credit	Balance Debit	Balance Credit
200X							
May	1	Balance	✓			1 5 0 00	

Account Clients' Trust Account — Account No. 121

Date		Item	Post Ref.	Debit	Credit	Balance Debit	Balance Credit
200X							
May	31		CR25	5 6 5 3 34		5 6 5 3 34	
	31		CP23		6 5 3 34	5 0 0 0 00	

Account Advances on Behalf of Clients — **Account No.** 131

Date		Item	Post Ref.	Debit	Credit	Balance Debit	Balance Credit
200X							
May	1	Balance	✓			850 00	
	15		CR25		650 00	200 00	
	28		CR25		25 00	175 00	
	29		CP23	720 00		895 00	
	31		CP23	25 00		920 00	

Account Office Supplies — **Account No.** 141

Date		Item	Post Ref.	Debit	Credit	Balance Debit	Balance Credit
200X							
May	1	Balance				1430 06	
	17		CP23	212 89		1642 95	
	31		CP23	15 78		1658 73	
	31	Adj. Entry	GJ13		243 73	1415 00	

Account Automobile — **Account No.** 185

Date		Item	Post Ref.	Debit	Credit	Balance Debit	Balance Credit
200X							
May	1	Balance	✓			16645 00	

Account Accumulated Depreciation—Automobile — **Account No.** 185.1

Date		Item	Post Ref.	Debit	Credit	Balance Debit	Balance Credit
200X							
May	1	Balance	✓				8460 85
	31	Adj. Entry	GJ13		975 00		9435 85

Account Office Equipment — **Account No.** 191

Date		Item	Post Ref.	Debit	Credit	Balance Debit	Balance Credit
200X							
May	1	Balance	✓			6376 40	
	16		CP23	443 37		6819 77	
	21		CP23	728 55		7548 32	

Account Accumulated Depreciation—Office Equipment — **Account No.** 191.1

Date		Item	Post Ref.	Debit	Credit	Balance Debit	Balance Credit
200X							
May	1	Balance	✓				3764 25
	31	Adj. Entry	GJ13		545 00		4309 25

Account *Liability for Trust Funds*   Account No. *221*

Date		Item	Post Ref.	Debit	Credit	Balance Debit	Balance Credit
200X							
May	31	Balance	CR25		5 6 5 3 34		5 6 5 3 34
	31	Adj. Entry	CP23	6 5 3 34			5 0 0 0 00

Account *Employees' Income Tax Payable*   Account No. *231*

Date		Item	Post Ref.	Debit	Credit	Balance Debit	Balance Credit
200X							
May	1	Balance	✓				3 6 8 00
	14		CP23	3 6 8 00			- 0 -
	31		CP23		3 8 4 00		3 8 4 00

Account *FICA Tax Payable—OASDI*   Account No. *232*

Date		Item	Post Ref.	Debit	Credit	Balance Debit	Balance Credit
200X							
May	1	Balance	✓				3 8 0 94
	14		CP23	3 8 0 94			- 0 -
	31		CP23		1 9 8 30		1 9 8 30
	31		GJ12		1 9 8 30		3 9 6 60

Account *FICA Tax Payable—HI*   Account No. *233*

Date		Item	Post Ref.	Debit	Credit	Balance Debit	Balance Credit
200X							
May	1	Balance	✓				7 6 36
	14		CP23	7 6 36			- 0 -
	31		CP23		3 9 65		3 9 65
	31		GJ12		3 9 65		7 9 30

Account *FUTA Tax Payable*   Account No. *241*

Date		Item	Post Ref.	Debit	Credit	Balance Debit	Balance Credit
200X							
May	1	Balance	✓				1 2 2 00
	31		GJ12		1 1 38		1 3 3 38

Account *SUTA Tax Payable*   Account No. *251*

Date		Item	Post Ref.	Debit	Credit	Balance Debit	Balance Credit
200X							
May	1	Balance	✓				8 1 60
	31		GJ12		3 8 39		1 1 9 99

Account *Wilson Simmons, Capital*   **Account No.** *311*

Date		Item	Post Ref.	Debit	Credit	Balance Debit	Balance Credit
200X							
May	1	Balance	✓				10 505 76
	31	Clos. Ent.	GJ13		57 868 38		68 374 14
	31	Clos. Ent.	GJ13	26 609 44			41 764 70

Account *Wilson Simmons, Drawing*   **Account No.** *312*

Date		Item	Post Ref.	Debit	Credit	Balance Debit	Balance Credit
200X							
May	1	Balance	✓			20 535 34	
	16		CP23	2 250 00		22 785 34	
	28		CP23	301 56		23 086 90	
	30		CP23	3 500 00		26 586 90	
	31		CP23	22 54		26 609 44	
	31		GJ13		26 609 44	- 0 -	

Account *Income Summary*   **Account No.** *331*

Date		Item	Post Ref.	Debit	Credit	Balance Debit	Balance Credit
200X							
May	31		GJ13		86 444 04		86 444 04
	31		GJ13	28 575 66			57 868 38
	31	Clos. Ent.	GJ13	57 868 38			- 0 -

Account *Legal Fees Revenue*   **Account No.** *411*

Date		Item	Post Ref.	Debit	Credit	Balance Debit	Balance Credit
200X							
May	1	Balance	✓				60 155 64
	31		CR25		21 335 00		81 490 64
	31	Clos. Ent.	GJ13	81 490 64			- 0 -

Account *Collection Fees Revenue*   **Account No.** *421*

Date		Item	Post Ref.	Debit	Credit	Balance Debit	Balance Credit
200X							
May	1	Balance	✓				4 626 73
	31		CR25		326 67		4 953 40
	31	Clos. Ent.	GJ13	4 953 40			- 0 -

Account *Rent Expense*   **Account No.** *541*

Date		Item	Post Ref.	Debit	Credit	Balance Debit	Balance Credit
200X							
May	1	Balance	✓			4 000 00	
	1		CP23	1 000 00		5 000 00	
	31	Clos. Ent.	GJ13		5 000 00	- 0 -	

Account *Salary Expense*   **Account No.** *542*

Date		Item	Post Ref.	Debit	Credit	Balance Debit	Balance Credit
200X							
May	1	Balance	✓			11 215 00	
	31		CP23	3 172 65		14 387 65	
	31	Clos. Ent.	GJ13		14 387 65	- 0 -	

Account *Office Supplies Expense*   **Account No.** *543*

Date		Item	Post Ref.	Debit	Credit	Balance Debit	Balance Credit
200X							
May	31	Adj. Entry	GJ13	2 43 73		2 43 73	
	31	Clos. Ent.	GJ13		2 43 73	- 0 -	

Account *Telephone Expense*   **Account No.** *545*

Date		Item	Post Ref.	Debit	Credit	Balance Debit	Balance Credit
200X							
May	1	Balance	✓			2 66 43	
	3		CP23	86 21		3 52 64	
	31	Clos. Ent.	GJ13		3 52 64	- 0 -	

Account *Automobile Expense*   **Account No.** *546*

Date		Item	Post Ref.	Debit	Credit	Balance Debit	Balance Credit
200X							
May	1	Balance	✓			1 076 45	
	4		CP23	1 01 46		1 177 91	
	31		CP23	32 55		1 210 46	
	31	Clos. Ent.	GJ13		1 210 46	- 0 -	

Account *Depreciation Expense—Automobile*   **Account No.** *547*

Date		Item	Post Ref.	Debit	Credit	Balance Debit	Balance Credit
200X							
May	31	Adj. Entry	GJ13	9 75 00		9 75 00	
	31	Clos. Ent.	GJ13		9 75 00	- 0 -	

Account *Depreciation Expense—Office Equipment*   **Account No.** *548*

Date		Item	Post Ref.	Debit	Credit	Balance Debit	Balance Credit
200X							
May	31	Adj. Entry	GJ13	5 45 00		5 45 00	
	31	Clos. Ent.	GJ13		5 45 00	- 0 -	

Account	*Law Library Expense*				Account No. *551*

Date		Item	Post Ref.	Debit	Credit	Balance Debit	Balance Credit
200X							
May	1	Balance	✓			1 7 0 3 64	
	10		CP23	1 3 6 8 79		3 0 7 2 43	
	31	Clos. Ent.	GJ13		3 0 7 2 43	- 0 -	

Account	*Payroll Taxes Expense*				Account No. *552*

Date		Item	Post Ref.	Debit	Credit	Balance Debit	Balance Credit
200X							
May	1	Balance	✓			1 0 0 5 33	
	31		GJ12	2 3 7 95		1 2 4 3 28	
	31		GJ12	4 9 77		1 2 9 3 05	
	31	Clos. Ent.	GJ13		1 2 9 3 05	- 0 -	

Account	*Charitable Contributions Expense*				Account No. *557*

Date		Item	Post Ref.	Debit	Credit	Balance Debit	Balance Credit
200X							
May	1	Balance	✓			4 5 0 00	
	11		CP23	1 0 0 00		5 5 0 00	
	31		CP23	3 0 00		5 8 0 00	
	31	Clos. Ent.	GJ13		5 8 0 00	- 0 -	

Account	*Miscellaneous Expense*				Account No. *572*

Date		Item	Post Ref.	Debit	Credit	Balance Debit	Balance Credit
200X							
May	1	Balance	✓			7 3 4 16	
	2		CP23	7 4 20		8 0 8 36	
	14		CP23	1 0 0 00		9 0 8 36	
	31		CP23	7 34		9 1 5 70	
	31	Clos. Ent.	GJ13		9 1 5 70	- 0 -	

Wilson Simmons, Attorney at Law
Work Sheet
For Five Months Ending May 31, 200X

	Account	Trial Balance Debit	Trial Balance Credit	Adjustments Debit	Adjustments Credit
1	Cash	29 9 4 4 75			
2	Petty Cash Fund	1 5 0 00			
3	Clients' Trust Account	5 0 0 0 00			
4	Advances on Behalf of Clients	9 2 0 00			
5	Office Supplies	1 6 5 8 73			(a) 2 4 3 73
6	Automobile	16 6 4 5 00			
7	Accum. Depreciation—Auto.		8 4 6 0 85		(b) 9 7 5 00
8	Office Equipment	7 5 4 8 32			
9	Accum. Depr.—Office Equip.		3 7 6 4 25		(c) 5 4 5 00
10	Liability for Trust Funds		5 0 0 0 00		
11	Employees' Income Tax Payable		3 8 4 00		
12	FICA Tax Payable—OASDI		3 9 6 60		
13	FICA Tax Payable—HI		7 9 30		
14	FUTA Tax Payable		1 3 3 38		
15	SUTA Tax Payable		1 1 9 99		
16	Wilson Simmons, Capital		10 5 0 5 76		
17	Wilson Simmons, Drawing	26 6 0 9 44			
18	Legal Fees Revenue		81 4 9 0 64		
19	Collection Fees Revenue		4 9 5 3 40		
20	Rent Expense	5 0 0 0 00			
21	Salary Expense	14 3 8 7 65			
22	Office Supplies Expense			(a) 2 4 3 73	
23	Telephone Expense	3 5 2 64			
24	Automobile Expense	1 2 1 0 46			
25	Depreciation Exp.—Automobile			(b) 9 7 5 00	
26	Depreciation Exp.—Office Equip.			(c) 5 4 5 00	
27	Law Library Expense	3 0 7 2 43			
28	Payroll Taxes Expense	1 2 9 3 05			
29	Charitable Contributions Expense	5 8 0 00			
30	Miscellaneous Expense	9 1 5 70			
31		115 2 8 8 17	115 2 8 8 17	1 7 6 3 73	1 7 6 3 73
32	Net Income				
33					
34					
35					
36					

Adjusted Trial Balance		Income Statement		Balance Sheet		
Debit	Credit	Debit	Credit	Debit	Credit	
29 9 4 4 75				29 9 4 4 75		1
1 5 0 00				1 5 0 00		2
5 0 0 0 00				5 0 0 0 00		3
9 2 0 00				9 2 0 00		4
1 4 1 5 00				1 4 1 5 00		5
16 6 4 5 00				16 6 4 5 00		6
	9 4 3 5 85				9 4 3 5 85	7
7 5 4 8 32				7 5 4 8 32		8
	4 3 0 9 25				4 3 0 9 25	9
	5 0 0 0 00				5 0 0 0 00	10
	3 8 4 00				3 8 4 00	11
	3 9 6 60				3 9 6 60	12
	7 9 30				7 9 30	13
	1 3 3 38				1 3 3 38	14
	1 1 9 99				1 1 9 99	15
	10 5 0 5 76				10 5 0 5 76	16
26 6 0 9 44				26 6 0 9 44		17
	81 4 9 0 64		81 4 9 0 64			18
	4 9 5 3 40		4 9 5 3 40			19
5 0 0 0 00		5 0 0 0 00				20
14 3 8 7 65		14 3 8 7 65				21
2 4 3 73		2 4 3 73				22
3 5 2 64		3 5 2 64				23
1 2 1 0 46		1 2 1 0 46				24
9 7 5 00		9 7 5 00				25
5 4 5 00		5 4 5 00				26
3 0 7 2 43		3 0 7 2 43				27
1 2 9 3 05		1 2 9 3 05				28
5 8 0 00		5 8 0 00				29
9 1 5 70		9 1 5 70				30
116 8 0 8 17	116 8 0 8 17	28 5 7 5 66	86 4 4 4 04	88 2 3 2 51	30 3 6 4 13	31
		57 8 6 8 38			57 8 6 8 38	32
		86 4 4 4 04	86 4 4 4 04	88 2 3 2 51	88 2 3 2 51	33
						34
						35
						36

| | General Journal | | | | | | | | | | Page 13 | | | | |

	Date		Description	Post Ref.	Debit					Credit						
1	200X		*Adjusting Entries*													1
2	May	31	Office Supplies Expense	543		2	4	3	73							2
3			Office Supplies	141							2	4	3	73		3
4																4
5		31	Depreciation Expense—Auto.	547		9	7	5	00							5
6			Accum. Depreciation—Auto.	181.5							9	7	5	00		6
7																7
8		31	Depreciation Expense—Office Equip.	548		5	4	5	00							8
9			Accum. Depr.—Office Equip.	191.1							5	4	5	00		9
10																10
11			*Closing Entries*													11
12		31	Legal Fees Revenue	411	81	4	9	0	64							12
13			Collection Fees Revenue	421	4	9	5	3	40							13
14			Income Summary	331						86	4	4	4	04		14
15																15
16		31	Income Summary	331	28	5	7	5	66							16
17			Rent Expense	541						5	0	0	0	00		17
18			Salary Expense	542						14	3	8	7	65		18
19			Office Supplies Expense	543							2	4	3	73		19
20			Telephone Expense	545							3	5	2	64		20
21			Automobile Expense	546						1	2	1	0	46		21
22			Depreciation Expense—Automobile	547							9	7	5	00		22
23			Depreciation Expense—Office Equip.	548							5	4	5	00		23
24			Law Library Expense	551						3	0	7	2	43		24
25			Payroll Taxes Expense	552						1	2	9	3	05		25
26			Charitable Contributions Expense	557							5	8	0	00		26
27			Miscellaneous Expense	572							9	1	5	70		27
28																28
29		31	Income Summary	331	57	8	6	8	38							29
30			Wilson Simmons, Capital	311						57	8	6	8	38		30
31																31
32		31	Wilson Simmons, Capital	311	26	6	0	9	44							32
33			Wilson Simmons, Drawing	312						26	6	0	9	44		33
34																34
35																35

Wilson Simmons, Attorney at Law
Income Statement
For Five Months Ending May 31, 200X

Revenue:

Legal fees revenue	$81,490.64	
Collection fees revenue	4,953.40	
Total revenue		$86,444.04

Expenses:

Salary expense	$14,387.65	
Rent expense	5,000.00	
Law library expense	3,072.43	
Payroll tax expense	1,293.05	
Automobile expense	1,210.46	
Depreciation expense—automobile	975.00	
Charitable contributions expense	580.00	
Depreciation expense—office equipment	545.00	
Telephone expense	352.64	
Office supplies expense	243.73	
Miscellaneous expense	915.70	
Total expenses		28,575.66
Net income		$57,868.38

Wilson Simmons, Attorney at Law
Statement of Owner's Equity
For Five Months Ending May 31, 200X

Wilson Simmons, capital, January 1, 200X		$10,505.76
Net income for the period	$57,868.38	
Less withdrawals	26,609.44	
Net increase in capital		31,258.94
Wilson Simmons, capital, May 31, 200X		$41,764.70

Wilson Simmons, Attorney at Law
Balance Sheet
May 31, 200X

Assets

Current Assets:		
Cash	$29,944.75	
Petty cash fund	150.00	
Clients' trust account	5,000.00	
Advances on behalf of clients	920.00	
Office supplies	1,415.00	
Total Current Assets		$37,429.75

Long-Term Assets:			
Automobile	$16,645.00		
Less accumulated depreciation—automobile	9,435.85	$ 7,209.15	
Office equipment	$ 7,548.32		
Less accumulated depreciation—office equipment	4,309.25	3,239.07	
Total Long-Term Assets			10,448.22
Total Assets			$47,877.97

Liabilities

Current Liabilities:		
Employees' income tax payable	$ 384.00	
FICA tax payable—OASDI	396.60	
FICA tax payable—HI	79.30	
FUTA tax payable	133.38	
SUTA tax payable	119.99	
Liability for trust funds	5,000.00	
Total Current Liabilities		$ 6,113.27

Owner's Equity

Wilson Simmons, capital	$41,764.70
Total liabilities and owner's equity	$47,877.97

Wilson Simmons, Attorney at Law Post-Closing Trial Balance May 31, 200X													
Account		**Debit**						**Credit**					
Cash	29	9	4	4	75								
Petty Cash Fund		1	5	0	00								
Clients' Trust Account	5	0	0	0	00								
Advances on Behalf of Clients		9	2	0	00								
Office Supplies	1	4	1	5	00								
Automobile	16	6	4	5	00								
Accum. Depreciation—Automobile							9	4	3	5	85		
Office Equipment	7	5	4	8	32								
Accum. Depreciation—Office Equipment							4	3	0	9	25		
Liability for Trust Funds							5	0	0	0	00		
Employees' Income Tax Payable								3	8	4	00		
FICA Tax Payable—OASDI								3	9	6	60		
FICA Tax Payable—HI									7	9	30		
FUTA Tax Payable								1	3	3	38		
SUTA Tax Payable								1	1	9	99		
Wilson Simmons, Capital							41	7	6	4	70		
	61	6	2	3	07		61	6	2	3	07		

Concept Questions

1. When are revenue and expenses recognized under the cash basis of accounting?
2. Explain how the accounts Clients' Trust Account and Liability for Trust Funds are used by the attorney.
3. When is the general journal used if an attorney is using a cash payments journal and a cash receipts journal?
4. What is the purpose of an office docket?
5. Explain how a collection docket is used.

CHAPTER SUMMARY

A personal service business such as an attorney in practice generally uses the modified cash basis of accounting. The modified cash basis of accounting recognizes revenue or expenses only when cash is received or paid. Adjusting entries are made for the depreciation of assets and for the use of supplies and insurance.

The special characteristics of accounting for an attorney include the use of a Clients' Trust Account and Liability for Trust Funds. These accounts are used when an attorney receives cash on behalf of a client.

An office docket is an auxiliary record which provides a complete record of each legal case. A collection docket is another auxiliary record that provides a record of money collected from the debtor and cash paid to the creditor.

Other auxiliary records used by an attorney include a petty cash payments record and an employee's earnings record.

The general books, or primary books, used by an attorney include a cash receipts journal, cash payments journal, general journal, and general ledger.

Key Terms

accrual basis, *203*

cash basis, *203*

cash payments journal, *208*

cash receipts journal, *207*

collection docket, *210*

defendant, *204*

modified cash basis, *204*

office docket, *209*

plaintiff, *204*

Exercises

EXERCISE 7-1

Match the terms with their respective descriptions:

1. ____ Accrual basis
2. ____ Cash basis
3. ____ Collection docket
4. ____ Defendant
5. ____ Office docket
6. ____ Plaintiff

a. The person or company being sued

b. An auxiliary record which provides a complete record of each legal case

c. Revenues and expenses are recognized when earned or occurred, regardless of when cash is received.

d. An auxiliary record which provides a record of the amounts collected from the debtor and the amounts paid to the creditor

e. Revenues and expenses are recognized only when cash is received or paid.

f. A person or company bringing a suit against someone else

EXERCISE 7-2

A blank lawyer's office docket used by Maxine Ogle, an attorney, is reproduced in the study guide/working papers. Enter the following information concerning the case of Douglas Davis vs. Johnson Architects Inc. on the office docket.

Client: Douglas Davis
Address: 9119 East Burnside, City
Number: 861
IN RE: Douglas Davis vs. Johnson Architects Inc.
Court: Gresham County District
Court File No.: 83175
Calendar No.: 416
Attorney for: Plaintiff
Nature of Matter: Lawsuit

July   3   Fee for preparing case $700
July   6   Retainer $300
July 10   Suit fee $50, issued Check No. 431
July 23   Payment on account, $200
July 30   Balance due, $250, is paid on this date.

EXERCISE 7-3

Refer to Exercise 7-2 and prepare the entries in the cash receipts and cash payments journals for these transactions.

EXERCISE 7-4

Harold Long, an attorney, has been engaged to collect a debt owed by Dick Ady to the Metro Department Store. A blank lawyer's collection docket is reproduced in the study guide/working papers. Enter the following information in the collection docket.

Debtor: Dick Ady
Address: 3419 Cromwell Avenue, City
Creditor: Metro Department Store
Address: 2215 Division Street, City
Date claim received: 9/10/200X
No.: 212
Date disposed of: 11/14/200X
Total amount: $1,860
Amount collected: $1,860
Fee: $620
Amount remitted: $1,240
Check No.: 60, 66, 75

Received from creditor

Date	For	Amount
9/24	Com.	$200
10/10	Com.	$300
11/7	Com.	$120

Received from debtor

Date	Amount
9/24	$600
10/10	$900
11/7	$360

Paid to creditor

Date	Check No.	Amount
10/1	60	$400
10/17	66	$600
11/14	75	$240

Remarks: Statement of account. Collection fee 33⅓%. No suit without further instructions.

EXERCISE 7-5

Refer to Exercise 7-4 and prepare the entries in the cash receipts and cash payments journals for these transactions.

Problems

PROBLEM 7-6

Laura Hamilton, an attorney, maintains her books on the modified cash basis of accounting. The following books of account are used in her business: cash receipts journal, cash payments journal, general journal, and a lawyer's office docket. The selected account names and numbers below were taken from the Laura Hamilton, Attorney at Law, Chart of Accounts.

Assets
111   Cash
115   Office Supplies
131   Advances on Behalf of Clients
Liabilities
211   Accounts Payable
Owner's Equity
311   Laura Hamilton, Capital
312   Laura Hamilton, Drawing

Revenue
411   Legal Fees Revenue
Expenses
541   Rent Expense
542   Salary Expense
551   Law Library Expense

The following selected transactions took place during February, 200X.

Feb

1   Issued Check No. 111 for February office rent, $1,300.

5   Hamilton has agreed to represent George Smith in a lawsuit to be known as Baker vs. Smith. Received a retainer of $400. Record the following on a lawyer's office docket:

> Client: George Smith
> Address: 351 Maplewood, City
> Office Docket No.: 285
> IN RE: Baker vs. Smith
> Court: District Court, Multnomah County
> Court File No.: 11367
> Calendar No.: 792
> Attorney for: Defendant
> Nature of Matter: Lawsuit
> Fee for Preparing Case: $2,100

Note: Record the $400 retainer in the cash receipts journal. Write "George Smith, Case No. 285" in the description column.

8   Issued Check No. 112 for purchase of office supplies, $112.25.

12   Issued Check No. 113 for the suit fee in the case of Baker vs. Smith, Case No. 285, $100 (Debit Advances on Behalf of Clients.)
Remember to update office docket, Case No. 285.

18   Purchased office equipment on account, $900. (Record in general journal.)

20   Received a check for $600 from George Smith, a client, to apply on account.

23   Issued Check No. 114 to American Law Publishing Company, $650. (Debit Law Library Expense.)

25   Received $400 from Morris Electric Co. for preparing and filing an electrician's lien.

27   Received the balance due from George Smith, a client, for services billed, $1,200 (Case No. 285).

28   Issued Check No. 115 for $1,182.90 to Kim Nethery for payment of salary to secretary, $1,400, less employee income tax payable, $110, less FICA Tax Payable—OASDI, $86.80, less FICA Tax Payable—HI, $20.30.

28   Issued Check No. 116 for owner's withdrawal, $4,000.

Required:

1.   Record the above transactions in the appropriate journals and office docket.

2. Foot the amount columns of the cash receipts and cash payments journals, and enter the footings in pencil figures immediately below the line on which the last entry appears.
3. Prove the equality of the debit and credit footings.

PROBLEM 7-7

John Bruso, Attorney at Law, maintains his books on the modified cash basis of accounting. The following books of account are used in his business: cash receipts journal; cash payments journal; general journal; checkbook used with Cash, Account No. 111; checkbook used with Clients' Trust Account, Account No. 121; and a lawyer's collection docket. The selected account names and numbers below were taken from the John Bruso, Attorney at Law, Chart of Accounts.

Assets
111 Cash
115 Office Supplies
121 Clients' Trust Account
Liabilities
211 Accounts Payable
221 Liability for Trust Funds
Owner's Equity
311 John Bruso, Capital
312 John Bruso, Drawing

Revenue
421 Collection Fees Revenue
Expenses
541 Rent Expense
542 Salary Expense
556 Utility Expense

The following selected transactions took place during July, 200X.

July

1 Issued Check No. 211 for July office rent, $1,600.
6 Received for collection from the Jackson Electrical Company a statement of its account with Tim Shockley. Shockley's account is over 12 months past due. Total amount owed is $2,400. Record the following on a lawyer's collection docket.

   Debtor: Tim Shockley
   Address: 8808 N.E. Davis, City
   Date Claim Received: July 6, 200X
   Collection No.: 47
   Creditor: Jackson Electrical Company
   Address: 700 S.W. 51st Avenue
   Total Amount: $2,400

Remarks: Statement of account. Collection fee 33⅓%. No suit without further instructions.

7 Received a check for $600 from Tim Shockley to apply on the account of Jackson Electrical Company, Collection No. 47. (Note: Debit Cash for $200 and debit Clients' Trust Account for $400. Credit Collection

Fees Revenue for $200 and credit Liability for Trust Funds for $400. In the description column of the cash receipts journal, write "Tim Shockley, Collection No. 47." Also make a memorandum entry of the amount received in the collection docket.)

8 Issued Check No. 57 from the Clients' Trust Account, Account No. 121, to Jackson Electrical Company for $400. (Note: Debit Liability for Trust Funds and credit Clients' Trust Account for $400 in the cash payments journal.)

10 Issued Check No. 212 for utility bill, $435.

14 Purchased office supplies on account, $425.

15 Received a check for $900 from Tim Shockley to apply on the account of Jackson Electrical Company, Collection No. 47. (See transaction on July 7.) *Remember: The collection fee is 33⅓%.*

16 Issued Check No. 58 from the Clients' Trust Account, Account No. 121, to Jackson Electrical Company for $600. (See transaction on July 8.)

23 Issued Check No. 213 for owner's withdrawal, $3,500.

26 Issued Check No. 214 for $1,217.25 to Andrea Fields, for payment of salary to secretary, $1,500, less employee income tax payable, $168, less FICA tax payable—OASDI, $93, less FICA tax payable—HI, $21.75.

30 Received a check for $900 from Tim Shockley for the balance due, Collection No. 47.

31 Issued Check No. 59 from the Clients' Trust Account, Account No. 121, to Jackson Electrical Company for $600.

Required:

1. Record the above transactions in the appropriate journals and collection docket.

2. Foot the amount columns of the cash receipts and cash payments journals, and enter the footings in pencil figures immediately below the line on which the last entry appears.

3. Prove the equality of the debit and credit footings.

PROBLEM 7-8

Thomas Durwood, Attorney at Law, maintains his books on the modified cash basis of accounting. The following books of account are used in his business: cash receipts journal, cash payments journal, general journal, and a lawyer's office docket. The selected account names and numbers shown were taken from the Thomas Durwood, Attorney at Law, Chart of Accounts.

Assets
111 Cash
115 Office Supplies
131 Advances on Behalf of Clients
Liabilities
211 Accounts Payable
Owner's Equity
311 Thomas Durwood, Capital
312 Thomas Durwood, Drawing

Revenue
411 Legal Fees Revenue
Expenses
541 Rent Expense
542 Salary Expense
551 Law Library Expense

The following selected transactions took place during February, 200X.

Feb

1 Issued Check No. 211 for February office rent, $1,900.

5 Durwood has agreed to represent Jim Warren in a lawsuit to be known as Fess vs. Warren. Received a retainer of $600. Record the following on a lawyer's office docket:

>   Client: Jim Warren
>   Address: 6512 N. Lake Shore Dr., City
>   Office Docket No.: 273
>   IN RE: Fess vs. Warren
>   Court: District Court, Clackamas County
>   Court File No.: 12461
>   Calendar No.: 649
>   Attorney for: Defendant
>   Nature of Matter: Lawsuit
>   Fee for Preparing Case: $2,700.

Note: Record the $600 retainer in the cash receipts journal. Write "Jim Warren, Case No. 273" in the description column.

8 Issued Check No. 212 for purchase of office supplies, $145.

12 Issued Check No. 213 for the suit fee in the case of Fess vs. Warren, Case No. 273, $100. (Debit Advances on Behalf of Clients.) *Remember to update office docket, Case No. 273.*

16 Purchased office equipment on account, $1,200. (Record in general journal.)

21 Received a check for $800 from Jim Warren, a client, to apply on account.

24 Issued Check No. 214 to American Law Publishing Company, $875. (Debit Law Library Expense.)

25 Received $965 from Stands Electric Co. for preparing and filing an electrician's lien.

28 Received the balance due from Jim Warren, a client, for services billed, $1,400 (Case No. 273).

28   Issued Check No. 215 for $1,536.47 to Jill Davis for payment of salary to secretary, $1,850, less employee income tax payable, $172, less FICA tax payable—OASDI, $114.70, less FICA tax payable—HI, $26.83.

28   Issued Check No. 216 for owner's withdrawal, $3,400.

Required:

1.   Record the above transactions in the appropriate journals and office docket.
2.   Foot the amount columns of the cash receipts and cash payments journals, and enter the footings in pencil figures immediately below the line on which the last entry appears.
3.   Prove the equality of the debit and credit footings.

PROBLEM 7-9

Charles McCord, Attorney at Law, maintains his books on the modified cash basis of accounting. The following books of account are used in his business: cash receipts journal; cash payments journal; general journal; checkbook used with Cash, Account No. 111; checkbook used with Clients' Trust Account, Account No. 121; and a lawyer's collection docket. The selected account names and numbers below were taken from the Charles McCord, Attorney at Law, Chart of Accounts.

Assets
111   Cash
115   Office Supplies
121   Clients' Trust Account
Liabilities
211   Accounts Payable
221   Liability for Trust Funds
Owner's Equity
311   Charles McCord, Capital
312   Charles McCord, Drawing

Revenue
421   Collection Fees Revenue
Expenses
541   Rent Expense
542   Salary Expense
556   Utility Expense

The following selected transactions took place during July, 200X.

July

1   Issued Check No. 111 for July office rent, $1,925.
7   Received for collection from Columbia Industries, a statement of its account with Robert Akers. Akers's account is over 12 months past due. Total amount owed is $3,900. Record the following on a lawyer's collection docket.

Debtor: Robert Akers
Address: 9119 East Burnside, City
Date Claim Received: July 7, 200X
Collection No.: 63

> Creditor: Columbia Industries
> Address: 3571 N. Marine Dr.
> Total amount: $3,900

Remarks: Statement of account. Collection fee 33⅓%. No suit without further instructions.

7   Received a check for $1,200 from Robert Akers to apply on the account of Columbia Industries, Collection No. 63. (Note: Debit Cash for $400 and debit Clients' Trust Account for $800. Credit Collection Fees Revenue for $400 and credit Liability for Trust Funds for $800. In the description column of the cash receipts journal, write "Robert Akers, Collection No. 63." Also make a memorandum entry of the amount received in the collection docket.)

9   Issued Check No. 82 from the Clients' Trust Account, Account No. 121, to Columbia Industries, $800. (Note: Debit Liability for Trust Funds and credit Clients' Trust Account for $800 in the cash payments journal.)

11 Issued Check No. 112 for utility bill, $820.

14 Purchased office supplies on account, $615.

15 Received a check for $900 from Robert Akers to apply on the account of Columbia Industries, Collection No. 47. (See transaction on July 7.) *Remember: The collection fee is 33⅓%.*

16 Issued Check No. 83 from the Clients' Trust Account, Account No. 121, to Columbia Industries for $600. (See transaction on July 9.)

23 Issued Check No. 113 for owner's withdrawal, $4,300.

27 Issued Check No. 114 for $1,605.35 to Rachel Hiner for payment of salary to secretary, $2,100, less employee income tax payable, $334, less FICA tax payable—OASDI, $130.20, less FICA tax payable—HI, $30.45.

30 Received a check for $1,800 from Robert Akers for the balance due, Collection No. 63.

31 Issued Check No. 84 from the Clients' Trust Account, Account No. 121, to Columbia Industries for $1,200.

Required:

1. Record the above transactions in the appropriate journals and collection docket.
2. Foot the amount columns of the cash receipts and cash payments journals, and enter the footings in pencil figures immediately below the line on which the last entry appears.
3. Prove the equality of the debit and credit footings.

Challenge Problem

The trial balance of Terry Potts, Attorney at Law, as of November 30, 200X, is provided below:

Account	Acct. No.	Dr.					Cr.				
Cash	111	25	3	4	3	00					
Petty Cash Fund	112		2	0	0	00					
Clients' Trust Account	121										
Advances on Behalf of Clients	131		6	1	5	00					
Office Supplies	141		9	7	5	00					
Prepaid Insurance	145	3	6	0	0	00					
Automobile	185	28	4	5	0	00					
Accumulated Depreciation—Automobile	185.1						6	0	0	0	00
Office Equipment	191	22	5	0	0	00					
Accum. Depreciation—Office Equipment	191.1						2	0	0	0	00
Accounts Payable	211						1	1	0	0	00
Employees' Income Tax Payable	231							3	5	0	00
FICA Tax Payable—OASDI	232							2	8	6	00
FICA Tax Payable—HI	233								6	6	00
Liability for Trust Funds	221										
Terry Potts, Capital	311						45	9	5	0	00
Terry Potts, Drawing	312	65	0	0	0	00					
Income Summary	331										
Legal Fees Revenue	411						155	3	0	0	00
Collection Fees Revenue	421						12	5	0	0	00
Rent Expense	541	22	0	0	0	00					
Salary Expense	542	39	5	9	4	50					
Office Supplies Expense	543										
Telephone Expense	545	1	7	1	0	00					
Automobile Expense	546	2	9	4	2	00					
Depreciation Expense—Automobile	547										
Depreciation Expense—Office Equipment	548										
Insurance Expense	549										
Law Library Expense	551	2	4	0	0	00					
Payroll Taxes Expense	552	2	8	5	7	50					
Charitable Contributions Expense	557	4	4	0	0	00					
Miscellaneous Expense	572		9	6	5	00					
		223	5	5	2	00	223	5	5	2	00

Terry Potts, Attorney at Law
Trial Balance
November 30, 200X

Terry Potts, Attorney at Law, maintains his books on the modified cash basis of accounting. The following books of account are used in his business: cash receipts journal; cash payments journal; general journal; lawyer's office docket; lawyer's collection docket; checkbook used with Cash, Account No. 111; checkbook used with Clients' Trust Account, Account No. 121; and a petty cash payments record.

The following transactions took place during December, 200X, the last month of the fiscal year.

Dec. 1 Issued Check No. 311 for December office rent, $2,100.

4 Potts has agreed to represent Bruce Brown in a lawsuit to be known as Brown vs. Weber. Received a retainer of $500. Record the following on a lawyer's office docket:

> Client: Bruce Brown
> Address: 3518 Macadam Avenue
> Office Docket No.: 421
> IN RE: Brown vs. Weber
> Court: Multnomah County, State Court
> Court File No.: 18967
> Calendar No.: 623
> Attorney for: Plaintiff
> Nature of Matter: Lawsuit
> Fee for Preparing Case: $2,100

Note: Record the $500 retainer in the cash receipts journal. Write "Bruce Brown, Case No. 421" in the description column.

5 Purchased office supplies on account, $400.

6 Issued Check No. 312 for the suit fee in the case of Brown vs. Weber, Case No. 421, $100.

8 Issued Check No. 313 for a one-year insurance policy, $1,400.

9 Received for collection from Jordan Enterprises, a statement of its account with Travis Hill. Hill's account is over 12 months past due. Total amount owed is $2,700. Record the following on a lawyer's collection docket:

> Debtor: Travis Hill
> Address: 703 N. Killingsworth, City
> Date Claim Received: December 9, 200X
> Collection No.: 85
> Creditor: Jordan Enterprises
> Address: 6714 Columbia Blvd., City
> Total amount: $2,700

Remarks: Statement of account. Collection fee is 33⅓%. No suit without further instructions.

11 On Potts' instruction, a $200 donation was given to a representative of the American Red Cross. Issued Check No. 314.

12 Received a check for $900 from Travis Hill to apply on the account of Jordan Enterprises, Collection No. 85. (Note: Debit Cash for $300 and debit Clients' Trust Account for $600. Credit Collection Fees Revenue for $300 and credit Liability for Trust Funds for $600. In the description column of the cash receipts journal, write "Travis Hill, Collection No. 85." Also update the collection docket.)

14 Issued Check No. 315 for $702 in payment of the following payroll taxes:

Employees' Income Tax Payable	$350
FICA Tax Payable—OASDI	286
FICA Tax Payable—HI	66

15 Issued Check No. 316 to Johnnie Ruth for $837 in payment of secretary's salary, $1,100, less $175 for employees' income tax payable, less $71.50 for FICA Tax Payable—OASDI, less $16.50 for FICA Tax Payable—HI.

16 Received a check for $4,700 from Davis Engineering Company, in full payment for work completed in the prior month.

Note: This remittance is in payment of the balance due for legal fees, $4,100, and $600 for payment for work done by an accountant paid by Potts and debited to Advances on Behalf of Clients. Debit Cash for $4,700, credit Advances on Behalf of Clients, $600, and credit Legal Fees Revenue, $4,100.

16 Issued Check No. 317 in payment of creditors on account, $900.

18 Received $1,025 from Kent Electric Co. for preparing and filing an electrician's lien.

21 Received a check for $1,000 from Bruce Brown, a client, to apply on account, Case No. 421.

23 Issued Check No. 91 from the Clients' Trust Account, Account No. 121, to Jordan Enterprises, $600. (Note: Debit Liability for Trust Funds and credit Clients' Trust Account for $600.)

26 Received a check for $1,800 from Travis Hill in full payment of amount owed to Jordan Enterprises, Collection No. 85.

29 Received the balance owed from Bruce Brown, a client, Case No. 421, $700. (Note: Debit Cash for $700, credit Advances on Behalf of Clients, $100, and credit Legal Fees Revenue, $600.)

30 Issued Check No. 318 for owner's withdrawal, $4,100.

31 Issued Check No. 319 to Johnnie Ruth for $837 in payment of secretary's salary, $1,100, less $175 for employees' income tax payable, less $71.50 for FICA Tax Payable—OASDI, less $16.50 for FICA Tax Payable—HI.

31　Issued Check No. 92 from the Clients' Trust Account, Account No. 121, to Jordan Enterprises, $1,200.

31　Entered in the general journal the payroll tax expense as follows:

FICA Tax Payable—OASDI	$143
FICA Tax Payable—HI	33

Note: There were no unemployment taxes.

31　Issued Check No. 320 to reimburse the petty cash fund, $194. The following expenditures were summarized from the petty cash payments record:

Automobile Expense	$102
Charitable Contributions Expense	35
Miscellaneous Expense	57

Required:

1. Enter the balances from the November 30 trial balance in the general ledger accounts. Write "balance" in the item column in the general ledger and use Dec. 1 in the date column. Enter all the accounts from the trial balance including those with a zero balance.
2. Record the above transactions in the appropriate journals and dockets.
3. Foot the amount columns of the cash receipts and cash payments journals, and enter the footings in pencil figures immediately below the line on which the last entry appears. Prove the equality of the debit and credit footings.
4. Complete the individual postings from the cash receipts journal, cash payments journal, and the general journal.
5. Complete the summary postings from the cash receipts journal and the cash payments journal. Be sure to include the general ledger account numbers in parentheses under the column totals for those accounts that were posted in total. Put a check mark in parentheses beneath the general columns.
6. Prepare a trial balance using the first pair of columns of a ten-column work sheet provided in the working papers. Include all accounts from the general ledger except the income summary account.
7. Use the following information to complete the year-end adjustments:
   a. Office supplies inventory as of December 31, 200X　　$ 310
   b. Insurance expired　　　　　　　　　　　　　　　　2,800
   c. Depreciation on automobile　　　　　　　　　　　3,100
   d. Depreciation on office equipment　　　　　　　　2,300
   Enter these adjustments on the work sheet. Identify each adjustment by letter.

8. Complete the work sheet.
9. Using the work sheet:
   a. Prepare an income statement for the year ended December 31, 200X.
   b. Prepare a statement of owner's equity for the year ended December 31, 200X.
   c. Prepare a balance sheet as of December 31, 200X.
10. Using the work sheet as a guide, journalize and post the adjusting entries, using page 4 of the general journal.
11. Using the work sheet as a guide, journalize and post the closing entries, using page 4 of the general journal.
12. Prepare a post-closing trial balance.

Chapter EIGHT

Accounting for Personal Services (Physicians and Dentists)

The following will be covered in this chapter

Accounting for Physicians and Dentists
Understand the cash basis and modified cash basis of accounting.
Understand the special characteristics of accounting for physicians and dentists.
Perform the tasks involved in accounting for physicians and dentists.

Accounting for Physicians and Dentists

Chapter 8 Objectives
Careful study of this chapter should enable you to:
1. Understand the cash basis, and modified cash basis of accounting.
2. Understand the special characteristics of accounting for physicians and dentists.
3. Perform the tasks involved in accounting for physicians and dentists.

The basis of accounting you have learned up through Chapter 6 is called the accrual basis of accounting. Under the **accrual basis**, revenue and expenses are recognized when earned or incurred, regardless of when cash is received.

> Remember the use of Accounts Receivable and Accounts Payable. A sale made on account involved a credit to revenue and a debit to Accounts Receivable. The revenue immediately accrues but cash will be received later. A bill received today but paid later involves a debit to an expense account and a credit to Accounts Payable. The expense immediately accrues but cash will be paid later.

Under a pure **cash basis** of accounting, revenue is recognized only when cash is received. Expenses are recognized only when paid in cash. There are no adjustments for depreciation of long-term assets or for the usage of supplies or other prepaid items. This accounting method violates the matching principle. The cash basis of accounting is acceptable for federal and state income tax purposes. However, very few (if any) businesses use a pure cash basis of accounting. Most businesses who use the cash basis will adjust for the depreciation of long-term assets and possibly adjust for the usage of supplies, insurance and other pre-paid items. This method of accounting is called the modified cash basis.

Under a **modified cash basis of accounting**, revenue and expenses are recognized only when cash is received or paid. However, assets purchased on account are entered in the journal with a credit to Accounts Payable. Prepaid assets such as supplies and prepaid insurance may be adjusted, at the end of the accounting period, to show how much was used. Also, long-term assets, such as equipment, are depreciated over their useful life. This method of accounting is used with personal service businesses such as attorneys, dentists, and physicians, whose income is earned from performing personal services.

The reason that physicians and dentists use the modified cash basis of accounting rather than the accrual basis is because of the nature of their receivables and how they are collected. Sometimes physician and dentist fees are quite large and the collection of these fees may be extended over a long period of time. In other cases, these fees may prove to be uncollectible and will never materialize as revenue. By using the modified cash basis of accounting, physicians and dentists will be taxed only on the amount of cash received.

Special Characteristics of Accounting for a Physician and Dentist. To illustrate some of the characteristics of accounting for the medical and dental professions, a basic system of accounting for Julie Cole and John Martin, Physicians and Surgeons, is presented. We will begin with the chart of accounts.

Exhibit 8.1
Chart of Accounts

Cole and Martin, Physicians and Surgeons
Chart of Accounts

Assets

111	Cash
112	Petty Cash Fund
113	Office Supplies
115	Prepaid Insurance
161	Automobiles
161.1	Accumulated Depreciation—Automobiles
171	Laboratory Equipment Expense
171.1	Accumulated Depreciation—Laboratory Equipment
181	Medical Equipment Expense

Revenue

| 411 | Professional Fees |
| 421 | **Other Income** |

Expenses

511	Automobile Expense
512	Charitable Contributions Expense
516	**Dues and Subscriptions Expense**
518	Electricity Expense
519	Insurance Expense
520	Office Supplies Expense

181.1   Accumulated Depreciation—Medical
       Equipment
191   Office Equipment
191.1   Accumulated Depreciation—Office
       Equipment

Liabilities
231   Employees' Income Tax Payable
232   FICA Tax Payable—OASDI
233   FICA Tax Payable—HI
241   FUTA Tax Payable Expense
251   SUTA Tax Payable

Owner's Equity
311   Julie Cole, Capital
312   Julie Cole, Drawing
321   John Martin, Capital
322   John Martin, Drawing
331   Income Summary

521   **Laundry Expense**
523   **Legal Expense**
527   **Medical Library Expense**
528   **Medical Supplies Expense**
532   Payroll Taxes Expense
535   **Postage Expense**
541   Rent Expense
543   Repairs and Maintenance Expense
551   Salary Expense
553   **Surgical Instruments Expense**
557   **Surgical Supplies Expense**
561   Telephone Expense
567   Traveling and Meetings Expense
571   Depr. Expense—Automobiles
572   Depr. Expense—Laboratory Equipment
573   Depr. Expense—Medical Equipment
574   Depr. Expense—Office Equipment
581   Miscellaneous Expense

Let's review new account titles that have not been used in previous chapters or modules.

Other Income, Account No. 421. Cole and Martin have subleased a large portion of the office building in which their practice is located. Terms of their lease permit them to sublease unused office space to other professionals until the space is needed by Cole and Martin. They currently sublease to Evan Deemis, an optometrist; Evelyn Crowe, an electrologist; Ron Guzik, a chiropractor; and Stewart Cross, a pharmacist and owner of Cross Pharmacy. Other sources of income include interest on the checking account and miscellaneous income from such activities as speaking engagements. All sources of income other than that from professional fees are credited to the Other Income account.

Medical Library Expense, Account No. 527. Most medical and dental offices maintain some kind of medical library for reference. Medical reference books are charged to the Medical Library Expense account when payment is made.

Medical Supplies Expense, Account No. 528; Surgical Instruments Expense, Account No. 553; Surgical Supplies Expense, Account No. 557. Because of the frequent need to be restocked or replaced, medical supplies and instruments are charged to these expense accounts when payment is made.

Other expense accounts introduced in this chapter and their uses include **Dues and Subscriptions Expense, Account No. 516** (for dues paid to professional organizations and for subscriptions to trade journals and office magazines); **Laundry Expense, Account No. 521** (for medical gowns, sheets, towels, etc.); **Legal Expense, Account No. 523** (for professional legal advice, collection of patients' accounts and other services); and **Postage Expense, Account No. 535,** (for mailing monthly statements, insurance claims, and other outgoing mail).

Books of Account

The illustration for Cole and Martin uses the following books of account:

1. General books
    a. Cash receipts journal - *all drs to Cash*
    b. Cash payments journal - *all crs to Cash*
    c. General journal
    d. General ledger
2. Auxiliary records
    a. Petty cash payments record
    b. Daily service record
    c. Patients' ledger
    d. Employee's earnings record
    e. Checkbook

Cash Receipts Journal. A **cash receipts journal** is used as the book of original entry for all cash that is received by the business. The cash receipts journal contains two credit columns and two debit columns, as shown in Exhibit 8.2 on page 255. The column headings for amounts are as follows:

1. General Dr.
2. Other Income 421 Cr.
3. Professional Fees 411 Cr.
4. Cash 111 Dr.

Every entry in the cash receipts journal includes:

1. Date of the cash receipt
2. Account and amount to be debited if the General Dr. column is used
3. Amounts to be credited if the special columns are used
4. Amount of the cash receipt, entered in the Cash Dr. column

Posting from this journal includes posting by column totals, called "summary posting," and posting from the general debit column, called "individual posting." The general and special columns for Other Income, Professional Fees, and Cash are totaled at the end of the month, or sooner if needed. These special column totals are posted in summary to the general ledger. This summary posting requires one debit entry to be posted to the Cash account, one credit entry to be posted to the Other Income account, and one credit entry to be posted to the Professional Fees account. Account numbers are written in parentheses below the column totals to indicate that the totals have been posted to the general ledger.

Exhibit 8.2

Cash Receipts Journal (Partial)

		Cash Receipts Journal											**Page 2**											
	Date		Description	Post Ref.	General Dr.					Other Income 421 Cr.					Prof. Fees 411 Cr.					Cash 111 Dr.					
1	200X																								
2	Feb.	2	Evan Deemis	✓							7	0	0	00							7	0	0	00
3		3	Speaking engagement	✓							6	2	5	00							6	2	5	00
4		4	Total receipts	✓											10	3	4	5	00	10	3	4	5	00
5										1	3	2	5	00	10	3	4	5	00	11	6	7	0	00
6																									
7					(✓)					(421)					(411)					(111)					

Each time the General Dr. column is used to enter a transaction, the account title must be written in the Description column. When posting the individual entries in the General Dr. column, conclude the posting process by writing the general ledger account number in the Post Reference column. To indicate that the total of the General Dr. column is not posted, a check mark (✔) is written in parentheses below the total. As a proof of the journal, the total of the two debit columns must equal the total of the two credit columns.

Cash Payments Journal. The **cash payments journal** is used as the book of original entry for all payments of cash. The cash payments journal used by Cole and Martin is shown on pages 270–273. It contains two debit columns and four credit columns. The column headings for amounts are as follows:

1. Debits
   a. General Dr.
   b. Salary Expense 551 Dr.
2. Credits
   a. Employees' Income Tax Payable 231 Cr.
   b. FICA Tax Payable—OASDI 232 Cr.
   c. FICA Tax Payable—HI 233 Cr.
   d. Cash 111 Cr.

Every entry in the cash payments journal includes:

1. Date and check number of the cash payment
2. Account name and amount to be debited if the General Dr. column is used
3. Amounts to be debited and/or credited if the special columns are used
4. Amount of the cash payment, entered in the Cash Cr. column

Summary and individual posting from this journal is similar to that from the cash receipts journal.

General Journal. The third book of original entry used by Cole and Martin is the two-column general journal. It is used for transactions that cannot be entered in the cash receipts journal or the cash payments journal. For example, the journal entry to record the employer's payroll tax expense is entered in the general journal as shown on page 274. Also, the end-of-period adjusting and closing entries are entered in the general journal.

General Ledger. Cole and Martin use a four-column account form for the general ledger accounts. The first pair of debit and credit columns shows the amount of the actual debit or credit from the special or general journal. The next pair of debit and credit columns shows the ending balance of the account.

Petty Cash Payments Record. Cole and Martin maintain a petty cash fund of $150.

Daily Service Record. A portion of the daily service record is illustrated in Exhibit 8.3 on page 257. Note that the daily service record is not set up as a double-entry record where debit entries equal the credit entries. Nothing offsets the Payments column under Patients' Accounts, but the total of the Office Visits and Surgery columns must equal the total of the Patients Charges and the Cash Services columns.

This proof of the daily service record can be done daily, weekly, or monthly, depending upon the volume of transactions. The February proof for the end of the month is shown below:

Office Visits	$ 3,180	Patient Accounts Charges	$37,260
Surgery	36,640	Cash Services	2,560
	$39,820		$39,820

Exhibit 8.3

Daily Service Record (Partial)

		Kinds of Services		Patients' Accounts		Cash	
Daily Service Record for Month of February, 200X							
Day	Name of Patient	Office Visits	Surgery	Charges	Payments	Cash Services	
1	Joan Hughes	50 00				50 00	
1	Paul Fuller		750 00	750 00			
1	Victor Fry	35 00				35 00	
1	Tim Duvall		2,000 00	2,000 00			
1	Craig Ebert	45 00		45 00			
1	Russ Eaton	25 00				25 00	
1	Blue Shield—K. Salk	35 00			1,600 00	35 00	
1	Deborah Deck		1,550 00	1,550 00			
1	Larry Davis		920 00	920 00			
2	Pauline Curtis	45 00				45 00	
2	Earl Cummings		625 00	625 00			
2	Roger Brett	25 00				25 00	
2	Cindy Creek	35 00				35 00	
2	Eric Bray	40 00		40 00			
2	Peter Arnold		1,200 00	1,200 00			
2	Jack Asher	35 00				35 00	
2	Brad Lewis		550 00	550 00			
2	Stacey Litman	50 00		50 00			
3	Donald Mac	30 00				30 00	
3	Roy Lyle	45 00				45 00	
3	Medicare—D. Madden				3,100 00		
3	Joseph Neill				450 00		
3	Prudential—C. Newman				1,465 00		
3	Rene Navarro				575 00		
3	Charles Stapinsky		450 00	450 00			
3	Paul Quay	40 00				40 00	
3	Vance Talbot				650 00		
3	Randall Sparks	25 00		25 00			
4	Clarence Wells	20 00		20 00			
4	Scott Weaver				1,765 00		
4	Daniel Hodges	25 00				25 00	
4	Kimberly Spence		150 00	150 00			
28	Wendy Hoffman	45 00				45 00	
28	Carla Johnson		225 00	225 00			
28	MONY—J. Gross				2,575 00		
28	Lee Knox		300 00	300 00			
	Totals	3,180 00	36,640 00	37,260 00	34,685 00	2,560 00	

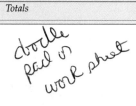

Each entry in the Kinds of Services column must also be entered in either the Patients' Accounts Charges or the Cash Services column. This information is posted to the appropriate patient's account in the patients' ledger as explained in the next paragraph. A daily or weekly bank deposit is made, and the total cash received is entered in the cash receipts journal by debiting Cash and crediting Professional Fees. The flowchart below summarizes the flow of accounting data through the daily service record.

Exhibit 8.4

Flow of Data Through the Daily Service Record

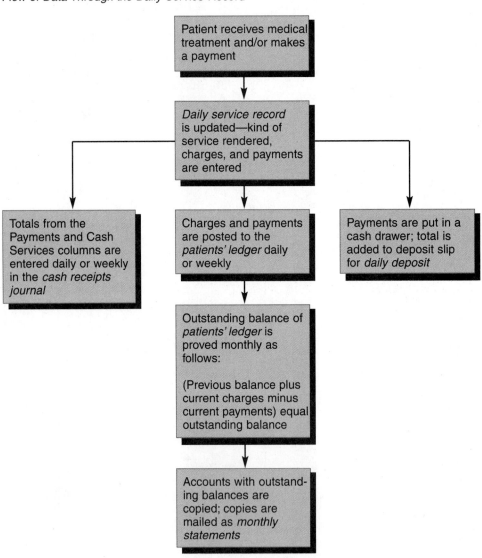

Patients' Ledger. The patients' accounts are kept on ledger cards and collectively they are known as the **patients' ledger**. The patients' ledger is generally not in a bound book but is kept as loose cards. This permits using a copying machine to reproduce the accounts with outstanding balances. The copies are then mailed as monthly statements. Having the accounts on loose cards also allows new accounts to be inserted and the ledger to be continually kept in alphabetical order. Charges and payments from the daily service record are usually posted daily or weekly to the patients' accounts. Information from the Cash Services column of the daily service record is also posted to the patients' accounts in both the Charges and Payments columns. A patient's account for Julia O'Donnell is shown in Exhibit 8.5 on page 260.

A description of the type of service performed is shown in the Professional Service column. Frequent types of services are listed on the bottom of the account form along with codes for each.

At the end of the month, the patients' ledger is totaled to show the balance of the outstanding accounts. The outstanding balance from the previous month, plus current charges minus payments from the daily service record, should equal the current total of the patients' ledger. This is called proving the patients' ledger. Patients' accounts receivable are not formally recorded in the general ledger under the modified cash basis of accounting.

Employee's Earnings Record. The employee's earnings record was discussed in Chapter 6. We will use the same format as that presented earlier.

Other Payments for Services. In the last few years, much of the burden of payment for services rendered by the medical and dental professions has shifted from the patient to private commercial insurance companies, company health plans, health maintenance organizations (HMOs), and government programs such as Medicare, Medicaid, and Champus. As a result, keeping the accounts in the patients' ledger has become much more complex.

Some patients pay their accounts in full and have their insurance carrier reimburse them for covered charges. On the other hand, the doctor or dentist may accept an assignment of the amounts due. Accepting **assignments** means that the patient will pay only those amounts due that are not covered by insurance. The balance will be paid by the insurance company to the doctor. For example, Rudy Wray's bill for services rendered, which totals $1,400, is covered by the

260   Chapter Eight   Accounting for Personal Services

Exhibit 8.5

Illustration of a Patient's Account

STATEMENT

COLE & MARTIN
PHYSICIANS & SURGEONS
6200 Monaco Parkway
Denver, CO 80210-6345

Julia O'Donnell
416 Amherst Ave., E.
Denver, CO 80203-6345

Date	Professional Service	Charge		Paid		Balance	
2/10	OV; X	75	00			75	00
2/13	OV	30	00			105	00
2/15	OV; LAB	100	00	50	00	155	00
2/18	M	60	00	100	00	115	00
2/20	Check–Blue Shield			212	00	(97	00)
2/25	OV	30	00			(67	00)
2/25	Refund			(67	00)	–0–	

PAY LAST AMOUNT IN THIS COLUMN ▲

1603

HV – Hospital Visit   M – Medical   X – X–ray
OV – Office Vist   S – Surgical   MISC – Miscellaneous
LAB – Laboratory

insurance company. The terms of his insurance policy specify that the patient must pay the first $100, referred to as a *deductible*. The insurance company will pay 80% of the remaining charges for covered illnesses. The patient is responsible for the remaining 20%. In this example, the insurance company will pay $1,040 ($1,400 − $100 = $1,300 × 80%). Rudy Wray must pay $360 ($1,400 − $1,040). Most medical and dental offices will automatically bill the insurance carrier. The patient is responsible for all charges not covered by insurance.

Cole and Martin have agreed to accept assignments and to complete the necessary insurance forms. The **Universal Health Insurance Claim Form** that was developed by the American Medical Association is used. This form has been adopted by most insurance carriers and programs. Special coding is used on the forms. Insurance companies have generally adopted the codes presented in the American Medical Association's Current Procedural Terminology, Fourth Edition (CPT-4), as the standard identification for medical procedures and treatments. The International Classification of Diseases, Revision Nine (ICD-9CM), has been adopted as the industry standard for diagnosis coding on forms. Hospital patients' illnesses are also classified into several groups; DRGs, Diagnosis-Related Groups, are codes to identify these illness groupings. A completed Universal Health Insurance Claim Form is shown in Exhibit 8.6 on page 262.

ACCOUNTING PROCEDURE

Following is a summary of transactions completed by Cole and Martin during the month of February, 200X. These transactions are recorded in the special journals and general journal on pages 270–290. Follow each transaction by frequently referring to the journals and auxiliary records. You will find the journal or auxiliary record listed at the end of each transaction.

Tuesday, February 1
1. Issued Check No. 700 for February rent, $4,250. *Cash Payments Journal.*
2. Issued Check No. 701 for $147.67 for automobile repairs. *Cash Payments Journal.*

Wednesday, February 2
3. Received $700 from Evan Deemis, an optometrist, for subleasing space. *Cash Receipts Journal.*

Exhibit 8.6

Universal Health Insurance Claim Form

HEALTH INSURANCE CLAIM FORM

READ INSTRUCTIONS BEFORE COMPLETING OR SIGNING THE FORM

☐ MEDICAID	☐ MEDICARE	☐ CHAMPUS	☒ OTHER	FORM APPROVED OMB NO. 06–R0012

PATIENT & INSURED (SUBSCRIBER) INFORMATION

1 PATIENT'S NAME (First name, middle initial, last name) George Hartzel	2 PATIENT'S DATE OF BIRTH 06 15 50	3 INSURED'S NAME (First name, middle initial, last name) George Hartzel
4 PATIENT'S ADDRESS (Street, city, state, zip code) 7593 Raleigh St. Denver, CO 80220–6345 TELEPHONE NO.	5 PATIENT SEX MALE X FEMALE 7 PATIENT RELATIONSHIP TO INSURED SELF SPOUSE CHILD OTHER X	6 INSURED'S I.D. MEDICARE AND OR MEDICAID NO. (Include any others) 206–50–3660 8 INSURED'S GROUP NO. (Or Group Name) CT 60598
9 OTHER HEALTH INSURANCE OVERAGE (Enter name of Policy Holder and Plan Name and Address and Policy or Medical Assistance Number) George Hartzel; United Surgical Plan; 53 Taft Road, Nashville, Tn 37206–1293; Group No. 6248	10 WAS CONDITION RELATED TO A. PATIENT'S EMPLOYMENT YES X NO B. ACCIDENT AUTO X OTHER	11 INSURED'S ADDRESS (Street, city, state, Zip code) 7593 Raleigh St. Denver, CO 80220–6345
12 PATIENT'S OR AUTHORIZED PERSON'S SIGNATURE (Read Doc before signing) I Authorize the Release of any Medical Information Necessary to Process this Claim and Request Payment of MEDICARE Benefits Either to Myself or to the Party Who Accepts Assignment Below. SIGNED *George Hartzel* DATE 5/16/xx		13 I AUTHORIZE PAYMENT OF MEDICAL BENEFITS TO UNDERSIGNED PHYSICIAN OR SUPPLIER FOR SERVICE DESCRIBED BELOW *George Hartzel* SIGNED (INSURED OR AUTHORIZED PERSON)

PHYSICIAN OR SUPPLIER INFORMATION

14 DATE OF 2/25/xx	ILLNESS (FIRST SYMPTOM) OR INJURY (ACCIDENT) OR PREGNANCY (LMP)	15 DATE FIRST CONSULTED YOU FOR THIS CONDITION 4/14/xx	16 HAS PATIENT EVER HAD SAME OR SIMILAR SYMPTOMS? YES X NO	16a IF AN EMERGENCY CHECK HERE ☐ DNA
17 DATE PATIENT ABLE TO RETURN TO WORK DNA	18 DATES OF TOTAL DISABILITY DNA THROUGH DNA		DATES OF PARTIAL DISABILITY FROM THROUGH	
19 NAME OF REFERRING PHYSICIAN OR OTHER SOURCE (e.g.: public health agency) Rose Gerrard, M.D.			20 FOR SERVICES RELATED TO HOSPITALIZATION GIVE HOSPITALIZATION DATES ADMITTED DNA DISCHARGED DNA	
21 NAME & ADDRESS OF FACILITY WHERE SERVICES RENDERED (If other than home or office) DNA			22 WAS LABORATORY WORK PERFORMED OUTSIDE YOUR OFFICE? YES X NO CHARGES DNA	

23 DIAGNOSIS OR NATURE OF ILLNESS OR INJURY RELATE DIAGNOSIS TO PROCEDURE IN COLUMN D BY REFERENCE NUMBERS 1 2 3 ETC OR DI CODE

A 1 Unstable arteriosclerotic heart disease, recent
2 heart irregularity   (412.9)
3 Hypercholesterolemia   (251.0)
4

B EPSDT YES DNA NO ☐
FAMILY PLANNING YES DNA NO ☐
PRIOR AUTHORIZATION NO

A DATE OF SERVICE	B PLACE OF SERVICE	C FULLY DESCRIBE PROCEDURES MEDICAL SERVICES OR SUPPLIES FURNISHED FOR EACH DATE GIVEN		D DIAGNOSIS CODE	E CHARGES	F DAYS/ UNITS	G TOS	H LEAVE BLANK
		PROCEDURE CODE (IDENTIFY)	(EXPLAIN UNUSUAL SERVICES OR CIRCUMSTANCES)					
5/14/xx	3	90060	Intermediate service	412.9 251.0	25 ¦00			
5/14/xx	3	71020	Chest X ray	412.9	30 ¦00			
5/14/xx	3	93000	Electrocardiogram	412.9	30 ¦00			
5/14/xx	3	82465	Cholesterol check	251.0	15 ¦00			

25 SIGNATURE OF PHYSICIAN OR SUPPLIER I certify that the statements on the reverse apply to this bill and are made a part thereof) *Julie Cole M.D.* 6/16/xx SIGNED DATE	26 ACCEPT ASSIGNMENT (GOVERNMENT CLAIMS ONLY) (SEE BACK) YES X NO 30 YOUR SOCIAL SECURITY NO. 206–60–4926	27 TOTAL CHARGE 100.00	28 AMOUNT PAID None	29 BALANCE DUE $100 ¦00
		31 PHYSICIANS OR SUPPLIERS NAME, ADDRESS, ZIP CODE & TELEPHONE NO. Cole & Martin Physicians and Surgeons 6200 Monaco Parkway Denver, CO 80210–6345 (808) 433–6219		
32 YOUR PATIENT ACCOUNT NO. 839	33 YOUR EMPLOYER ID NO. 2083899022			

• PLACE OF SERVICE AND TYPE OF SERVICE (T.O.S.) CODES ON THE BACK

REMARKS

APPROVED BY AMA COUNCIL ON MEDICAL SERVICE 5-80
APPROVED BY THE HEALTH CARE
FINANCING ADMINISTRATION & CHAMPUS

Form AMA–OP–407
Form HCFA–1500 (4–80)
Form CHAMPUS–501

Thursday, February 3

4. Received $625 for serving as speakers on the program at a professional meeting. *Cash Receipts Journal.*
5. Issued Check No. 702 to The Electric Company for electricity consumed during January, $288.54. *Cash Payments Journal.*
6. Issued Check No. 703 for telephone service, $133.65. *Cash Payments Journal.*
7. Issued Check No. 704 for laundry service, $246.24. *Cash Payments Journal.*
8. Issued Check No. 705 for medical supplies, $175.87. *Cash Payments Journal.*

Friday, February 4

9. Issued Check No. 706 for equipment repair, $89. *Cash Payments Journal.*
10. Issued Check No. 707 for physician's liability insurance policy, $4,400. *Cash Payments Journal.*

Note: Cole and Martin have given the account of Ralph Curtis in the amount of $1,623 and the account of Clara Walker in the amount of $660 to Bess Talley, an attorney, for collection. Talley's collection fee is 33⅓%. No entry is needed at this time.

END-OF-WEEK WORK

a. Footed the amount columns in the daily service record, and proved the totals.
b. Posted all entries in the Patients' Accounts Charges and Payments columns and Cash Services to the appropriate individual accounts in the patients' ledger.
c. Recorded the total cash received from the Payments and Cash Services columns ($10,345) in the cash receipts journal by entering the words "Total receipts" in the Description column and the amount in both the Cash Dr. column and the Professional Fees Cr. column.
d. Footed the amount columns of the cash receipts and cash payments journals, and proved the journals by comparing total debits with total credits. Checked the cash balance in the checkbook ($78,571.66) by starting with the checkbook balance on February 1 ($76,632.63) and adding the total of the Cash Dr. column ($11,670.00) from the cash receipts journal and subtracting the total of the Cash Cr. column ($9,730.97) from the cash payments journal.
e. Completed the individual postings from the General Dr. columns of the cash receipts and cash payments journals and from the general journal.

Monday, February 7
11. Issued Check No. 708 for surgical instruments purchased in January, $342.58. *Cash Payments Journal.*

Tuesday, February 8
12. Issued Check No. 709 to *The New England Journal of Medicine* for a subscription to this professional journal, $90. *Cash Payments Journal.*

Wednesday, February 9
13. Issued Check No. 710 for surgical supplies, $153.78. *Cash Payments Journal.*

Thursday, February 10
14. Issued Check No. 711 to University Publishing Company for medical books, $267.65. *Cash Payments Journal.*
15. Issued Check No. 712 to Adolpho's Department Store in payment of Cole's personal account, $98. *Cash Payments Journal.*

Friday, February 11
16. Cole withdrew $2,600 for personal use. Check No. 713. *Cash Payments Journal.*
17. Martin withdrew $2,600 for personal use. Check No. 714. *Cash Payments Journal.*
18. Issued Check No. 715 for $776.50 to Evelyn Hopkins, R.N., in payment of salary in the amount of $980, less $130 withheld for federal income tax, less $61.25 withheld for FICA—OASDI tax, and less $12.25 withheld for FICA—HI tax. *Cash Payments Journal.*
19. Issued Check No. 716 for $710.25 to Richard Robbins, office manager, in payment of salary in the amount of $850, less $76 withheld for federal income tax, less $53.13 withheld for FICA—OASDI tax, and less $10.62 withheld for FICA—HI tax. *Cash Payments Journal.*
20. Issued Check No. 717 for $652.50 to Sharon Rommel, secretary, in payment of salary in the amount of $820, less $106 withheld for federal income tax, less $51.25 withheld for FICA—OASDI tax, and less $10.25 withheld for FICA—HI tax. *Cash Payments Journal.*
21. Issued Check No. 718 for $751 to Joyce Schultz, laboratory technologist, in payment of salary in the amount of $920, less $100 withheld for federal income tax, less $57.50 withheld for FICA—OASDI tax, and less $11.50 withheld for FICA—HI tax. *Cash Payments Journal.*

Note: Cole and Martin are subject to the federal unemployment tax and state unemployment tax. The liability for these taxes and the employer's matching portion of the FICA—OASDI tax and FICA—HI tax is entered at the end of the month.

END-OF-WEEK WORK

a. Footed the amount columns in the daily service record, and proved the totals.

b. Posted all entries in the Patients' Accounts Charges and Payments columns and Cash Services to the appropriate individual accounts in the patients' ledger.

c. Recorded the total cash received from the Payments and Cash Services columns ($9,677) in the cash receipts journal.

d. Footed the amount columns of the cash receipts and cash payments journals, and proved the totals. Checked the cash balance in the checkbook ($79,206.40).

e. Completed the individual postings from the General Dr. columns of the cash receipts and cash payments journals.

Monday, February 14

22. Issued Check No. 719 for office equipment, $204.70. *Cash Payments Journal.*

23. Issued Check No. 720 to Mile High National Bank in payment of the following payroll taxes based on wages paid during the month of January.

Employees' income tax withheld from wages		$ 854.00
FICA—OASDI	$925.00	
FICA—HI	185.00	1,110.00
Amount of check		$1,964.00

24. Issued Check No. 721 for stationery and office supplies, $86.11. *Cash Payments Journal.*

25. Issued Check No. 722 for medical supplies, $217.65. *Cash Payments Journal.*

26. Received a check for $950 for rent payment from Evelyn Crowe, an electrologist who subleases from Cole and Martin. *Cash Receipts Journal.*

Wednesday, February 16

27. Issued Check No. 723 to United Fund, $650. *Cash Payments Journal.*

28. Received a check for $900 for rent payment from Ron Guzik, a chiropractor who subleases from Cole and Martin. *Cash Receipts Journal.*

Thursday, February 17

29. Issued Check No. 724 for an insurance policy for Martin's car, $660, which is used exclusively for business purposes. *Cash Payments Journal.*

Friday, February 18

30. Issued Check No. 725 to Mile High National Bank, $40, in payment of the annual rental of a safe deposit box for use by the partnership. *Cash Payments Journal.*

END-OF-WEEK-WORK

a. Footed the amount columns in the daily service record, and proved the totals.

b. Posted all entries in the Patients' Accounts Charges and Payments columns and Cash Services to the appropriate individual accounts in the patients' ledger.

c. Recorded the total cash received from the Payments and Cash Services columns ($8,618) in the cash receipts journal.

d. Footed the amount columns of the cash receipts and cash payments journals, and proved the totals. Checked the cash balance in the checkbook ($85,851.94).

e. Completed the individual postings from the General Dr. columns of the cash receipts and cash payments journals.

Monday, February 21

31. Issued Check No. 726 to American Cancer Society, $450. *Cash Payments Journal.*

32. Entered $72 of interest earned on the partnership checking account. *Cash Receipts Journal.*

33. Issued Check No. 727 for automobile expense, $188.48. *Cash Payments Journal.*

Tuesday, February 22

34. Issued Check No. 728 for Medical Equipment, $2,794.85. *Cash Payments Journal.*

35. Received $1,082 from Bess Talley representing collection of the account of Ralph Curtis in the amount of $1,623. Talley deducted the fee of $541 and remitted the balance, $1,082.

Note: This transaction was entered in the cash receipts journal by debiting Cash for $1,082 and Legal Expense for $541, and by crediting Professional Fees for $1,623. In order to avoid duplication of the $1,581 credit to Professional Fees, this payment was not entered in the daily service record. An entry was made, however, in Curtis's account in the patients' ledger crediting the account for $1,623.

Wednesday, February 23
36. Issued Check No. 729 for typewriter repairs, $84.31. *Cash Payments Journal.*

Thursday, February 24
37. Issued Check No. 730 for Traveling and Meetings Expense, $955.45. *Cash Payments Journal.*

Friday, February 25
38. Received $280 from Bess Talley to apply on the account of Clara Walker. Talley collection $420 from Walker and remitted $280 after deducting the fee of $140. *Cash Receipts Journal.*

Note: Since the next workday is the end of the month, the usual end-of-week procedures were not completed.

Monday, February 28
39. Cole withdrew $2,600 for personal use. Check No. 731. *Cash Payments Journal.*
40. Martin withdrew $2,600 for personal use. Check No. 732. *Cash Payments Journal.*
41. Issued Check No. 733 for $776.50 to Evelyn Hopkins, R.N., in payment of salary in the amount of $980, less $130 withheld for federal income tax, less $61.25 withheld for FICA—OASDI tax, and less $12.25 withheld for FICA—HI tax. *Cash Payments Journal.*
42. Issued Check No. 734 for $710.25 to Richard Robbins, office manager, in payment of salary in the amount of $850, less $76 withheld for federal income tax, less $53.13 withheld for FICA—OASDI tax, and less $10.62 withheld for FICA—HI tax. *Cash Payments Journal.*
43. Issued Check No. 735 for $652.50 to Sharon Rommel, secretary, in payment of salary in the amount of $820, less $106 withheld for federal income tax, less $51.25 withheld for FICA—OASDI tax, and less $10.25 withheld for FICA—HI tax. *Cash Payments Journal.*
44. Issued Check No. 736 for $751 to Joyce Schultz, laboratory technologist, in payment of salary in the amount of $920, less $100 withheld for federal income tax, less $57.50 withheld for FICA—OASDI tax, and less $11.50 withheld for FICA—HI tax. *Cash Payments Journal.*
45. Received a check for $1,100 for rent payment from Cross Pharmacy, which subleases from Cole and Martin. *Cash Receipts Journal.*

END-OF-MONTH WORK

a. Footed the amount columns in the daily service record, and proved the totals.

b. Posted all entries in the Patients' Accounts Charges and Payments columns and Cash Services to the appropriate individual accounts in the patients' ledger.

c. Recorded the total cash received from the Payments and Cash Services columns ($8,605) in the cash receipts journal.

d. Made an entry in the general journal for the payroll taxes imposed on Cole and Martin for the month of February by debiting Payroll Taxes Expense for $785.40, crediting FICA—OASDI Tax Payable for $446.25, and crediting FICA—HI Tax Payable for $89.25, FUTA Tax Payable for $57.12, and SUTA Tax Payable for $192.78.

e. Issued Check No. 737 for $107 to replenish the petty cash fund. The following information was taken from the petty cash payments record:

Julie Cole, Drawing	$ 18.50
John Martin, Drawing	22.25
Automobile Expense	18.50
Office Supplies	5.75
Postage Expense	20.00
Travel and Meetings Expense	22.00
	$107.00

Note: There was $43.00 remaining in the petty cash fund. This information was entered in the cash payments journal.

f. Footed the amount columns of the cash receipts and cash payments journals, and proved the totals. Checked the cash balance in the checkbook ($84,320.60).

g. Completed the individual postings from the General Dr. and Cr. columns of the cash receipts journal, cash payments journal, and the general journal. Completed the summary postings from the cash receipts and cash payments journals.

END-OF-YEAR WORK

We have just completed the transactions for February which is the second month of a calendar year. In order to demonstrate the entire accounting cycle, we are going to perform the end-of-year accounting procedures that are normally done at the end of the year. The following steps were done to complete the accounting cycle for Julie Cole and John Martin, Physicians and Surgeons:

1. A trial balance was taken from the general ledger accounts and appears on the work sheet, page 276–278.
2. The following adjustments were entered on the work sheet:
    a. The ending inventory of office supplies, as of February 28, was $84.
    b. The amount of insurance expired was $600.
    c. Depreciation for two months on the automobiles was $643.
    d. Depreciation for two months on the laboratory equipment was $332.
    e. Depreciation for two months on the medical equipment was $500.
    f. Depreciation for two months on the office equipment was $112.
3. Completed the work sheet.
4. Using the work sheet, financial statements were prepared. The income statement, statement of owner's equity, and balance sheet are shown on pages 278 and 280–281.
5. The adjusting entries were entered on page 2 of the general journal and are shown on page 274.
6. The closing entries were entered on page 3 of the general journal and are shown on page 275.
7. The adjusting and closing entries were posted to the general ledger.
8. A post-closing trial balance was prepared and is shown on page 290.

Cash Payments Journal

Date	Check No.	Description	Post Ref.	General Dr.	Salary Expense 551 Dr.
200X					
Feb. 1	700	Rent Expense	541	4 2 5 0 00	
1	701	Automobile Expense	511	1 4 7 67	
3	702	Electricity Expense	518	2 8 8 54	
3	703	Telephone Expense	561	1 3 3 65	
3	704	Laundry Expense	521	2 4 6 24	
3	705	Medical Supplies Expense	528	1 7 5 87	
4	706	Repairs and Maintenance Expense	543	8 9 00	
4	707	Prepaid Insurance	115	4 4 0 0 00	
				9 7 3 0 97	
7	708	Surgical Instruments Expense	553	3 4 2 58	
8	709	Dues and Subscriptions Expense	516	9 0 00	
9	710	Surgical Supplies Expense	557	1 5 3 78	
10	711	Medical Library Expense	527	2 6 7 65	
10	712	Julie Cole, Drawing	312	9 8 00	
11	713	Julie Cole, Drawing	312	2 6 0 0 00	
11	714	John Martin, Drawing	322	2 6 0 0 00	
11	715	Evelyn Hopkins	✓		9 8 0 00
11	716	Richard Robbins	✓		8 5 0 00
11	717	Sharon Rommel	✓		8 2 0 00
11	718	Joyce Shultz	✓		9 2 0 00
				15 8 8 2 98	3 5 7 0 00
14	719	Office Equipment	191	2 0 4 70	
14	720	FICA Tax Payable—OASDI	232	9 2 5 00	
		FICA Tax Payable—HI	233	1 8 5 00	
		Employees' Income Tax Payable	231	8 5 4 00	
14	721	Office Supplies	113	8 6 11	
14	722	Medical Supplies Expense	528	2 1 7 65	
16	723	Charitable Contributions Expense	512	6 5 0 00	
17	724	Prepaid Insurance	115	6 6 0 00	
18	725	Miscellaneous Expense	581	4 0 00	
				19 7 0 5 44	3 5 7 0 00
21	726	Charitable Contributions Expense	512	4 5 0 00	
21	727	Automobile Expense	511	1 8 8 48	
22	728	Medical Equipment	181	2 7 9 4 85	
23	729	Repairs and Maintenance Expense	543	8 4 31	
24	730	Travel and Meeting Expense	567	9 5 5 45	
28	731	Julie Cole, Drawing	312	2 6 0 0 00	
28	732	John Martin, Drawing	322	2 6 0 0 00	

Temp footings accum. totals

	Emp. Inc. Tax Pay. 231 Cr.	FICA Tax Pay. OASDI 232 Cr.	FICA Tax Pay. HI 233 Cr.	Cash Cr.	
1					
2				4 2 5 0 00	
3				1 4 7 67	
4				2 8 8 54	
5				1 3 3 65	
6				2 4 6 24	
7				1 7 5 87	
8				8 9 00	
9				4 4 0 0 00	
10				9 7 3 0 97	
11				3 4 2 58	
12				9 0 00	
13				1 5 3 78	
14				2 6 7 65	
15				9 8 00	
16				2 6 0 0 00	
17				2 6 0 0 00	
18	1 3 0 00	6 1 25	1 2 25	7 7 6 50	
19	7 6 00	5 3 13	1 0 62	7 1 0 25	
20	1 0 6 00	5 1 25	1 0 25	6 5 2 50	
21	1 0 0 00	5 7 50	1 1 50	7 5 1 00	
22	4 1 2 00	2 2 3 13	4 4 62	18 7 7 3 23	
23				2 0 4 70	
24					
25					
26				1 9 6 4 00	
27				8 6 11	
28				2 1 7 65	
29				6 5 0 00	
30				6 6 0 00	
31				4 0 00	
32	4 1 2 00	2 2 3 13	4 4 62	22 5 9 5 64	
33				4 5 0 00	
34				1 8 8 48	
35				2 7 9 4 85	
36				8 4 31	
37				9 5 5 45	
38				2 6 0 0 00	
39				2 6 0 0 00	

Page 3

Cash Payments Journal (continued)

	Date		Check No.	Description	Post Ref.	General Dr.	Salary Expense 551 Dr.
40	Feb.	28	733	Evelyn Hopkins	✓		980 00
41		28	734	Richard Robbins	✓		850 00
42		28	735	Sharon Rommel	✓		820 00
43		28	736	Joyce Shultz	✓		920 00
44		28	737	Julie Cole, Drawing	312	18 50	
45				John Martin, Drawing	322	22 25	
46				Automobile Expense	511	18 50	
47				Office Supplies	113	5 75	
48				Postage Expense	535	20 00	
49				Travel and Meetings Expense	567	22 00	
50						29485 53	7140 00
51						(✓)	(551)
52							

Cash Receipts Journal — Page 2

	Date		Description	Post Ref.	General Dr.	Other Income 421 Cr.	Prof. Fees 411 Cr.	Cash 111 Dr.
1	200X							
2	Feb.	2	Evan Deemis	✓		700 00		700 00
3		3	Speaking engagement	✓		625 00		625 00
4		4	Total receipts	✓			10345 00	10345 00
5						1325 00	10345 00	11670 00
6		11	Total receipts	✓			9677 00	9677 00
7						1325 00	20022 00	21347 00
8		14	Evelyn Crowe	✓		950 00		950 00
9		16	Ron Guzik	✓		900 00		900 00
10		18	Total receipts	✓			8618 00	8618 00
11						3175 00	28640 00	31815 00
12		21	Interest on checking acct.	✓		72 00		72 00
13		22	Legal expense	523	541 00		1623 00	1082 00
14		25	Legal expense	523	140 00		420 00	280 00
15		28	Cross Pharmacy	✓		1100 00		1100 00
16		28	Total receipts	✓			8605 00	8605 00
17					681 00	4347 00	39288 00	42954 00
18					(✓)	(421)	(411)	(111)

	Emp. Inc. Tax Pay. 231 Cr.				FICA Tax Pay. OASDI 232 Cr.				FICA Tax Pay. HI 233 Cr.				Cash Cr.				
																	Page 4
	1	3	0	00		6	1	25		1	2	25	7	7	6	50	40
		7	6	00		5	3	13		1	0	62	7	1	0	25	41
	1	0	6	00		5	1	25		1	0	25	6	5	2	50	42
	1	0	0	00		5	7	50		1	1	50	7	5	1	00	43
																	44
																	45
																	46
																	47
																	48
														1	0	7	00	49
	8	2	4	00		4	4	6	26		8	9	24	35	2	6	6	03	50
		(231)					(232)				(233)				(111)			51
																	52

	Date		Description	Post. Ref.	Debit				Credit				
1	200X												1
2	Feb.	28	Payroll Taxes Expense	532	7	8	5	40					2
3			FICA Tax Payable—OASDI	232					4	4	6	26	3
4			FICA Tax Payable—HI	233						8	9	24	4
5			FUTA Tax Payable	241						5	7	12	5
6			SUTA Tax Payable	251					1	9	2	78	6
7			Employer's payroll tax expense										7
8			for February										8
9													9
10			Adjusting Entries										10
11		28	Office Supplies Expense	520		9	6	32					11
12			Office Supplies	113						9	6	32	12
13													13
14		28	Insurance Expense	519	6	0	0	00					14
15			Prepaid Insurance	115					6	0	0	00	15
16													16
17		28	Depreciation Expense—Automobiles	571	6	4	3	00					17
18			Accum. Depreciation—Automobiles	161.1					6	4	3	00	18
19													19
20		28	Depreciation Exp.—Lab. Equip.	572	3	3	2	00					20
21			Accum. Depr.—Lab. Equip.	171.1					3	3	2	00	21
22													22
23		28	Depreciation Exp.—Medical Equip.	573	5	0	0	00					23
24			Accu. Depr.—Medical Equip.	181.1					5	0	0	00	24
25													25
26		28	Depreciation Exp.—Office Equip.	574	1	1	2	00					26
27			Accum. Depr.—Office Equip.	191.1					1	1	2	00	27
28													28

General Journal Page 2

General Journal — Page 3

	Date	Description	Post. Ref.	Debit	Credit
1	200X	Closing Entries			
2	Feb. 28	Professional Fees	411	78 1 2 2 00	
3		Other Income	421	9 2 0 9 25	
4		Income Summary	331		87 3 3 1 25
5					
6	28	Income Summary	331	33 4 5 6 97	
7		Automobile Expense	511		4 1 0 65
8		Charitable Contributions Expense	512		1 1 0 0 00
9		Dues and Subscriptions Expense	516		9 0 00
10		Electricity Expense	518		2 8 8 54
11		Insurance Expense	519		6 0 0 00
12		Office Supplies Expense	520		9 6 32
13		Laundry Expense	521		2 4 6 24
14		Legal Expense	523		1 2 9 1 00
15		Medical Library Expense	527		2 6 7 65
16		Medical Supplies Expense	528		3 9 3 52
17		Payroll Taxes Expense	532		1 5 9 9 40
18		Postage Expense	535		7 5 00
19		Rent Expense	541		8 5 0 0 00
20		Repairs and Maintenance Expense	543		2 1 9 31
21		Salary Expense	551		14 5 4 0 00
22		Surgical Instruments Expense	553		3 4 2 58
23		Surgical Supplies Expense	557		2 6 3 00
24		Telephone Expense	561		1 3 3 65
25		Travel and Meeting Expense	567		1 2 6 3 45
26		Depreciation Exp.—Automobiles	571		6 4 3 00
27		Depr. Exp.—Laboratory Equip.	572		3 3 2 00
28		Depreciation Exp.—Medical Equip.	573		5 0 0 00
29		Depreciation Exp.—Office Equip.	574		1 1 2 00
30		Miscellaneous Expense	581		1 4 9 66
31					
32	28	Income Summary	331	53 8 7 4 28	
33		Julie Cole, Capital	311		26 9 3 7 14
34		John Martin, Capital	321		26 9 3 7 14
35					
36	28	Julie Cole, Capital	311	10 7 8 1 90	
37		Julie Cole, Drawing	312		10 7 8 1 90
38					
39	28	John Martin, Capital	321	10 8 5 7 85	
40		John Martin, Drawing	322		10 8 5 7 85

Julie Cole and John Martin,
Work
For Two Months Ending

Account Title	Trial Balance Debit	Trial Balance Credit	Adjustments Debit	Adjustments Credit
1 Cash	84 3 2 0 60			
2 Petty Cash Fund	1 5 0 00			
3 Office Supplies	1 8 0 32			(a) 9 6 32
4 Prepaid Insurance	5 0 6 0 00			(b) 6 0 0 00
5 Automobiles	25 0 0 0 00			
6 Accum. Depr.—Automobiles		7 7 2 2 72		(c) 6 4 3 00
7 Laboratory Equipment	18 4 6 0 00			
8 Accum. Depr.—Laboratory Equip.		3 9 8 5 00		(d) 3 3 2 00
9 Medical Equipment	32 3 2 6 85			
10 Accum. Depr.—Medical Equip.		5 9 6 0 00		(e) 5 0 0 00
11 Office Equipment	5 8 8 4 70			
12 Accum. Depr.—Office Equip.		1 3 5 0 00		(f) 1 1 2 00
13 Employees' Income Tax Payable		8 2 4 00		
14 FICA Tax Payable—OASDI		8 9 2 52		
15 FICA Tax Payable—HI		1 7 8 48		
16 FUTA Tax Payable		1 1 6 32		
17 SUTA Tax Payable		3 9 2 58		
18 Julie Cole, Capital		56 7 6 8 00		
19 Julie Cole, Drawing	10 7 8 1 90			
20 John Martin, Capital		58 6 7 5 00		
21 John Martin, Drawing	10 8 5 7 85			
22 Professional Fees		78 1 2 2 00		
23 Other Income		9 2 0 9 25		
24 Automobile Expense	4 1 0 65			
25 Charitable Contributions Exp.	1 1 0 0 00			
26 Dues and Subscriptions Exp.	9 0 00			
27 Electricity Expense	2 8 8 54			
28 Insurance Expense			(b) 6 0 0 00	
29 Office Supplies Expense			(a) 9 6 32	
30 Laundry Expense	2 4 6 24			
31 Legal Expense	1 2 9 1 00			
32 Medical Library Expense	2 6 7 65			
33 Medical Supplies Expense	3 9 3 52			
34 Payroll Taxes Expense	1 5 9 9 40			
35 Postage Expense	7 5 00			
36 Balance carried forward	198 7 8 4 22	224 1 9 5 87	6 9 6 32	2 2 8 3 32
37				

Physicians & Surgeons
Sheet
February 28, 200X   Page 1

Adjusted Trial Balance Debit	Adjusted Trial Balance Credit	Income Statement Debit	Income Statement Credit	Balance Sheet Debit	Balance Sheet Credit	#
84 320 60				84 320 60		1
150 00				150 00		2
84 00				84 00		3
4 460 00				4 460 00		4
25 000 00				25 000 00		5
	8 365 72				8 365 72	6
18 460 00				18 460 00		7
	4 317 00				4 317 00	8
32 326 85				32 326 85		9
	6 460 00				6 460 00	10
5 884 70				5 884 70		11
	1 462 00				1 462 00	12
	824 00				824 00	13
	892 52				892 52	14
	178 48				178 48	15
	116 32				116 32	16
	392 58				392 58	17
	56 768 00				56 768 00	18
10 781 90				10 781 90		19
	58 675 00				58 675 00	20
10 857 85				10 857 85		21
	78 122 00		78 122 00			22
	9 209 25		9 209 25			23
410 65		410 65				24
1 100 00		1 100 00				25
90 00		90 00				26
288 54		288 54				27
600 00		600 00				28
96 32		96 32				29
246 24		246 24				30
1 291 00		1 291 00				31
267 65		267 65				32
393 52		393 52				33
1 599 40		1 599 40				34
75 00		75 00				35
198 784 22	225 782 87	6 458 32	87 331 25	192 325 90	138 451 62	36
						37

Work Sheet　　(continued)

	Account Title	Trial Balance Debit	Trial Balance Credit	Adjustments Debit	Adjustments Credit
1	Balance brought forward	198,784 22	224,195 87	696 32	2,283 32
2	Rent Expense	8,500 00			
3	Repairs and Maintenance Exp.	219 31			
4	Salary Expense	14,540 00			
5	Surgical Instruments Expense	342 58			
6	Surgical Supplies Expense	263 00			
7	Telephone Expense	133 65			
8	Travel and Meetings Expense	1,263 45			
9	Depreciation Exp.—Automobiles			(c) 643 00	
10	Depr. Exp.—Laboratory Equipment			(d) 332 00	
11	Depreciation Exp.—Medical Equip.			(e) 500 00	
12	Depreciation Exp.—Office Equip.			(f) 112 00	
13	Miscellaneous Expense	149 66			
14		224,195 87	224,195 87	2,283 32	2,283 32
15	Net Income				
16					
17					

Julie Cole and John Martin, Physicians and Surgeons
Statement of Owners' Equity
For Two Months Ending February 28, 200X

Julie Cole, Capital:

Capital, January 1, 200X		$56,768.00	
One half of net income	$26,937.14		
Less withdrawals	10,781.90		
Net increase in capital		16,155.24	
Capital, February 28, 200X			$ 72,923.24

John Martin, Capital:

Capital, January 1, 200X		$58,675.00	
One half of net income	$26,937.14		
Less withdrawals	10,857.85		
Net increase in capital		16,079.29	
Capital, February 28, 200X			74,754.29
Total owners' equity			$147,677.53

	Adjusted Trial Balance		Income Statement		Balance Sheet			Page 2
	Debit	Credit	Debit	Credit	Debit	Credit		
1	198 784 22	225 782 87	6 458 32	87 331 25	192 325 90	138 451 62		1
2	8 500 00		8 500 00					2
3	219 31		219 31					3
4	14 540 00		14 540 00					4
5	342 58		342 58					5
6	263 00		263 00					6
7	133 65		133 65					7
8	1 263 45		1 263 45					8
9	643 00		643 00					9
10	332 00		332 00					10
11	500 00		500 00					11
12	112 00		112 00					12
13	149 66		149 66					13
14	225 782 87	225 782 87	33 456 97	87 331 25	192 325 90	138 451 62		14
15			53 874 28			53 874 28		15
16			87 331 25	87 331 25	192 325 90	192 325 90		16
17								17

Julie Cole and John Martin, Physicians and Surgeons
Income Statement
For Two Months Ending February 28, 200X

Revenue:

Professional fees	$78,122.00	
Other income	9,209.25	
Total revenue		$87,331.25

Expenses:

Salary expense	$14,540.00	
Rent expense	8,500.00	
Payroll tax expense	1,599.40	
Legal expense	1,291.00	
Travel and meetings expense	1,263.45	
Charitable contributions expense	1,100.00	
Depreciation expense—automobiles	643.00	
Insurance expense	600.00	
Depreciation expense—medical equipment	500.00	
Automobile expense	410.65	
Medical supplies expense	393.52	
Surgical instruments expense	342.58	
Depreciation expense—laboratory equipment	332.00	
Electricity expense	288.54	
Medical library expense	267.65	
Surgical supplies expense	263.00	
Laundry expense	246.24	
Repairs and maintenance expense	219.31	
Telephone expense	133.65	
Depreciation expense—office equipment	112.00	
Office supplies expense	96.32	
Dues and subscriptions expense	90.00	
Postage expense	75.00	
Miscellaneous expense	149.66	
Total expenses		33,456.97
Net income		$53,874.28

Julie Cole and John Martin, Physicians and Surgeons
Balance Sheet
February 28, 200X

Assets

Current Assets:			
Cash		$84,320.60	
Petty cash fund		150.00	
Office supplies		84.00	
Prepaid insurance		4,460.00	
Total Current Assets			$ 89,014.60
Long-Term Assets:			
Automobiles	$25,000.00		
Less accum. depreciation—automobiles	8,365.72	$16,634.28	
Laboratory equipment	$18,460.00		
Less accum. depreciation—laboratory equip.	4,317.00	14,143.00	
Medical equipment	$32,326.85		
Less accum. depreciation—medical equip.	6,460.00	25,866.85	
Office equipment	$ 5,884.70		
Less accum. depreciation—office equip.	1,462.00	4,422.70	
Total Long-Term Assets			61,066.83
Total Assets			$150,081.43

Liabilities

Current Liabilities:		
Employees' income tax payable	$ 824.00	
FICA tax payable—OASDI	892.52	
FICA tax payable—HI	178.48	
FUTA tax payable	116.32	
SUTA tax payable	392.58	
Total Current Liabilities		$ 2,403.90

Owners' Equity

Julie Cole, capital	$72,923.24	
John Martin, capital	74,754.29	
Total Owners' Equity		147,677.53
Total Liabilities and Owners' Equity		$150,081.43

Account *Cash*   **Account No.** *111*

Date		Item	Post Ref.	Debit	Credit	Balance Debit	Balance Credit
200X							
Feb.	1	Balance	✓			76 6 3 2 63	
	28		CR2	42 9 5 4 00		119 5 8 6 63	
	28		CP3		35 2 6 6 03	84 3 2 0 60	

Account *Petty Cash Fund*   **Account No.** *112*

Date		Item	Post Ref.	Debit	Credit	Balance Debit	Balance Credit
200X							
Feb.	1	Balance	✓			1 5 0 00	

Account *Office Supplies*   **Account No.** *113*

Date		Item	Post Ref.	Debit	Credit	Balance Debit	Balance Credit
200X							
Feb	1	Balance	✓			8 8 46	
	15		CP3	8 6 11		1 7 4 57	
	28		CP3	5 75		1 8 0 32	
	28	Adj. Entry	GJ2		9 6 32	8 4 00	

Account *Prepaid Insurance*   **Account No.** *115*

Date		Item	Post Ref.	Debit	Credit	Balance Debit	Balance Credit
200X							
Feb.	4		CP3	4 4 0 0 00		4 4 0 0 00	
	17		CP3	6 6 0 00		5 0 6 0 00	
	28		GJ2		6 0 0 00	4 4 6 0 00	

Account *Automobiles*   **Account No.** *161*

Date		Item	Post Ref.	Debit	Credit	Balance Debit	Balance Credit
200X							
Feb.	1	Balance	✓			25 0 0 0 00	

Account *Accumulated Depreciation—Automobiles*   **Account No.** *161.1*

Date		Item	Post Ref.	Debit	Credit	Balance Debit	Balance Credit
200X							
Feb.	1	Balance	✓				7 7 2 2 72
	28	Adj. Entry	GJ2		6 4 3 00		8 3 6 5 72

Account *Laboratory Equipment* — **Account No.** *171*

Date		Item	Post Ref.	Debit	Credit	Balance Debit	Balance Credit
200X							
Feb.	1	Balance	✓		18 460 00		

Account *Accumulated Depreciation—Laboratory Equip.* — **Account No.** *171.1*

Date		Item	Post Ref.	Debit	Credit	Balance Debit	Balance Credit
200X							
Feb.	1	Balance	✓				3 985 00
	28	Adj. Entry	GJ2		332 00		4 317 00

Account *Medical Equipment* — **Account No.** *181*

Date		Item	Post Ref.	Debit	Credit	Balance Debit	Balance Credit
200X							
Feb.	1	Balance	✓			29 532 00	
	22		CP3	2 794 85		32 326 85	

Account *Accumulated Depreciation—Medical Equip.* — **Account No.** *181.1*

Date		Item	Post Ref.	Debit	Credit	Balance Debit	Balance Credit
200X							
Feb.	1	Balance	✓				5 960 00
	28	Adj. Entry	GJ2		500 00		6 460 00

Account *Office Equipment* — **Account No.** *191*

Date		Item	Post Ref.	Debit	Credit	Balance Debit	Balance Credit
200X							
Feb.	1	Balance	✓			5 680 00	
	14		CP3	204 70		5 884 70	

Account *Accumulated Depreciation—Office Equip.* — **Account No.** *191.1*

Date		Item	Post Ref.	Debit	Credit	Balance Debit	Balance Credit
200X							
Feb.	1	Balance	✓				1 350 00
	28	Adj. Entry	GJ2		112 00		1 462 00

Account *Employees' Income Tax Payable* — **Account No.** *231*

Date		Item	Post Ref.	Debit	Credit	Balance Debit	Balance Credit
200X							
Feb.	1	Balance	✓				854 00
	15		CP3	854 00			- 0 -
	28		CP3		824 00		824 00

Account FICA Tax Payable—OASDI   **Account No.** 232

Date		Item	Post Ref.	Debit	Credit	Balance Debit	Balance Credit
200X							
Feb.	1	Balance	✓				9 2 5 00
	15		CP3	9 2 5 00			- 0 -
	28		GJ2		4 4 6 26		4 4 6 26
	28		CP3		4 4 6 26		8 9 2 52

Account FICA Tax Payable—HI   **Account No.** 233

Date		Item	Post Ref.	Debit	Credit	Balance Debit	Balance Credit
200X							
Feb	1	Balance	✓				1 8 5 00
	15		CP3	1 8 5 00			- 0 -
	28		CJ3		8 9 24		8 9 24
	28		GP3		8 9 24		1 7 8 48

Account FUTA Tax Payable   **Account No.** 241

Date		Item	Post Ref.	Debit	Credit	Balance Debit	Balance Credit
200X							
Feb.	1	Balance	✓				5 9 20
	28		GJ2		5 7 12		1 1 6 32

Account SUTA Tax Payable   **Account No.** 251

Date		Item	Post Ref.	Debit	Credit	Balance Debit	Balance Credit
200X							
Feb.	1	Balance	✓				1 9 9 80
	28		GJ2		1 9 2 78		3 9 2 58

Account Julie Cole, Capital   **Account No.** 311

Date		Item	Post Ref.	Debit	Credit	Balance Debit	Balance Credit
200X							
Feb.	1	Balance	✓				56 7 6 8 00
	28	Clos. Ent.	GJ3		26 9 3 7 14		83 7 0 5 14
	28	Clos. Ent.	GJ3	10 7 8 1 90			72 9 2 3 24

Account Julie Cole, Drawing   **Account No.** 312

Date		Item	Post Ref.	Debit	Credit	Balance Debit	Balance Credit
200X							
Feb	1	Balance	✓			5 4 6 5 40	
	10		CP3	9 8 00		5 5 6 3 40	
	11		CP3	2 6 0 0 00		8 1 6 3 40	
	28		CP3	2 6 0 0 00		10 7 6 3 40	
	28		CP3	1 8 50		10 7 8 1 90	
	28	Clos. Ent.	GJ3		10 7 8 1 90	- 0 -	

Account	John Martin, Capital										Account No. 321			
Date	Item	Post Ref.	Debit		Credit		Balance							
							Debit			Credit				
200X														
Feb. 1	Balance	✓								58	6	7	5	00
28	Clos. Ent.	GJ3			26	9 3 7 14				85	6	1	2	14
28	Clos. Ent.	GJ3	10	8 5 7 85						74	7	5	4	29

Account	John Martin, Drawing										Account No. 322			
200X														
Feb 1	Balance	✓					5	6 3 5 60						
11		CP3	2	6 0 0 00			8	2 3 5 60						
28		CP3	2	6 0 0 00			10	8 3 5 60						
28		CP3		2 2 25			10	8 5 7 85						
28	Clos. Ent.	GJ3			10	8 5 7 85		- 0 -						

Account	Income Summary										Account No. 331			
200X														
Feb. 28		GJ3			87	3 3 1 25				87	3	3	1	25
28		GJ3	33	4 5 6 97						53	8	7	4	28
28	Clos. Ent.	GJ3	53	8 7 4 28							-	0	-	

Account	Professional Fees										Account No. 411			
200X														
Feb. 1	Balance	✓								38	8	3	4	00
28		CR2			39	2 8 8 00				78	1	2	2	00
28	Clos. Ent.	GJ3	78	1 2 2 00							-	0	-	

Account	Other Income										Account No. 421			
200X														
Feb. 1	Balance	✓									4	8	6	2 25
28		CR2			4	3 4 7 00					9	2	0	9 25
28	Clos. Ent.	GJ3	9	2 0 9 25								-	0	-

Account	Automobile Expense										Account No. 511			
200X														
Feb 1	Balance	✓						5 6 00						
1		CP3		1 4 7 67				2 0 3 67						
21		CP3		1 8 8 48				3 9 2 15						
28		CP3		1 8 50				4 1 0 65						
28	Clos. Ent.	GJ3				4 1 0 65		- 0 -						

Account *Charitable Contributions Expense*   Account No. *512*

Date		Item	Post Ref.	Debit	Credit	Balance Debit	Balance Credit
200X							
Feb.	16		CP3	6 50 00		6 50 00	
	21		CP3	4 50 00		1 1 00 00	
	28	Clos. Ent.	GJ3		1 1 00 00	- 0 -	

Account *Dues and Subscriptions Expense*   Account No. *516*

Date		Item	Post Ref.	Debit	Credit	Balance Debit	Balance Credit
200X							
Feb.	8		CP3	9 0 00		9 0 00	
	28	Clos. Ent.	GJ3		9 0 00	- 0 -	

Account *Electricity Expense*   Account No. *518*

Date		Item	Post Ref.	Debit	Credit	Balance Debit	Balance Credit
200X							
Feb.	3		CP3	2 88 54		2 88 54	
	28	Clos. Ent.	GJ3		2 88 54	- 0 -	

Account *Insurance Expense*   Account No. *519*

Date		Item	Post Ref.	Debit	Credit	Balance Debit	Balance Credit
200X							
Feb.	28	Adj. Ent.	GJ2	6 00 00		6 00 00	
	28	Clos. Ent.	GJ3		6 00 00	- 0 -	

Account *Office Supplies Expense*   Account No. *520*

Date		Item	Post Ref.	Debit	Credit	Balance Debit	Balance Credit
200X							
Feb.	28	Adj. Entry	GJ3	9 6 32		9 6 32	
	28	Clos. Ent.	GJ3		9 6 32	- 0 -	

Account *Laundry Expense*   Account No. *521*

Date		Item	Post Ref.	Debit	Credit	Balance Debit	Balance Credit
200X							
Feb.	3		CP3	2 46 24		2 46 24	
	28	Clos. Ent.	GJ3		2 46 24	- 0 -	

Account *Legal Expense*   Account No. *523*

Date		Item	Post Ref.	Debit	Credit	Balance Debit	Balance Credit
200X							
Feb	1	Balance	✓			6 1 0 00	
	22		CR2	5 41 00		1 1 51 00	
	25		CR2	1 40 00		1 2 91 00	
	28	Clos. Ent.	GJ3		1 2 91 00	- 0 -	

Account *Medical Library Expense*   **Account No.** *527*

Date		Item	Post Ref.	Debit	Credit	Balance Debit	Balance Credit
200X							
Feb.	10		CP3	2 6 7 65		2 6 7 65	
	28	Clos. Ent.	GJ3		2 6 7 65	- 0 -	

Account *Medical Supplies Expense*   **Account No.** *528*

Date		Item	Post Ref.	Debit	Credit	Balance Debit	Balance Credit
200X							
Feb.	3		CP3	1 7 5 87		1 7 5 87	
	15		CP3	2 1 7 65		3 9 3 52	
	28	Clos. Ent.	GJ3		3 9 3 52	- 0 -	

Account *Payroll Taxes Expense*   **Account No.** *532*

Date		Item	Post Ref.	Debit	Credit	Balance Debit	Balance Credit
200X							
Feb.	1	Balance	✓			8 1 4 00	
	15		GJ2	7 8 5 40		1 5 9 9 40	
	28	Clos. Ent.	GJ3		1 5 9 9 40	- 0 -	

Account *Postage Expense*   **Account No.** *535*

Date		Item	Post Ref.	Debit	Credit	Balance Debit	Balance Credit
200X							
Feb.	1	Balance	✓			5 5 00	
	28		CP3	2 0 00		7 5 00	
	28	Clos. Ent.	GJ3		7 5 00	- 0 -	

Account *Rent Expense*   **Account No.** *541*

Date		Item	Post Ref.	Debit	Credit	Balance Debit	Balance Credit
200X							
Feb.	1	Balance	✓			4 2 5 0 00	
	1		CP3	4 2 5 0 00		8 5 0 0 00	
	28	Clos. Ent.	GJ3		8 5 0 0 00	- 0 -	

Account *Repairs and Maintenance Expense*   **Account No.** *543*

Date		Item	Post Ref.	Debit	Credit	Balance Debit	Balance Credit
200X							
Feb	1	Balance	✓			4 6 00	
	4		CP3	8 9 00		1 3 5 00	
	23		CP3	8 4 31		2 1 9 31	
	28	Clos. Ent.	GJ3		2 1 9 31	- 0 -	

Account *Salary Expense* — **Account No.** *551*

Date		Item	Post Ref.	Debit	Credit	Balance Debit	Balance Credit
200X							
Feb.	1	Balance	✓			7 4 0 00	
	28		CP3	7 1 4 0 00		14 5 4 0 00	
	28	Clos. Ent.	GJ3		14 5 4 0 00	- 0 -	

Account *Surgical Instruments Expense* — **Account No.** *553*

Date		Item	Post Ref.	Debit	Credit	Balance Debit	Balance Credit
200X							
Feb.	7		CP3	3 4 2 58		3 4 2 58	
	28	Clos. Ent.	GJ3		3 4 2 58	- 0 -	

Account *Surgical Supplies Expense* — **Account No.** *557*

Date		Item	Post Ref.	Debit	Credit	Balance Debit	Balance Credit
200X							
Feb.	1	Balance	✓			1 0 9 22	
	9		CP3	1 5 3 78		2 6 3 00	
	28	Clos. Ent.	GJ3		2 6 3 00	- 0 -	

Account *Telephone Expense* — **Account No.** *561*

Date		Item	Post Ref.	Debit	Credit	Balance Debit	Balance Credit
200X							
Feb.	3		CP3	1 3 3 65		1 3 3 65	
	28	Clos. Ent.	GJ3		1 3 3 65	- 0 -	

Account *Travel and Meetings Expense* — **Account No.** *567*

Date		Item	Post Ref.	Debit	Credit	Balance Debit	Balance Credit
200X							
Feb	1	Balance	✓			2 8 6 00	
	24		CP3	9 5 5 45		1 2 4 1 45	
	28		CP3	2 2 00		1 2 6 3 45	
	28	Clos. Ent.	GJ3		1 2 6 3 45	- 0 -	

Account *Depreciation Expense—Automobiles* — **Account No.** *571*

Date		Item	Post Ref.	Debit	Credit	Balance Debit	Balance Credit
200X							
Feb.	28	Adj. Entry	GJ2	6 4 3 00		6 4 3 00	
	28	Clos. Entry	GJ3		6 4 3 00	- 0 -	

Account	Depreciation Expense—Laboratory Equipment						Account No. 572	
Date	Item	Post Ref.	Debit	Credit	Balance			
					Debit		Credit	
200X								
Feb. 28	Adj. Entry	GJ2	3 3 2 00		3 3 2 00			
28	Clos. Entry	GJ3		3 3 2 00	- 0 -			

Account	Depreciation Expense—Medical Equipment						Account No. 573	
200X								
Feb. 28	Adj. Entry	GJ2	5 0 0 00		5 0 0 00			
28	Clos. Entry	GJ3		5 0 0 00	- 0 -			

Account	Depreciation Expense—Office Equipment						Account No. 574	
200X								
Feb. 28	Adj. Entry	GJ2	1 1 2 00		1 1 2 00			
28	Clos. Entry	GJ3		1 1 2 00	- 0 -			

Account	Miscellaneous Expense						Account No. 581	
200X								
Feb. 1	Balance	✓			1 0 9 66			
18		CP3	4 0 00		1 4 9 66			
28	Clos. Ent.	GJ3		1 4 9 66	- 0 -			

Julie Cole and John Martin, Physicians and Surgeons
Post-Closing Trial Balance
February 28, 200X

Account	Debit	Credit
Cash	84 3 2 0 60	
Petty Cash Fund	1 5 0 00	
Office Supplies	8 4 00	
Prepaid Insurance	4 4 6 0 00	
Automobiles	25 0 0 0 00	
Accum. Depreciation—Automobiles		8 3 6 5 72
Laboratory Equipment	18 4 6 0 00	
Accum. Depreciation—Laboratory Equipment		4 3 1 7 00
Medical Equipment	32 3 2 6 85	
Accum. Depreciation—Medical Equipment		6 4 6 0 00
Office Equipment	5 8 8 4 70	
Accum. Depreciation—Office Equipment		1 4 6 2 00
Employees' Income Tax Payable		8 2 4 00
FICA Tax Payable—OASDI		8 9 2 52
FICA Tax Payable—HI		1 7 8 48
FUTA Tax Payable		1 1 6 32
SUTA Tax Payable		3 9 2 58
Julie Cole, Capital		72 9 2 3 24
John Martin, Capital		74 7 5 4 29
	170 6 8 6 15	170 6 8 6 15

Concept Questions

1. How is the daily service record used in a medical or dental office?
2. The "office visits" and "surgery" columns on the daily service record must equal the total of what two columns?
3. Explain how the patients' ledger is organized.
4. What items are posted daily or weekly from the daily service record to the patients' ledger?
5. What does it mean when a doctor or dentist accepts an "assignment of the amount due" from a patient?
6. How does the use of the cash receipts journal and the cash payments journal save time in journalizing and posting transactions, as compared to the use of a general journal?

CHAPTER SUMMARY

 Most physicians and dentists use a modified cash basis of accounting. The cash receipts and cash payments journals are used as books of original entry. The daily service record is used to record the kinds of services, charges to patients' accounts, cash services, and cash payments received from patients. The total of the "Kinds of Services" columns must equal the total of Patients' Accounts Charges and Cash Services columns. The patients' ledger is generally not in a bound book but kept as loose cards to allow photocopying. Charges and payments from the daily service record are usually posted daily or weekly to the patients' accounts. Information from the Cash Services column of the daily services record is also posted to the patients' accounts in both the Charges and Payments columns. Accepting assignments means that the patient will pay only those amounts due that are not covered by insurance. The balance will be paid by the insurance company to the doctor or dentist. The Universal Health Insurance Claim Form has been adopted by most insurance carriers and programs.

Chapter 8

Key Terms

accrual basis, *251*
assignment, *259*
cash basis, *251*
cash payments journal, *255*
cash receipts journal, *254*

daily service record, *256*
modified cash basis of accounting, *252*
patients' ledger, *259*
Universal Health Insurance
   Claim Form, *261*

Chapter 8

Exercises

EXERCISE 8-1

Norma Staples incurred medical expenses of $7,345. All the charges were covered by her insurance. The deductible on her policy is $200, and the coverage that her insurance company will pay is 80%.

   1. How much of the debt must Norma Staples pay?   *1629*
   2. How much of the debt will the insurance company pay? *5716*

 ### EXERCISE 8-2

Complete a statement of account for Almeda Ogden, 6241 East Wales Boulevard, Portland, OR, 97208-6431, using the following information:

Date	Service Performed	Amount
June 6	Complete blood count	$ 90
June 8	Complete physical; electrocardiogram	250
June 14	Office visit	50
June 16	X-ray	115
June 21	Emergency room treatment	325
June 24	Hospital visit	90
June 25	Surgery	3,250
June 26	Hospital visit	90
July 2	Office visit	50

Payments were received as follows:

July 8 Check was received from Blue Shield for 80% of the balance owed by Ms. Ogden, less $200 deductible.

14 Check was received from Ms. Ogden for balance due on her account.

EXERCISE 8-3

Give the general journal entry to reimburse the petty cash fund. The petty cash fund was established for $250. There is $35 remaining in the fund. The following statement provides the information needed to enter this transaction.

Vidal and Neilson, Physicians
Statement of Petty Cash Payments for April 6, 200X

S. Vidal, Drawing	$ 48
R. Neilson, Drawing	32
Automobile Expense	51
Postage Expense	33
Traveling and Meetings Expense	29
Telephone Expense	15
Miscellaneous Expense	7
Total Payments	$215

EXERCISE 8-4   11/11/99

Dr. Dochia Nix is a practicing physician and surgeon. Enter the following selected transactions in the cash receipts and cash payments journal during March 200X.

Mar. 3 Footed the amount columns in the daily service record and obtained the following totals. Entered the total cash received.

Kind of Service:

Office Visits	$ 528	Patients' Accounts Charges	$9,267
Surgery	9,144	Cash Services	405
Total	$9,672	Total	$9,672

The total cash received from patients for the week was found to be:

Payments	$8,755
Cash Services	405
Total	$9,160

8 Issued Check No. 701 for $125 to American Medical Association for subscription to professional journal.

9 Issued Check No. 702 to Precision Supply Company for surgical supplies, $315.

13 Issued Check No. 703 to Shoppe Center in payment of Dochia Nix's personal account, $248.

15 Issued Check No. 704 to Friendly National Bank in payment of the following payroll taxes based on wages paid during the month of February:

Employees' income tax withheld from wages		$ 556
FICA tax payable—OASDI	$372.36	
FICA tax payable—HI	74.64	
Total FICA Tax		447
Amount of check		$1,003

21 Issued Check No. 705 to William Wallace, laboratory technician, in payment of salary in the amount of $845, less $134 withheld for federal income tax, $52.39 withheld for FICA—OASDI tax, and $12.25 withheld for FICA—HI tax.

26 Received $600 from Margaret Lyon, Attorney, representing collection of the account of Steve Feider in the amount of $850. Lyon deducted the fee of $250 and remitted the balance.

30 Issued Check No. 706 for $814 to Gilligan for reimbursement of expenses incurred in attending a medical convention earlier this month.

Problems

PROBLEM 8-5

Dr. Jeanine Herzog is a dentist. The books of original entry include a cash payments journal, cash receipts journal and general journal. The accounts are kept in a general ledger. Herzog has two employees: Evan Talbot, a dental hygienist, and Christine Bell, a secretary-bookkeeper. There is an auxiliary record for Herzog's patients and for Talbot's patients, but these records are not involved in this problem. The books are kept on the modified cash basis. Herzog requests that patients pay cash for the services of the hygienist, and most patients do. The trial balance as of March 31 is shown below.

Account	Acct. No.	Dr. Balance	Cr. Balance
Dr. Jeanine Herzog, Dentist Trial Balance March 31, 200X			
Cash	111	20 2 3 4 65	
Office Supplies	113	1 4 2 0 00	
Professional Supplies	114	9 8 0 00	
Professional Equipment	161	30 1 0 0 00	
Accum. Depr.—Professional Equip.	161.1		12 4 0 0 00
Office Equipment	171	16 4 3 5 00	
Accum. Depr.—Office Equip.	171.1		1 8 0 0 00
Employees' Income Tax Payable	231		4 4 0 00
FICA Tax Payable—OASDI	232		4 7 7 53
FICA Tax Payable—HI	233		9 5 51
FUTA Tax Payable	241		9 1 68
SUTA Tax Payable	251		3 0 9 42
Jeanine Herzog, Capital	311		30 3 4 6 00
Jeanine Herzog, Drawing	312	15 9 9 0 00	
Professional Fees—Dentistry	411		52 8 6 0 00
Professional Fees—Oral Hygiene	412		13 4 8 0 00
Laboratory Expense	511	13 1 5 1 28	
Laundry Expense	512	4 9 7 00	
Payroll Taxes Expense	532	1 2 6 0 60	
Rent Expense	541	4 8 0 0 00	
Salary Expense	551	5 7 3 0 00	
Telephone Expense	561	6 2 4 98	
Utilities Expense	567	9 7 8 53	
Miscellaneous Expense	581	9 8 10	
		112 3 0 0 14	112 3 0 0 14

Narrative of Transactions for April

April 1   Issued Check No. 275 for April rent, $1,700. CP
        2   Issued Check No. 276 for water bill for March, $254.75. CP
        5   Issued Check No. 277 to Hemotek Services for laboratory work performed in March, $3,992. CP
        9   The amount columns in the daily services record kept by Herzog and Talbot for the week ended April 9 contained the following totals:

Kind of Service:		
Dentistry—Herzog	CR	$4,502.00
Oral Hygiene—Talbot		921.00
Total		$5,423.00

Patients' Accounts—Charges	$2,276.00
Cash Services	3,147.00
Total	$5,423.00

The total cash received from patients during the week ended April 9 was:

Dentistry	$2,285.00
Oral Hygiene	862.00
Total	$3,147.00

       12   Issued Check No. 278 for laundry bill for March, $73.66. CP
       13   Paid the following bills:

Electricity	$441.48	CP
Gas	125.55	CP

(Issued Check Numbers 279 and 280 by debiting Utilities Expense twice.)

       16   The amount columns in the daily services record kept by Herzog and Talbot for the week ended April 16 contained the following totals:

Kind of Service:		
Dentistry—Herzog	CR	$4,835.00
Oral Hygiene—Talbot		880.00
Total		$5,715.00

Patients' Accounts—Charges	$2,850.00
Cash Services	2,865.00
Total	$5,715.00

The total cash received from patients during the week ended April 16 was:

Dentistry	$2,040.00
Oral Hygiene	825.00
Total	$2,865.00

16 Issued Check No. 281 to Evan Talbot for salary, $1,025, less income tax payable, $213, less FICA tax payable—OASDI, $63.55, less FICA tax payable—HI, $14.86.   CP

16 Issued Check No. 282 to Christine Bell for salary, $985, less income tax payable, $127, less FICA tax payable—OASDI, $61.07, less FICA tax payable—HI, $14.28.   CP

16 Issued Check No. 283 to Washington National Bank for March payroll taxes, $1,013.04:

Employees' income tax withheld	$ 440.00
FICA tax payable—OASDI	477.53
FICA tax payable—HI	95.51
	$1,013.04

CP

19 Issued Check No. 284 for professional supplies, $315.77.   CP

20 Issued Check No. 285 for dues to the state dental society, $300 (Debit Miscellaneous Expense).   CP

23 The amount columns in the daily services record kept by Herzog and Talbot for the week ended April 23 contained the following totals:

Kind of Service:	
Dentistry—Herzog	$3,457.00
Oral Hygiene—Talbot	852.00
Total	$4,309.00

CR

Patients' Accounts—Charges	$1,439.00
Cash Services	2,870.00
Total	$4,309.00

The total cash received from patients during the week ended April 23 was:

Dentistry	$2,085.00
Oral Hygiene	785.00
Total	$2,870.00

27 Issued Check No. 286 for office supplies, $43.79.   CP

28 Issued Check No. 287 for subscriptions to magazines for the waiting room, $87 (debit Miscellaneous Expense).   CP

28 Issued Check No. 288 for state unemployment tax for the first quarter of the year, $309.42.   CP

30   The amount columns in the daily services record kept by Herzog and Talbot for the week ended April 30 contained the following totals:

Kind of Service:

Dentistry—Herzog	$3,215.00
Oral hygiene—Talbot	900.00
Total CR	$4,115.00
Patients' Accounts—Charges	$1,195.00
Cash Services	2,920.00
Total	$4,115.00

The total cash received from patients during the week ended April 30 was:

Dentistry	$2,020.00
Oral Hygiene	900.00
Total	$2,920.00

30   Issued Check No. 289 to Evan Talbot for salary for second half of month, $1,025, less income tax payable, $213, less FICA tax payable—OASDI, $63.55, less FICA tax payable—HI, $14.86. CP

30   Issued Check No. 290 to Christine Bell for salary for second half of month, $985, less income tax payable, $127, less FICA tax payable—OASDI, $61.07, less FICA tax payable—HI, $14.28. CP

30   Issued Check No. 291 to Jeanine Herzog for personal use, $3,300. CP

30   Made an entry in the general journal for the employer's unemployment taxes and the matching portion of the FICA tax for the month of April. Payroll Taxes Expense is debited for the total taxes and FICA tax payable—OASDI credited for $249.24, FICA tax payable—HI credited for $58.28, FUTA tax payable credited for $33.28, and SUTA tax payable credited for $123.64.   GJ

Required:

1.   Record each transaction in the cash payments journal, cash receipts journal, and general journal. Number the journal pages as follows: cash receipts, page 23; cash payments, page 31; and general, page 13.

2.   At the end of the month, prove the cash receipts and cash payments journals by footing the amount columns and then totaling and ruling the journals.

3.   Open the necessary general ledger accounts using the account forms provided. Record the April 1 balances as shown in the March 31 trial balance and complete the posting from the journals. All posting is done at the end of the month in order to simplify the problem. Post the General Dr. columns of the cash receipts and cash payments

journals (if applicable) before posting the general journal and the special columns of the cash receipts and cash payments journals.

4.   Prepare a trial balance as of April 30 using the two-column paper.

PROBLEM 8-6

Dr. Jan Hamilton is a practicing physician and surgeon. The books of original entry include a cash payments journal, cash receipts journal and general journal. The accounts are kept in a general ledger. Dr. Hamilton employs a secretary-bookkeeper. There is a patients' ledger, but it is not involved in this problem. The books are kept on the modified cash basis. The trial balance as of November 30 is shown below.

Account	Acct. No.	Dr. Balance	Cr. Balance
Cash	111	25 2 5 2 25	
Medical Supplies	114	12 3 5 0 00	
Prepaid Insurance	118	8 3 0 0 00	
Medical Equipment	161	65 6 0 0 00	
Accumulated Depr.—Medical Equipment	161.1		8 2 0 0 00
Office Equipment	171	18 4 5 0 00	
Accumulated Depr.—Office Equipment	171.1		2 4 0 0 00
Employees' Income Tax Payable	231		2 4 0 00
FICA Tax Payable—OASDI	232		1 8 7 52
FICA Tax Payable—HI	233		3 7 52
Jan Hamilton, Capital	311		65 7 5 0 23
Jan Hamilton, Drawing	312	60 0 0 0 00	
Income Summary	331		
Professional Fees	411		167 4 4 1 00
Laundry Expense	512	9 9 4 00	
Payroll Taxes Expense	532	1 1 0 1 52	
Rent Expense	541	28 8 0 0 00	
Medical Supplies Expense	543		
Depreciation Expense—Medical Equip.	547		
Depreciation Expense—Office Equip.	548		
Insurance Expense	549		
Salary Expense	551	18 0 0 0 00	
Telephone Expense	561	7 3 0 00	
Legal Expense	564	6 4 0 00	
Utilities Expense	567	4 0 0 0 00	
Miscellaneous Expense	581	3 8 50	
		244 2 5 6 27	244 2 5 6 27

Dr. Jan Hamilton, Physician and Surgeon
Trial Balance
November 30, 200X

Narrative of Selected Transactions for December

Dec. 1   Issued Check No. 175 for December rent, $1,900.
  2   Issued Check No. 176 to Precision Medical Supply for medical supplies, $950.
  5   Issued Check No. 177 for medical liability insurance, $2,800.
  6   Issued Check No. 178 to Columbia Power Co. for utility expenses for November, $720.
  8   Footed the amount columns in the daily service record and obtained the following totals. Entered the total cash received.

Kind of Service:

Office Visits	$ 415	Patients' Accounts Charges	$4,230
Surgery	4,265	Cash Services	450
Total	$4,680	Total	$4,680

The total cash received from patients for the week was found to be:

Payments	$3,628
Cash Services	450
Total	$4,078

  12   Issued Check No. 179 for magazine subscriptions to be used in the waiting room, $85 (debit Miscellaneous Expense).
  15   Issued Check No. 180 to Franklin Colonial Bank for November payroll taxes:

Employees' income tax withheld	$240.00
FICA tax payable—OASDI	187.52
FICA tax payable—HI	37.52
Total amount of check	$465.04

  15   Issued Check No. 181 for $573.74 to Raynette Wray for salary for secretary-bookkeeper, $750, less income tax payable, $120, less FICA tax payable—OASDI, $46.88, less FICA tax payable—HI, $9.38.
  16   Issued Check No. 182 to Mt. Hood Bell Co. for November telephone bill, $186.00.
  16   Issued Check No. 183 to Chin Lee Laundry Service for November Laundry Expense, $93.00.
  17   Footed the amount columns in the daily service record and obtained the following totals. Entered the total cash received.

Kind of Service:

Office Visits	$ 396	Patients' Accounts Charges	$4,486
Surgery	4,625	Cash Services	535
Total	$5,021	Total	$5,021

The total cash received from patients for the week was found to be:

Payments	$4,160
Cash Services	535
Total	$4,695

21 Received $900 from Dennis Cardoso, Attorney, representing collection of the account of Nicole Lawrence in the amount of $1,200. Cardoso deducted the fee of $300 and remitted the balance.

26 Issued Check No. 184 to Jan Hamilton for a personal withdrawal, $6,000.

28 Footed the amount columns in the daily service record and obtained the following totals. Entered the total cash received.

Kind of Service:

Office Visits	$ 418	Patients' Accounts Charges	$4,968
Surgery	5,165	Cash Services	615
Total	$5,583	Total	$5,583

The total cash received from patients for the week was found to be:

Payments	$4,270
Cash Services	615
Total	$4,885

31 Issued Check No. 185 for $573.74 to Raynette Wray for salary for secretary-bookkeeper, $750, less income tax payable, $120, less FICA tax payable—OASDI, $46.88, less FICA tax payable—HI, $9.38.

31 Recorded employers' payroll tax expense for the month of December in the general journal:

FICA tax payable—OASDI	$93.76
FICA tax payable—HI	18.76

Note: There were no unemployment taxes.

Required:

1. Enter the balances from the November 30 trial balance in the general ledger accounts. Write *balance* in the item column in the general ledger and use Dec. 1 in the date column. Enter all the accounts from the trial balance including those with a zero balance.

2. Record each transaction in the cash payments journal, cash receipts journal, and general journal. Number the journal pages as follows: cash receipts, page 19; cash payments, page 23; and general, page 7.

3. At the end of the month, prove the cash receipts and cash payments journals by footing the amount columns and then totaling and ruling the journals.

4. All posting is done at the end of the month in order to simplify the problem. Post the General Dr. columns of the cash receipts and cash payments journals (if applicable) before posting the general journal and the special columns of the cash receipts and cash payments journal. Be sure to include the general ledger account numbers in parentheses under the column totals for those accounts that were posted in total. Put a check mark in parentheses beneath the general columns.

5. Prepare a trial balance using the first pair of columns of a ten-column work sheet provided in the working papers. Include all accounts from the general ledger except the income summary account.

6. Use the following information to complete the year-end adjustments:
   a. Medical supplies inventory as of December 31, 200X $3,100
   b. Insurance expired   4,200
   c. Depreciation on medical equipment   2,500
   d. Depreciation on office equipment   1,200
   Enter these adjustments on the work sheet. Identify each adjustment by letter.

7. Complete the work sheet.

8. Using the work sheet:
   a. Prepare an income statement for the year ended December 31, 200X.
   b. Prepare a statement of owner's equity for the year ended December 31, 200X.
   c. Prepare a balance sheet as of December 31, 200X.

9. Using the work sheet as a guide, journalize and post the adjusting entries, using page 7 of the general journal.

10. Using the work sheet as a guide, journalize and post the closing entries, using page 8 of the general journal.

11. Prepare a post-closing trial balance as of December 31, 200X.

PROBLEM 8-7

Dr. Cheryl Klobas is a dentist. The books of original entry include a cash payments journal, cash receipts journal and general journal. The accounts are kept in a general ledger. Klobas has two employees: Tavis Hill, a dental hygienist, and Shannon Massey, a secretary-bookkeeper. There is an auxiliary record for Klobas's patients and for Hill's patients, but these records are not involved in this problem. The books are kept on the modified cash basis. Klobas requests that patients pay cash for the services of the hygienist, and most patients do. The trial balance as of March 31 is shown on the following page.

Dr. Cheryl Klobas, Dentist Trial Balance March 31, 200X			
Account	Acct. No.	Dr. Balance	Cr. Balance
Cash	111	19 4 8 5 45	
Office Supplies	113	1 3 1 0 00	
Professional Supplies	114	8 5 0 00	
Professional Equipment	161	32 5 0 0 00	
Accum. Depr.—Professional Equip.	161.1		15 3 0 0 00
Office Equipment	171	18 2 6 5 00	
Accum. Depr.—Office Equip.	171.1		3 6 7 5 00
Employees' Income Tax Payable	231		4 1 0 00
FICA Tax Payable—OASDI	232		4 6 5 18
FICA Tax Payable—HI	233		9 4 46
FUTA Tax Payable	241		8 9 88
SUTA Tax Payable	251		2 9 7 56
Cheryl Klobas, Capital	311		32 8 9 9 59
Cheryl Klobas, Drawing	312	17 1 5 0 00	
Professional Fees—Dentistry	411		49 9 7 5 00
Professional Fees—Oral Hygiene	412		12 7 2 0 00
Laboratory Expense	511	12 7 4 5 78	
Laundry Expense	512	5 2 3 00	
Payroll Taxes Expense	532	1 4 3 0 90	
Rent Expense	541	4 5 0 0 00	
Salary Expense	551	5 6 3 0 00	
Telephone Expense	561	5 9 4 30	
Utilities Expense	567	8 9 5 52	
Miscellaneous Expense	581	4 6 72	
		115 9 2 6 67	115 9 2 6 67

Narrative of Transactions for April

April 1   Issued Check No. 175 for April rent, $1,600.

2   Issued Check No. 176 for water bill for March, $99.30.

5   Issued Check No. 177 to Mercury Services for laboratory work performed in March, $2,988.

9   The amount columns in the daily services record kept by Klobas and Hill for the week ended April 9 contained the following totals:

Kind of Service:

Dentistry—Klobas	$3,284.00
Oral Hygiene—Hill	897.00
Total	$4,181.00

Patients' Accounts—Charges	$1,196.00
Cash Services	2,985.00
Total	$4,181.00

The total cash received from patients during the week ended April 9 was:

Dentistry	$2,370.00
Oral Hygiene	615.00
Total	$2,985.00

12 Issued Check No. 178 for laundry bill for March, $52.25.

13 Paid the following bills:

Electricity	$129.83
Gas	55.90

(Issued Check Numbers 179 and 180 by debiting Utilities Expense twice.)

16 The amount columns in the daily services record kept by Klobas and Hill for the week ended April 16 contained the following totals:

Kind of Service:

Dentistry—Klobas	$3,715.00
Oral Hygiene—Hill	820.00
Total	$4,535.00

Patients' Accounts—Charges	$1,420.00
Cash Services	3,115.00
Total	$4,535.00

The total cash received from patients during the week ended April 16 was:

Dentistry	$2,220.00
Oral Hygiene	895.00
Total	$3,115.00

16 Issued Check No. 181 to Tavis Hill for salary, $1,000, less income tax payable, $125, less FICA tax payable—OASDI, $62.50, less FICA tax payable—HI, $12.50.

16 Issued Check No. 182 to Shannon Massey for salary, $950, less income tax payable, $98, less FICA tax payable—OASDI, $59.38, less FICA tax payable—HI, $11.88.

16 Issued Check No. 183 to Washington National Bank for March payroll taxes, $969.64:

Employees' income tax withheld	$410.00
FICA tax payable—OASDI	465.18
FICA tax payable—HI	94.46
	$969.64

19 Issued Check No. 184 for professional supplies, $197.68.

20 Issued Check No. 185 for dues to the state dental society, $200 (Debit Miscellaneous Expense).

23 The amount columns in the daily services record kept by Klobas and Hill for the week ended April 23 contained the following totals:

Kind of Service:	
Dentistry—Klobas	$3,710.00
Oral Hygiene—Hill	794.00
Total	$4,504.00
Patients' Accounts—Charges	$1,494.00
Cash Services	3,010.00
Total	$4,504.00

The total cash received from patients during the week ended April 23 was:

Dentistry	$2,185.00
Oral Hygiene	825.00
Total	$3,010.00

27 Issued Check No. 186 for office supplies, $43.50

28 Issued Check No. 187 for subscriptions to magazines for the waiting room, $58 (debit Miscellaneous Expense).

28 Issued Check No. 188 for state unemployment tax for the first quarter of the year, $297.56.

30 The amount columns in the daily services record kept by Klobas and Hill for the week ended April 30 contained the following totals:

Kind of Service:	
Dentistry—Klobas	$3,075.00
Oral Hygiene—Hill	885.00
Total	$3,960.00

Patients' Accounts—Charges	$ 910.00
Cash Services	3,050.00
Total	$3,960.00

The total cash received from patients during the week ended April 30 was:

Dentistry	$1,950.00
Oral Hygiene	1,100.00
Total	$3,050.00

30   Issued Check No. 189 to Tavis Hill for salary for second half of month, $1,000, less income tax payable, $125, less FICA tax payable—OASDI, $62.50, less FICA tax payable—HI, $12.50.

30   Issued Check No. 190 to Shannon Massey for salary for second half of month, $950, less income tax payable, $98, less FICA tax payable—OASDI, $59.38, less FICA tax payable—HI, $11.88.

30   Issued Check No. 191 to Cheryl Klobas for personal use, $3,200.

30   Made an entry in the general journal for the employer's unemployment taxes and the matching portion of the FICA tax for the month of April. Payroll Taxes Expense is debited for the total taxes and FICA tax payable—OASDI credited for $243.76, FICA tax payable—HI credited for $48.76, FUTA tax payable credited for $31.20, and SUTA tax payable credited for $99.90.

Required:

1.   Record each transaction in the cash payments journal, cash receipts journal, and general journal. Number the journal pages as follows: cash receipts, page 21; cash payments, page 28; and general, page 11.

2.   At the end of the month, prove the cash receipts and cash payments journals by footing the amount columns, and then totaling and ruling the journals.

3.   Open the necessary general ledger accounts using the account forms provided. Record the April 1 balances as shown in the March 31 trial balance and complete the posting from the journals. All posting is done at the end of the month in order to simplify the problem. Post the General Dr. columns of the cash receipts and cash payments journals (if applicable) before posting the general journal and the special columns of the cash receipts and cash payments journals.

4.   Prepare a trial balance as of April 30 using the two-column paper.

PROBLEM 8-8

Dr. Andrea Fields is a practicing physician and surgeon. The books of original entry include a cash payments journal, cash receipts journal and general journal. The accounts are kept in a general ledger. Dr. Fields employs a secretary-bookkeeper. There is a patients' ledger, but it is not involved in this problem. The books are kept on the modified cash basis. The trial balance as of November 30 is shown below.

Dr. Andrea Fields, Physician and Surgeon
Trial Balance
November 30, 200X

Account	Acct. No.	Dr. Balance	Cr. Balance
Cash	111	27 3 0 0 00	
Medical Supplies	114	14 1 2 5 00	
Prepaid Insurance	118	9 1 0 0 00	
Medical Equipment	161	66 8 2 0 00	
Accumulated Depr.—Medical Equipment	161.1		10 4 0 0 00
Office Equipment	171	21 5 0 0 00	
Accumulated Depr.—Office Equipment	171.1		3 1 0 0 00
Employees' Income Tax Payable	231		2 8 0 00
FICA Tax Payable—OASDI	232		2 2 5 00
FICA Tax Payable—HI	233		4 5 00
Andrea Fields, Capital	311		67 8 2 0 00
Andrea Fields, Drawing	312	52 0 0 0 00	
Income Summary	331		
Professional Fees	411		169 4 9 2 00
Laundry Expense	512	5 6 5 00	
Payroll Taxes Expense	532	8 1 5 00	
Rent Expense	541	32 0 0 0 00	
Medical Supplies Expense	543		
Depreciation Expense—Medical Equip.	547		
Depreciation Expense—Office Equip.	548		
Insurance Expense	549		
Salary Expense	551	21 1 0 0 00	
Telephone Expense	561	6 8 0 00	
Legal Expense	564	8 1 0 00	
Utilities Expense	567	4 5 0 0 00	
Miscellaneous Expense	581	4 7 00	
		251 3 6 2 00	251 3 6 2 00

Narrative of Selected Transactions for December

Dec. 1 Issued Check No. 275 for December rent, $2,100.

2 Issued Check No. 276 to Precision Medical Supply for medical supplies, $1,120.

5 Issued Check No. 277 for medical liability insurance, $3,200.

6 Issued Check No. 278 to Clackamas Power Co. for utility expenses for November, $755.

8 Footed the amount columns in the daily service record and obtained the following totals. Entered the total cash received.

Kind of Service:

Office Visits	$ 959	Patients' Accounts Charges	$4,429
Surgery	3,995	Cash Services	525
Total	$4,954	Total	$4,954

The total cash received from patients for the week was found to be:

Payments	$3,865
Cash Services	525
Total	$4,390

12 Issued Check No. 279 for magazine subscriptions to be used in the waiting room, $85 (debit Miscellaneous Expense).

15 Issued Check No. 280 to Washington Colonial Bank for November payroll taxes:

Employees' income tax withheld	$280.00
FICA tax payable—OASDI	225.00
FICA tax payable—HI	45.00
Total amount of check	$550.00

15 Issued Check No. 281 to Sheree Smith, secretary-bookkeeper, for salary of $900, less income tax payable, $135, less FICA tax payable—OASDI, $56.25, less FICA tax payable—HI, $11.25.

16 Issued Check No. 282 to Western Bell Co. for November telephone bill, $193.

16 Issued Check No. 283 to Clean Laundry Service for November Laundry Expense, $132.

17 Footed the amount columns in the daily service record and obtained the following totals. Entered the total cash received.

Kind of Service:

Office Visits	$ 405	Patients' Accounts Charges	$4,570
Surgery	4,745	Cash Services	580
Total	$5,150	Total	$5,150

The total cash received from patients for the week was found to be:

Payments	$4,260
Cash Services	580
Total	$4,840

21 Received $800 from Brandon Lohse, Attorney, representing collection of the account of Mayumi Yoshizawa in the amount of $1,200. Lohse deducted the fee of $400 and remitted the balance.

26 Issued Check No. 284 to Andrea Fields for a personal withdrawal, $5,500.

28 Footed the amount columns in the daily service record and obtained the following totals. Entered the total cash received.

Kind of Service:

Office Visits	$ 530	Patients' Accounts Charges	$5195
Surgery	5,375	Cash Services	710
Total	$5,905	Total	$5,905

The total cash received from patients for the week was found to be:

Payments	$4,690
Cash Services	710
Total	$5,400

31 Issued Check No. 285 to Sheree Smith, secretary-bookkeeper, for salary of $900, less income tax payable, $135, less FICA tax payable—OASDI, $56.25, less FICA tax payable—HI, $11.25.

31 Recorded employer's payroll tax expense for the month of December in the general journal:

| FICA tax payable—OASDI | $112.50 |
| FICA tax payable—HI | 22.50 |

Note: There were no unemployment taxes.

Required:

1. Enter the balances from the November 30 trial balance in the general ledger accounts. Write *balance* in the item column in the general ledger and use Dec. 1 in the date column. Enter all the accounts from the trial balance including those with a zero balance.

2. Record each transaction in the cash payments journal, cash receipts journal, and general journal. Number the journal pages as follows: cash receipts, page 19; cash payments, page 23; and general, page 7.

3. At the end of the month, prove the cash receipts and cash payments journals by footing the amount columns and then totaling and ruling the journals.

4. All posting is done at the end of the month in order to simplify the problem. Post the General Dr. columns of the cash receipts and cash payments journals (if applicable) before posting the general journal and the special columns of the cash receipts and cash payments journal. Be sure to include the general ledger account numbers in parentheses under the column totals for those accounts that were posted in total. Put a check mark in parentheses beneath the general columns.

5. Prepare a trial balance using the first pair of columns of a ten-column work sheet provided in the working papers. Include all accounts from the general ledger except the income summary account.

6. Use the following information to complete the year-end adjustments:
   a. Medical supplies inventory as of December 31, 200X $2,600
   b. Insurance expired   5,700
   c. Depreciation on medical equipment   3,400
   d. Depreciation on office equipment   1,500
   Enter these adjustments on the work sheet. Identify each adjustment by letter.

7. Complete the work sheet.

8. Using the work sheet:
   a. Prepare an income statement for the year ended December 31, 200X.
   b. Prepare a statement of owner's equity for the year ended December 31, 200X.
   c. Prepare a balance sheet as of December 31, 200X.

9. Using the work sheet as a guide, journalize and post the adjusting entries, using page 7 of the general journal.

10. Using the work sheet as a guide, journalize and post the closing entries, using page 8 of the general journal.

11. Prepare a post-closing trial balance as of December 31, 200X.

Challenge Problem

Tony Chen has a dental practice and employs Sheree Smith as the office manager and Christine Vickers as the dental assistant. Below is the chart of accounts for Chen's dental practice. The transactions for the first week of April 200X, along with the information to be entered in the daily service record, are also shown.

Tony Chen, Dentist
Chart of Accounts

Assets

111   Cash
115   Prepaid Insurance
161   Automobile
161.1 Accumulated Depreciation—
        Automobile
171   Equipment
171.1 Accumulated Depreciation—
        Equipment

Liabilities

231   Employees' Income Tax Payable
232   FICA Tax Payable—OASDI
233   FICA Tax Payable—HI
241   FUTA Tax Payable
251   SUTA Tax Payable

Owner's Equity

311   Tony Chen, Capital
312   Tony Chen, Drawing

Revenue

411   Professional Fees
421   Other Income

Expenses

512   Charitable Contributions Expense
515   Depreciation Expense
516   Dues and Subscriptions
        Expense
518   Laboratory Expense
521   Laundry Expense
523   Legal Expense
528   Medical Supplies Expense
531   Office Plants Expense
532   Payroll Taxes Expense
541   Rent Expense
551   Salary Expense
561   Utilities Expense

April 1 Issued Check No. 520 for $1,200 to Professional Property Management in payment of the monthly rent.

1 Issued Check No. 521 in payment of the annual subscription for a medical journal, $95.

1 Received notice from Pine Hills National Bank that $73 of interest had been added to the business checking account.

1 Entered and coded in the daily service record the following information related to services rendered:

> Joseph Baker, Examination, Radiographs, $85; paid $85
> Jason Billings, Oral Surgery, $350; paid $75
> Rose Stockwell, Root Canal, $325; paid $200
> Carol Falk, Emergency Treatment, $300; paid $225
> Charles Steed, Study Models, $30; paid $30
> Lin Mieko, Consultation, $20; paid $20

2 Issued Check No. 522 to Matthews and Todd Insurance Agency for annual premium on Chen's automobile which is used exclusively for business, $850.

2 Issued Check No. 523 to Townsend Office Equipment in payment of a new office copier, $3,964.73.

2 Received $902.44 from Rod Tate, Attorney. Tate collected $1,303.66 from a delinquent patient and retained $401.22 for his fee.

2 Entered and coded in the daily service record the following information related to services rendered:

Joan Petit, Radiographs, Extraction, $50 each; no payment
George Kelp, Crown, $425; paid $325
James Baird, Partial Denture, $750; paid $400
Received check from Blue Shield for T. Carris for $325
Josephine Parker, Complete Denture, $2,100; paid $600
Jacob Stien, Partial Denture, $750; paid $150
Anton Dimitri, Root Canal, $350; paid $100

3 Issued Check No. 524 to Bonns Department Store in payment of Chen's personal charge account, $80.
3 Issued Check No. 525 payable to the United Fund Charities, $500.
3 Issued Check No. 526 to Conner Center Laboratories in payment of laboratory expense for the month, $824.78.
3 Entered and coded in the daily service record the following information related to services rendered:

Ralph Mobley, Amalgam, $75; paid $75
David Stevenson, Sealants, $30; paid $30
Misty Cawkins, Examination, $20; Radiographs, $50; Study Models, $20; paid $90
Ali Hassan, Prophylaxis, $40, Fluoride, $15; paid $55
Ruth Stefano, Amalgam, $45; paid $45
Janice Lancio, Extraction, $50; paid $50
Francis Norris, Sealants, $30; paid $30

4 Issued Check No. 527 to Business Laundry Service, $280.65.
4 Issued Check No. 528 to Preferred Medical Supplies, $505.46.
4 Issued Check No. 529 to Natures Nursery for the monthly maintenance of the office plants, $95.
4 Issued Check No. 530 to City Lighting Power in payment of the electricity bill, $315.26.
4 Entered and coded in the daily service record the following information related to services rendered:

Reina Berger, Space Retainer, $175; paid $125
Received check from Blue Shield for V. O'Malley for $1,458
Stacy Karem, Control Visit, $25; paid $25
Troy Block, Emergency Treatment, $30; paid $30
Katrina Davis, Pulpotomy, $35; paid $35
Collin Striker, Oral Surgery, $150; paid $75
Jennifer Ward, Crown, $475; paid $125

5 Issued Check No. 531 to Tony Chen for personal use, $1,350.
5 Issued the following checks in payment of the weekly salaries:
   Check No. 532 to Sheree Smith for $279.75, for gross salary of $350,
      less income tax payable, $44, less FICA tax payable—OASDI,
      $21.88, less FICA taxpayable—HI, $4.37.
   Check No. 533 to Christine Vickers $264.25, for gross salary of
      $330, less income tax payable, $41, less FICA tax payable—
      OASDI, $20.63, less FICA tax payable—HI, $4.12.
5 Received $450 for Chen's presentation at a professional meeting.
5 Issued Check No. 534 to Hometown Bell for the telephone bill,
   $273.89.
5 Entered and coded in the daily service record the following information related to services rendered:

   Received check from Teachers Insurance for B. Young for $1,782
   Kyla Bankroft, Examination, $20, Radiographs, $75; Control
      Visit, $20; paid $115
   Jack Pursell, Extraction, $60; paid $60
   Boris Stuart, Pulpotomy, $35; paid $35
   Frank Lewis, Post and Core, $95; paid $35
   Greg Troup, Emergency Treatment, $300; paid $80
   Anna Rodriguez, Stainless Steel Crown, $300; paid $100
   Eryn Neal, Fluoride, $15; paid $15

5 Footed the daily service record and obtained the following totals:

Kind of Service
   Diagnostic $ 370
   Preparative   2,035
   Reconstructive   4,595
   Restoration   420
   Preventive   350
   Miscellaneous   0
      Total $7,770

Patients' Accounts—Charges $4,330
Cash Services   3,440
      Total $7,770

The total cash received from patients for
   the week was:
Payments $3,565
Cash Services   3,440
      Total $7,005

Required:

1. Enter the transactions and information provided in the cash receipts journal, cash payments journal, and daily service record. The daily service record is to be completed daily and the total cash received will be entered in the cash receipts journal at the end of the week.

    In entering data in the daily service record, the Charge column is used to record the amount of the current services for which payment was not made, and the Cash Services column is used to enter all cash paid for current services. All payments received for previous services (from insurance carriers and individuals) is recorded in the Payments column.

2. The following codes are to be written in parentheses next to the patient's name to identify the procedure performed:

Diagnostic

EX	Examination
R	Radiographs
SM	Study Models
CO	Consultation

Reconstructive

C	Crown
CB	Crown & Bridge
PD	Partial Denture
CD	Complete Denture
RE	Reline, Rebase, Repair
PC	Post and Core
SS	Stainless Steel Crown

Preventive

CV	Control Visit
P	Prophylaxis
F	Fluoride
S	Sealants
SR	Space Retainer

Preparative

OS	Oral Surgery
PR	Periodontal Treatment
PP	Pulpotomy
RC	Root Canal
OT	Orthodontics
EC	Extraction
ET	Emergency Treatment

Restoration

AM	Amalgam
CM	Composite
GI	Gold Inlay
PT	Pin Restoration

3. Foot the journals and prove the balances.

Check Figures

Appendix A

EXERCISE
or
PROBLEM   CHECK FIGURE

Chapter 8

8-1   1. $1,629

8-2   Bank statement entry, 7/8 CK—Blue Shield,
        (Paid) $3,288

8-5   Cash receipts journal, total cash debit,
        $11,802.00; Cash payments journal, total
        cash credit, $14,988.94

8-6   Cash receipts journal, total cash debit,
        $14,558; Cash payments journal, total cash
        credit, $14,346.52; Net income, $104,998.46

8-7   Cash receipts journal, total cash debit,
        $12,160.00; Cash payments journal, total
        cash credit, $13,053.14

8-8   Cash receipts journal, total cash debit,
        $15,430.00; Cash payments journal, total
        cash credit, $15,030.00; Net income,
        $95,960.00

CP   Cash receipts journal, total cash debit,
        $8,430.44; Cash payments journal, total cash
        credit, $10,878.77

Glossary

A

accountant A professional with the education and experience to design an accounting system, prepare reports, and interpret results.

account form A form of balance sheet which lists assets on the left side and liabilities and owner's equity on the right side of the paper.

accounting The process of analyzing, recording, classifying, summarizing, reporting, and interpreting.

accounting cycle Steps involved in accounting for business activities during a time period. The cycle begins with analyzing source documents and ends with preparing a post-closing trial balance.

accounting equation The relationship between the three basic account elements: assets = liabilities + owner's equity.

accrual basis Revenue and expenses are recognized when earned or incurred, regardless of when cash is received.

accrued Earned but not yet received; incurred but not yet paid.

adjusting entries The process of journalizing the adjustments which are necessary at the end of the period, and which are shown in the adjustments columns of the work sheet.

adjustments Computations of changes within prepaid asset accounts, depreciation expense, accrued wages, or other entries needed to match revenue with expenses. The adjustments appear in the second set of columns titled "adjustments" on the work sheet.

ARA (American Bankers Association) Number A number expressed as a fraction, printed on the upper right-hand corner of a check. The numerator is used to identify a check being deposited.

analyzing The first phase of the accounting process. Examining a transaction or event to determine its importance to the business.

assets Items of value owned by a business that will provide future benefits. Examples include cash, office supplies, and accounts receivable.

assignment Accepting assignments means that the patient will pay only those amounts due that are not covered by insurance.

B

balance sheet A financial statement which lists assets, liabilities, and owner's equity of a business as of a specified date.

bank reconciliation The process of bringing the book and bank balances into agreement.

bank statement A statement of account, mailed by the bank to each depositor, which itemizes transactions during the month for the account.

basic accounting elements Assets, liabilities, and owner's equity (they exist in every business entity).

blank endorsement A type of check endorsement where the depositor simply signs his or her name on the back of the check.

bookkeeper A person who records accounting information, posts, and prepares financial statements at the end of the period.

book of original entry The book into which the first accounting record of a transaction is made from a source document. The general journal is often called a book of original entry.

book value The difference between the asset account and its related accumulated depreciation (contra-asset) account.

business entity An individual, association, or other organization that engages in business activities.

Glossary

C

cancelled checks Checks which have already been paid by the bank and are returned to the depositor.

cash basis Revenue is recognized only when it is received. Expenses are recognized only when paid in cash.

cash in bank The name for a business's bank account which contains cash deposits.

cash items Checks, drafts, credit card receipts, and money orders which are to be deposited in a bank.

cash payments Cash and cash items which are paid by a business.

cash payments journal Used as the book of original entry for all payments of cash.

cash receipts Cash and cash items which are received by a business.

cash receipts journal Used as the book of original entry for all cash receipts.

cash short and over The difference between the cash count and the daily deposit. An account used to keep track of daily shortages and overages of cash.

change fund A pre-existing amount which is used to make change for transactions during the day, such as $200.

Chart of Accounts A list of all general ledger accounts used by a business.

check A document that orders a bank to pay cash from a depositor's account.

classifying Phase three of the accounting process. Grouping of like transactions together rather than keeping a narrative record of many transactions.

close, closed, closing, closing entries The process of bringing temporary accounts (revenue, expense, and drawing) to a zero balance at the end of the accounting cycle so that income is matched with expenses for the period, and accounts can begin the new cycle.

collection docket A form used by lawyers who collect accounts for clients.

collections When the bank collects money for a depositor, such as on a promissory note left with the bank for collection.

contra-asset account An offsetting account. For example, Accumulated Depreciation is a contra-asset account which accounts for depreciation that has been recorded to date against the book value of an asset. It has a credit balance.

cost principle The actual amount paid or received is the amount recorded in a business's accounting books.

credit memos Notices from the bank that money is being deposited in the depositor's account.

cross-reference A link between the journal and the ledger. These are found in the posting reference column of the journal where account numbers show that amounts have been posted, and in the posting reference column of ledger accounts that show the journal and page from which the posting came.

current assets Assets which will be used up within the year or accounting cycle, such as cash, accounts receivable, supplies, and pre-paid insurance.

current liabilities Debts that will be paid in less than a year or within the accounting cycle, such as accounts payable and salaries payable.

D

daily service record An office record showing patient's name, dates of services, kinds of services, charges, payments, and cash strategies.

debit memos Notices from the bank that money has been taken from the depositor's account.

deductions Money taken from a depositor's account for pre-authorized reasons, such as a bank payment.

defendant The person or company being sued.

Glossary

deposit ticket Form used by banks to summarize coins, currency, and checks being deposited.

deposits in transit Deposits recorded in the depositor's books but not yet received or recorded in the bank's records.

depreciation The process of allocating the cost of an asset over its useful life. The using up of a fixed or plant asset. An adjusting entry is used to record depreciation expense at the end of the accounting period.

double-entry accounting A system of accounting which provides that every transaction affects at least two accounting elements. The accounting equation is in balance after each transaction.

drawer The person being paid cash when a check is written.

drawee The bank on which a check is written.

drawing A personal expense account, rather than a business expense. Also a temporary owner's equity (reducing owner's equity) account.

E

employee A person who works for an employer for salary or wages.

employee's earnings record A record which provides cumulative information for each employee for each pay period.

endorsement Stamping or writing the depositor's name on the back of a check.

errors Errors made by the bank or the depositor.

expenses Temporary owner's equity accounts which record decreases to owner's equity incurred in the ordinary course of business.

F

Fair Labor Standards Act Wage and hour law that provides overtime wage requirements.

Federal Unemployment Tax (FUTA) The federal program whereby employers pay a tax, based on the payroll, to provide federal benefits for qualified, unemployed workers.

Federal Insurance Contributions Tax (FICA) Federal taxes withheld from an employee's earnings which contribute to federal programs for old age, survivors, disability insurance (OASDI), and health insurance (HI), or Medicare.

fiscal year Any accounting period of twelve months' duration.

G

gross earnings Total salary or wages earned, prior to deductions.

I

income Temporary owner's equity accounts which record increases to owner's equity from revenues in the ordinary course of business.

income statement A financial statement which shows total revenue, total expenses, and net income or net loss for a period of time.

income summary account A temporary owner's equity account used in the closing process. Also known as Expense and Revenue Summary, Profit and Loss Summary, or Profit and Loss. This account is also closed during the closing process.

independent contractor A person who performs service for a fee, but is not subject to the control of those for whom the service is performed.

interim financial statements Statements covering less than a year.

internal control Methods designed to safeguard assets, such as requiring cash and cash items to be deposited daily in a bank.

interpreting The final phase of the accounting process. Determining relationships through ratios and comparisons.

Glossary

J

journalizing Entering a transaction in a journal, beginning with the account being debited.

L

ledger A book of accounts that contains a separate account for each account listed on the Chart of Accounts.

liabilities Amounts owed to others which are usually paid in cash.

long-term assets Assets that will last more than one year or accounting cycle. They are generally depreciated. Examples are buildings, automobiles and trucks, office equipment, and machinery.

long-term liabilities Debts that will be paid after a year or more, such as notes payable and mortgage payable.

M

matching concept (or principle) Expenses incurred to earn revenues are matched with those revenues to see what it "cost" to get the income.

merit rating system A tax-saving incentive system whereby employers are given a credit toward state unemployment taxes. The incentive is based on the employer's record of laying off workers.

modified cash basis Revenue and expenses are recognized only when cash is received or paid. Adjustments are entered for depreciation of assets and usage of supplies and insurance.

N

net income When total revenue of the period exceeds total expense.

net loss When total expenses of the period exceed total revenue.

not-sufficient funds (NSF) checks Checks rejected by the bank because the depositor has insufficient funds to cover the check.

O

office docket A form used to maintain a memorandum record of each legal case with a client.

outstanding checks Checks written by a depositor that have not yet cleared the bank for payment.

overtime Hours worked over 40 hours per week, which require payment of a wage premium, such as one and one-half times the regular rate of pay.

owner's equity The amount by which a business's assets exceed its liabilities.

P

patients ledger Patient accounts that are kept on ledger cards.

payee The person being paid cash when a check is written.

payroll register A multi-column form used to collect and compute payroll data for employees.

permanent accounts Asset, liability, and owner's equity accounts which appear on the balance sheet, and which have ongoing balances from one accounting period to the next.

petty cash fund A small amount of cash that is kept in a drawer or other safe place and is used to pay small expenses that do not justify a check either by time or by amount.

petty cash payments record A special multi-column form which is used to keep track of monies used to buy petty cash items. The petty cash payments record is not a book of original entry. An entry is made in the general journal to account for petty cash when it is replenished.

Glossary

plaintiff A person or company bringing a lawsuit against another person or company.

post-closing trial balance A listing of all accounts which are still open following the closing entries, together with their debit or credit balances. Accounts with debit balances must equal accounts with credit balances (the accounting equation must be in balance).

posting The process of entering the journal amounts into the appropriate general ledger accounts.

R

recording The second phase of the accounting process. Writing or entering into a computer the transactions affecting a business.

recording the payroll The process of recording gross earnings by employees and their withholdings.

regular wages Computed by multiplying regular hours worked by the hourly wage.

report form A form of balance sheet which lists accounts along the left side, with assets first, followed by liabilities and owner's equity.

reporting Communicating results through some combination of tables of numbers and/or narrative reports.

restrictive endorsement A kind of check endorsement where the depositor writes the words "For Deposit Only," or "Pay to Mike Smith Only." This restricts payment of the check.

revenue An increase in assets because a service was rendered.

reversing entries Used to eliminate balances in asset or liability accounts for new accounting period; the adjusting entry is reversed; that is, the account debited in adjusting entry is credited and the account credited in adjusting entry is debited.

S

salary A regular paycheck in equal installments, for services rendered as an employee.

service charges Bank charges for services such as check processing and printing.

signature card A card kept on file to verify the depositor's signature.

source document A receipt, invoice, sales docket, cash register tape, or other evidence of a transaction.

statement of owner's equity A financial statement which reveals what happened to the owner's capital account during the accounting period. Net income for the period increases owner's equity, while withdrawals (drawing) by the owner decrease owner's equity.

State Unemployment Tax (SUTA) Money paid by employers, based on payroll, to fund payments of benefits to qualified, unemployed workers by state governments.

summarizing The process of bringing together various items of information to determine or explain a result.

T

temporary accounts Revenue accounts, expense accounts, and the drawing account, which are closed at the end of an accounting period. These accounts appear on either the income statement or statement of owner's equity.

transaction Any activity of a business which affects the accounting equation.

trial balance A listing of all accounts showing the title and the ending balance (before adjusting or closing entries).

Glossary

U

Universal Health Insurance Claim Form
Developed by the American Medical Association and used by most insurance carriers and programs.

W

wage-bracket method Use of withholding tax tables to determine income taxes to be withheld.

wages Earnings by employees based on the number of hours worked or number of units produced.

withholding allowance An amount on which no federal income tax will be withheld.

work sheet An accountant's informal tool used to determine adjustments, net income or loss, and whether the books balance.

Z

zero out To reduce, with closing entries, all temporary owner's equity accounts to zero balances. All revenue, expense, and drawing accounts must have zero balances to begin the new accounting cycle.

Index

325

Index

Index

Index

Rules of Debit and Credit

Balance Sheet Accounts

ASSETS

Asset Accounts

Debit to enter increases **(+)**	**Credit** to enter decreases **(−)**

LIABILITIES

All Revenue Accounts

Debit to enter decreases **(−)**	**Credit** to enter increases **(+)**

OWNER'S EQUITY

Owner's Equity Accounts

Debit to enter decreases **(−)**	**Credit** to enter increases **(+)**

Income Statement Accounts

Debit for decreases in owner's equity

Credit for increases in owner's equity

Expense Accounts

Debit to enter increases **(+)**	**Credit** to enter decreases **(−)**

Revenue Accounts

Debit to enter decreases **(−)**	**Credit** to enter increases **(+)**